REVELATION EXPLAINED

Revelation Explained

by
Lerry W. Fogle

Distributed by
Logos International
Plainfield, New Jersey 07060

All Scripture references are from the King James Version unless otherwise noted.

"And there were certain Greeks among them that came up to worship at the feast: The same came therefore to Philip . . . and desired him, saying, Sir, we would see Jesus."

John 12:20-21

Contents

Acknowledgments

I wish to offer my sincere thanks to those who helped in many ways in the preparation of this book. I praise the Lord for the patience and love of my family during this time. I want to acknowledge the editorial work of my mother and two very close friends in the Lord. Above all, I want to thank the Lord for His blessings and the strength given me in this task.

May the Lord by His grace cover any mistakes or shortcomings in this work.

Introduction

Lord, why me? You know that scores and maybe hundreds of books have been written on the book of Revelation. My small library alone has eight volumes on the subject, several written within the last ten years. And every one of them was probably written by an author more learned and knowledgeable of theology and biblical doctrine than I! Is it really necessary that I devote a vast amount of time researching and writing another manuscript on that most difficult-to-understand last book of the Bible?

Those and a dozen other questions like these filled my mind the night I began to pen this book. I had become a Christian six and a half years earlier, falling to my knees in repentance after reading the Revelation of Jesus Christ in The Living Bible. I had a growing hunger for the Word of God and the truth it reveals. I had taken seminary courses on a variety of subjects and had done some Christian writing in the past. But I felt totally inadequate for the task as I pondered the endless hours of work that would be involved.

I had just read through the Revelation again and testified to our prayer group how God was revealing Jesus to me through it. A sister in the Lord had just given me several articles on eschatology, the subject of "end" times, which is so often related to or even viewed synonymously with the Revelation. Those articles confirmed again in my heart what God was showing me and established again the need for a fresh look at God's "revelation" of His Son.

Nearly every work I had ever read concerning the book of Revelation started with the intent of showing Jesus being revealed but would end up casting each chapter or section of the Revelation into a time frame, very often developing a chronology of events when possible. Many had neatly arranged the past, present and future into eras called dispensations. Others came just short of attaching dates to the events of the end times, particularly the second coming of Jesus, which, Jesus said, He could not even do (Matt. 24:36).

This approach had always confused me as a baby Christian trying to understand God's Word. How could all those authors develop a schedule of future happenings from the book of Revelation, when myself and many others were having a difficult time understanding a book which did not seem to have a natural sequence or progression?

Additionally was the problem with different interpretations of the Revelation most always related to the "rapture." There are the pretribs, the midtribs, the posttribs and about a half dozen other views of theology which speculate as to the sequence of the great tribulation and the "rapture" of God's Church. Would the Church be "snatched away" before tribulation on the earth, during this awful time of judgment on the earth or after it was all over at Jesus' coming? These questions added to the confusion and misunderstanding of the prophecy.

Now God was impressing me to write another view. Would it help or would it just add to the confusion? The answer had already been given to me months earlier when our fellowship had studied the book of Revelation. As we allowed the Holy Spirit to illuminate the truth to us, we saw the great need for the Body of Christ to know that truth. The only confusion that existed was in the minds of men. Because mankind may have different views on the Word of God does not mean that the truth is confusing. What it does suggest is that man's thinking and intellect has often superseded the truth of God's Word as revealed by the Holy Spirit. While I do not have a "corner" on or exclusive rights to the truth of the Word, I am assured that God's Spirit, which dwells within every Christian, does speak to me as well. And if God has shown some truth to me by His Spirit, then it should be shared and made available to the Body of Christ.

At this point I must give credit where credit is due. Much of what you will read in this book was not developed by me as an individual believer. It came through many years of studying the Bible and seeking the truth together with a group of believers who meet regularly in the fellowship of which I'm a part. There are specific individuals who have given me great insight into spiritual things that God had already shown them, but it was from the Body of Christ assembled and seeking to know God's will that the idea and context of this volume evolved. Jesus told the disciples that "the Holy Ghost, whom the Father will send in my name, he shall teach you all things" (John 14:26). It is the Holy Spirit who reveals Jesus, speaking the truth to individuals and the Body as a whole. He has given this book to the Church.

There is no personal motivation of my own involved in this project; I am not writing just for the sake of writing a book. The Lord knows how I've struggled against it. But I am convinced now that He just wants a willing vessel to document the continuing revelation of Jesus Christ. My testimony concerning this work could be, "I can do all things through Christ which strengtheneth me" (Phil. 4:13). It would be utterly impossible to do it without the guidance of the Spirit and the strength of our Lord.

I'm not proposing that I have all the answers to the Revelation. Nor do I believe that any one person or group within the universal Body of Christ does. All the pieces of our understanding have to be shared and brought together in order that we "May be made perfect in one"

(John 17:23).

I have endeavored to be as thorough as possible by introducing other viewpoints which are spiritually based and by providing ample scriptural references as well as references to other works on the subject. The ultimate test of this text comes in lining it up with all of God's Word. The revealing of Jesus is not unique to the book of Revelation but begins in Genesis 1 and winds its way through Scripture to Revelation 22. "Try the spirits" says John (1 John 4:1) and, in another place Paul tells Timothy, "Study to shew thyself approved unto God, a workman that needeth not to be ashamed, rightly dividing the word of truth" (2 Tim. 2:15). That should be our procedure for all study of the Scriptures and other resources. It is my hope that I have been faithful in doing that and that you will be in reading this.

There are many places in the text of each chapter where I could have gone into much greater detail. I have chosen, however, to introduce spiritual aspects of the Revelation which are not usually considered. I have dwelt less on matters where there is either unity in the Body of Christ on that subject or where brief coverage tended to suffice in getting the reader thinking and studying on his own. The serious student of the Revelation will read other volumes where these details have been explored in depth.

Although I have done much of the preparatory work on this book utilizing several translations of the Scriptures, you will note that all of the Revelation text (set in italics with quotation marks), as well as other Scripture noted, is from the King James Version unless specifically noted otherwise.

Finally, I want to give all the glory to God and to His Son, Jesus Christ, who has saved me by His grace. I would not even be writing this introduction, let alone a book, were it not for His miraculous touch on my life in 1972. I profess Jesus Christ as Savior and Lord and pray that my labor will serve to illuminate and glorify Him. May we all live with our hearts' greatest desire being that of the Greeks who told the disciple Philip, "We would see Jesus" (John 12:21).

1
The Main Theme
(1:1-3)

The opening words from the book of the Revelation establish from the very beginning the main theme of what is to follow, *"the Revelation of Jesus Christ."* God, by His Spirit, has a way of getting right to the point. There should be no confusion as to what God is going to communicate to His Church: He is going to communicate Jesus.

About sixty years had passed since Jesus had ascended into the heavenly places. Some authorities say that it wasn't quite that long until God gave the message to his servant John. But regardless of the precise number of years, time had passed, and the circumstances in which the Church found itself had changed. The city of Jerusalem was no longer the only place where Christians lived and assembled. Having spread the good news of Jesus under the direction of the Holy Spirit they found themselves in many localities, some quite distant from Jerusalem. This was wholly compatible with Jesus' prophetic words at His ascension, "Ye shall be witnesses unto me both in Jerusalem, and in all Judaea, and in Samaria, and unto the uttermost part of the earth" (Acts 1:8). The dispersion of the Church to all the earth was by divine appointment. It was God's will that believers in every place would gather to build themselves up in the faith and add new believers to their number.

The passing of time, though, had brought about some unhealthy signs in the Church. Some Christians had become apathetic and indifferent. Some had become totally unfaithful. The fervor with which the work of the Church had begun was starting to wane. The imminent return of

1

Jesus, which the early Christians fully expected in their lifetime, had not happened. As a consequence, even many of the faithful were probably discouraged.

Realizing the needs of the Church, God moved to reassure it by sending a fresh revelation of Jesus, the very Head of the Church. The physical body of man cannot function without the head. It is the center of the mind, the intellect and all that controls the activities of the body. So it is with the Church of Jesus Christ. Without its Head, Jesus, it cannot perform or, for that matter, have life at all. The Body of Christ, at the time of the Revelation, had gotten to the point where it needed to reestablish communication with Jesus, the Head.

The Church needed to see that, though He was yet to come, Jesus was in their midst even "where two or three" were gathered in His name (Matt. 18:20). It needed to see, through spiritual eyes, that the relationship of Jesus to the Church had already been established, and that Jesus was and would always be, by the Holy Spirit, with the Church.

The message of the Revelation served that purpose, as John was faithful to receive it and record it. As it also became part of the written canonized Word, it would touch the lives of countless millions of Christians through the centuries.

The Unveiling

"The Revelation of Jesus Christ." The Greek word from which "revelation" is translated means "revealing" or the "unveiling." The Church could not see Jesus, so God was going to unveil Him. He was there all the time; He simply wasn't visible in their lives. He is present by faith, not by sight.

When the sculptor finishes his new work of art, the work is done and ready for viewing, but it is not visible until the unveiling takes place. The work of Calvary and

Pentecost had established Jesus Christ as Lord and Head of the Church. Jesus had ascended to heaven to sit on the right hand of God, His redemptive work finished for the Lord. But He wasn't far away from the Church. He was still as close to us as God the Father is. In fact, considering the Trinity, which makes the Father, Son and Holy Spirit one, He was dwelling in Christians by the Holy Spirit. The believers were the temple of the Holy Spirit (1 Cor. 3:16-17). That fact had to be unveiled to the Church afresh.

God had prefigured Jesus through aspects of the Old Covenant, which we'll see later in chapter 4 of this commentary. He had shown Jesus to mankind in the flesh. He had revealed the resurrected Jesus to mankind before His ascension. He had revealed more of Jesus with the coming of the Holy Spirit. And now He was unveiling Jesus still further to the world through the Revelation to John.

The Revelation was not given just to detail the final events of Jesus' coming, though many details of His coming are contained therein. It was given that we might see Jesus, now as well as in the future, in the life of every believer and the Church as a whole.

Revelation, Not Mystery

"The Revelation of Jesus Christ." Notice again that the message begins by indicating something was to be revealed. Many readers of the book of the Revelation might find the word mystery to be more appropriate. Diligence is often taken to read and study the book through, with the end result being the veiling of Jesus instead of an unveiling. The risen Jesus is no more visible than He was before the book was read. Why is that so? How can a book which intends to reveal something shroud it in so much mystery?

Several answers need to be considered. All of them

serve to show that the Revelation is not a mystery. First, the book is an apocalyptic writing, a literary style used from around 200 B.C. to A.D. 200. Though the book is prophetic in nature and even termed as such in 1:3, the writing is still very obviously apocalyptic. It draws heavily on the use of symbolism, dualism and other means which visually or graphically get the message across to the reader without actually writing the message directly.

In the case of John, the experience was actually an extended vision in which, he says many times, he was carried away "in the Spirit." Over and over, God was showing John spiritual truth and reality. What he was getting a glimpse of must have been incomprehensible. The glory of God and the beauty of heavenly places was something John could only describe in the terms with which he was familiar, namely, earthly terms. How frustrating and exasperating it must have been to attempt descriptions of God's presence, the reality of spiritual beings such as angels and the wonder of the finished work of Christ and the Church using terms which apply to natural things! But by the Spirit of God, he did. Consequently, he describes things like the *"sea of glass"* (4:6), a *"woman clothed with the sun"* (12:1) and *"a beast rise up out of the sea"* (13:1).

When a man writes a love letter or poem to the one who has captured his heart, he describes her eyes as pools of blue water, her hair as strands of golden silk and her lips as having the sweet taste of ripe cherries. He doesn't actually see water, golden silk or cherries. He is so awestruck and completely dazzled by his love that he cannot describe her except that he use analogous terms reflecting pleasant realities and experiences. That's exactly what John must have done after he regained his composure and began to write what he had seen. More will be said about this later.

Secondly, John's experiences are probably documented

4

in topical sequences as they were shown to him and not necessarily in a chronological sequence from one point in time to another. Herein lies a key point in understanding the Revelation. Many passages and entire chapters of the Revelation have been given different interpretations because an attempt was made to make them fit chronologically. If we realize that what John saw in the vision was presented in overlapping segments, which were sometimes repeated in slightly different ways, then maybe these unexplainable passages would be more explainable.

The use of flashbacks in movies and television stories might be a good example of this. As the events of a span of time are revealed to the viewing audience, the details are given in small segments, with many of the succeeding segments repeated or reviewed, until the whole sequence is known and the plot is revealed. Some of the segments may cover greater amounts of time than others. But added up in their entirety, they reveal the complete story. So it is with the book of the Revelation.

Chapter 1, verse 19, has been used many times to support the idea of a chronology. John is told to *"write the things which thou hast seen, and the things which are, and the things which shall be hereafter."* Chronologists would say that the *"things which thou hast seen"* refer to what occurred in history before John was given the vision or what had occurred up to that point in the vision (recorded in chapter 1). The *"things which are"* apply to the condition of the Church at that time, as revealed to John in chapters 2 and 3. Finally, the *"things which shall be hereafter"* are generally related to all future history, as depicted by chapters 4 through 22. The sum of all this suggests the depicting of past, present and future, which seems to be a rational idea. But maybe this idea should be carried one step further.

What if the elements of past, present and future were applied to the entire prophecy or revelation? John's immediate revelation of Jesus Christ in chapter 1 could surely embrace all three elements of time, considering Heb. 13:8, "Jesus Christ the same yesterday, and to day, and for ever." The messages to the seven churches of Asia do not seem to be unique to them and most probably apply to the Church as a whole before John's vision, at the time of John's vision and in the centuries ahead beyond it. Revelation 4 to 22 often mixes the past, future and present. Chapter 12 is a good example. Here we see a highly symbolic story of the birth, ministry and ascension of Jesus to the very throne of God (past); the victory saints have over Satan by the blood of the Lamb and the word of their testimony (present and future); and the keeping power of God for the Church (present and future). Much more will be shared concerning this chapter when it is addressed later. Suffice it to say at this time that the elements of past, present and future are found throughout that chapter, as well as throughout the entire book. Chapter 12 just does not fit chronologically between chapters 11 and 13. It does, however, in past, present and future tenses, reveal Jesus Christ, the subject of the book.

Finally, the book of Revelation is often misunderstood when an attempt is made to understand it in a literal sense or in the natural only. As mentioned before, John was carried away "in the Spirit" to observe much of the Revelation. The truth about Christ and the Church that God wanted to reveal could only be comprehended "in the Spirit."

The apostle Paul tells the Corinthians in his first letter that the natural man "receiveth not the things of the Spirit of God: for they are foolishness unto him: neither can he know them, because they are spiritually discerned" (2:14). The entire section of 1 Cor. 2:9-16 relates the fact that we can have no understanding of God, His will or any other spiritual truth except the Holy Spirit, the Teacher of all spiritual truth, reveal it to us. And so it is with the

Revelation. To try to understand it in literal terms or in the flesh will do little except to cast it into the realm of a mystery. A mystery it is not; it is a revelation!

It has been reasoned by many who date it around A.D. 70 that this vision which reveals Jesus was given in symbolic or apocalyptic terms so that only Christians "in the Spirit" could understand its edifying message. Tribulation and persecution of Christians had already begun in the Church, whether the book is dated then or later near the end of the century, as others believe. The Romans or others who would come against God's elect could in no way understand this writing should it fall into their hands. But any Christian abiding and walking in the Spirit could be expected to wait on the Lord and see its great spiritual truths. The same applies today.

The Method of Transcription

How did this message from God get into our hands today? The first verse tells us that God gave it to Jesus, *"The Revelation of Jesus Christ, which God gave unto him."* He is our access to the Father (John 14:6). God demonstrates this by giving the message first to His Son. Jesus is our Lord and Savior. All power and authority has been given to him by God, the Father. This is why God hands it over to Jesus to pass on to the Church.

Skipping one small phrase, which we'll return to directly, John says, *"And he sent and signified it by his angel unto his servant John."* Having received the essence of the vision from the Father, Jesus passes on the revelation of himself through his angel. Angels are spiritual creations of God utilized throughout Scripture as messengers (Matt. 1:20) and ministers to the saints (Heb. 1:14). This particular angel is designated as one which ministered to and for the Lord Jesus himself.

The key word to focus on here is *signified.* *"He sent and signified it by his angel."* The English word *signified*

7

comes from the root word *sign*. The Greek shows a similar relationship. What is actually being said here is that the revelation was sent and *sign*-ified by His angel. In other words, the message was made known to John in signs and symbols, which he records for the saints of all time to read and be blessed by as they absorb it "in the Spirit." That was the method of transcription that God used to get the vision to the Church.

A Blessing for the Servants of God

We now return to that one small phrase, *"to shew unto his servants things which must shortly come to pass"* (1:1). The word *"servants"* specifically implies a freewill slave. A servant who was a freewill slave was one who loved his master so much that, when given his freedom, he chose to work for his master without being paid. It was to a person of that caliber and devotion that God directs this revelation, those people that make up the universal Church of Jesus Christ, His servants forever.

Though we have established that the emphasis of the Revelation is both past, present and future, the specific emphasis here is on what was about to transpire in the life of the Church from that point forward. John continues his opening remarks in verse 3, *"Blessed is he that readeth, and they that hear the words of this prophecy, and keep those things which are written therein: for the time is at hand."*

The Revelation, as we can see from this verse, was intended to be a blessing. It can, in no way, be a blessing to anyone who simply cannot understand it. The most enjoyable reading is that which we can comprehend personally and relate to. The Revelation interpreted as a literal, chronological story is not personally comprehendible. Neither is it a blessing as such. The Revelation as seen from the perspective of revealing Jesus to the Church, using signs and symbols to represent His glory and authority, is very personable and is certainly a blessing.

The Revelation was always intended to be a blessing for the servants of God, the Church. It could never be a blessing to an unbeliever. Why is that so? Verse 3 indicates a condition that had to be met if the prophecy was going to be a blessing. Whether it was read (*"he that readeth"*) or heard (*"and they that hear the words of this prophecy"*), it had to be kept (*"and keep those things which are written therein"*). It would not be a blessing just to read it or hear it. On the contrary, it might, for many, be quite difficult to swallow and cause the fearful and unbelieving to search their hearts. To be a blessing, the reader or person hearing it must keep it. This is the key to all of the Scriptures. God demands an active and positive response to His will as revealed in the Word. The servants of God could do that, but it would be hard to imagine the unrighteous keeping the words of a prophecy intended to reveal Jesus, the Righteous.

An example of keeping *"those things"* which are written would be the aspect of praise, which is such a predominant feature of the Revelation. The Church and even the entire creation in Revelation 5 are seen round about the throne or presence of God singing songs of praise, ascribing honor, glory and majesty to the Father, Son and Holy Spirit. Later, we'll examine this in detail, but it's important to see here that God is to be praised, especially by His children. The Revelation, and indeed all Scripture, reveals this. The blessings of God always follow the biblical principle of obedience. So it is with those who would examine the Revelation and *"keep those things"* with respect to praise.

Another area in which the reader or hearer of this prophecy would be blessed is that of remaining faithful to the Lord God and not being drawn away by the evil so present in the world. Revelation 13 begins a lengthy discourse on the powers of evil which, in the life of the Church, will endeavor to allure the Bride of Christ into committing spiritual fornication or adultery. The beasts of chapters 13 and following are ruthless in their pursuit to accomplish that. They cause a "mark" to be placed on all of mankind and then move to cause economic and financial ruin to all who will not receive the "mark" and be drawn away from the righteousness of God. The blessing of the Revelation comes (for those called "overcomers") in keeping that loyalty to Almighty God and Jesus, His revealed Son.

There are many other words of the prophecy to be kept, but these few examples highlight the types of response demanded of those who read or hear it. The fearful and unbelieving will not be blessed with its content, for they will not keep it. The faithful and loving servants of God, moving in obedience to the Word of God, will definitely be blessed.

An Invitation

With all of these things in mind, I invite you to see Jesus as we move on. If you see Him and respond to Him, He will bless you. If you are a servant of the living God, a freewill slave to His will, the Revelation can be an exciting experience of seeing divine love toward you. If you are not sure of your commitment to the Lord Jesus Christ, you can make one now before you read on. Open your heart to him, confess your sins and accept him as Savior and Lord. Do it now and be blessed with *the Revelation of Jesus Christ.*

2
A Message to the Church
(1:4-8)

Upon identifying the theme of the book, John momentarily shifts to some additional salutations and greetings but, in doing so, continues to reveal the majesty of God, with the emphasis on Jesus Christ. In these next five verses is also found the indication of who is to be the recipient of the message. It clearly reveals that the Church is being addressed, the Bride of the Lord Jesus, which needs the constant assurance of His love.

To the Church
"John to the seven churches which are in Asia" (1:4). At first glance it would appear that this Revelation was being given to a select group of churches which existed at the time John received it. The churches are generally identified here as those in Asia. They are introduced corporately in chapter 1 of the Revelation and individually, by name, in chapters 2 and 3. Why does God choose these seven local churches? Is there something unique about them which caused the Spirit of God to confront them as He does? What about all the other local churches that existed at that time?

The clue to providing the answers is found in the number of local churches that are addressed—seven. *"John to the* seven *churches which are in Asia."* The number seven in Scripture is very significant, particularly in the Revelation, a book of signs and symbols. Whenever it is used, seven seems to indicate, or *sign*-ify, completeness and perfection. This is the first place we find the number seven in the Revelation, but certainly not the last. It occurs fifty-three more times, twelve times in the first chapter alone. Each time it occurs, the definition of completeness and perfection holds true.

The seven churches mentioned here are representative of the Church of all time. They, as an aggregate, characterize the nature and actions of all the churches before, at the time of and after the vision which John received, i.e., past, present and future. Some of the specific assemblies are quite recognizable to the reader of the New Testament. Many are not. The churches most recognizable to us in Scripture, such as Corinth, Thessalonica, Rome or even Antioch, are not to be found. But the ability to relate to these specific churches in their locality is not important. The important thing for us to see is that in them, we can find ourselves—in their actions, in their shortcomings, in their victories.

These seven were selected by God. When viewed on a map, they form a circle, which is symbolic of completeness. A circle is a continuum, whose line has no end. Such is the Church. The Church had its beginning in Jesus Christ and, because of His obedience to God the Father, in Him it has no end. It will abide and live in Him forever. Through these seven assemblies God speaks a message of exhortation, encouragement and love to the whole Church.

About the Author

Little has been said about the man that God chose as a vessel to relay the Revelation to the Church. That man was John. Verse 1 identifies him as the servant of God to whom the angel passed the message. Here in verse 4 we see John faithfully relating what he had observed, *"John to the seven churches which are in Asia."*

There is much speculation as to which John this might be. Putting together all the information that we find about this John in the opening verses of the book would strongly indicate that this was the apostle John *"who bare*

12

record of the word of God, and of the testimony of Jesus Christ, and of all things that he saw" (1:2). The gospel writer John, the loving disciple of Jesus, was the very one who had termed Jesus as the "Word" (John 1:1). It doesn't seem to be coincidental that he identifies himself as the one *"who bare record of the* word *of God."* Here is a man who had walked with Jesus, heard His teaching and had come to a loving and close relationship to his Lord. He had seen *"the testimony of Jesus Christ"* and was intimately familiar with it, to the point where he had documented through the Gospel message and the Epistles the message of Jesus Christ, the Word of God. This same man was now being shown a vision which would not only reveal Jesus, whom he knew, but would make clear Jesus' relationship to the Church. Who could better describe these things to the Church than the one who had seen and loved Jesus so much?

Much more could be said about this John. Lengthy studies have been done to confirm or deny his authorship. But the particular man chosen to write the vision's message is of little consequence compared to its content. God used this John, whether the apostle or some other, to do the recording. God could have used anyone. He chose, however, this man named John.

The Greeting (1:4-6)

The salutation having been addressed, *"John* [the messenger] *to the seven churches* [the Church, the recipient] *which are in Asia,"* words of greeting are given. That greeting itself is full of spiritual truth and revelation. It contains some keys to understanding what follows. The greeting conveys grace and peace from God, who is identified first as *"him which is, and which was, and which is to come"* (1:4). In the sense of present, past and future, God greets His Church. Though the order is slightly different, God the Father is shown as being the Eternal, the Ancient of Days, the Almighty, the Everlasting—the Past, Present and Future. He has always been, is today and will ever be the God of the universe. Seeing it from that perspective, how privileged we are to be granted grace and peace from the Everlasting God, the Father of all life.

The greeting could end there but goes on by giving greetings from the other two persons of the Trinity—the Holy Spirit and Jesus. The Holy Spirit is described as the *"seven spirits which are before his throne"* (1:4). Again we see the number seven, which indicates completeness or perfection. The Holy Spirit is really one entity with diverse manifestations, even as God is one in three.

Isaiah the prophet may have been given this truth about the Holy Spirit when in his prophecy he says, "And the spirit of the Lord shall rest upon him, the spirit of wisdom and understanding, the spirit of counsel and might, the spirit of knowledge and of the fear of the Lord" (Isa. 11:2). Counting the phrase "of the Lord," we see here the Holy Spirit of God described in seven ways, probably the same seven we now observe before the throne of God in the Revelation. This Holy Spirit, full of the nature and character of God, the same that rested on Jesus and now the Church, also sent grace and peace.

To complete the greeting from the Trinity, it says, *"and from Jesus Christ"* (1:5). All of the Godhead has been identified, Father, Son and Spirit. From all three come the greetings of grace and peace.

The remainder of verse 5 and all of verse 6 describe Christ and the Church. Jesus is first called *"the faithful witness."* This is in direct reference to Jesus' ministry of witnessing the love of God as He came to earth in the flesh. He was God's witness, telling of Him and pointing all to the Father. He was faithful in doing that. He took no glory for himself but preferred always to give God the preeminence. He was truly a faithful witness.

The Greek word here translated "witness" can be

14

transliterated "martyr." The word *martyr* carries the connotation of witnessing to the point of death. Although the Greek doesn't necessarily communicate our English connotations, Jesus' ministry certainly was not only one of witnessing to the love of the Father, but also one of obedience unto death for the salvation of souls. In this aspect, Jesus is seen as a martyr, put to death in obedience to God's will and in concert with His master plan. Viewed as "witness" or "martyr," Jesus was faithful.

He is also described as *"the first begotten of the dead."* Here, Jesus is declared to be the first of many who would, through obedience, rise from the dead. Paul had already described Jesus that way, "In Christ shall all be made alive. But every man in his own order: Christ the first-fruits; afterward they that are Christ's at his coming" (1 Cor. 15:22-23). First fruits were a select part of the crop soon to be gathered and were a token of the great harvest to come. Jesus was the first fruits of a great crop of souls that would be given life though dead.

Next Jesus is acclaimed to be *"the prince of the kings of the earth"* (1:5). Many see this as the reign of Jesus during a future time called the "millennium," an era that will feature divine rule on the face of the earth, with Jesus Christ as the highest authority. Without getting too deep into the considerations of the kingdom of God and so as not to cover material which will be given in later chapters concerning the "millennium" and the rule of Jesus, let us consider just one thought concerning Jesus as *"the prince of the kings of the earth."*

The *"kings of the earth"* are the world rulers (17:2). Just as Jesus is Lord of the Church, He is Lord over *"the kings of the earth"* as well (17:14).

Jesus is Lord over the actions of sinful men. He is at work in the world, bringing tribulation to those who oppose the good news, in order to bring them to repentance. Even though the Church might be tempted to think that God is not in control, as they are persecuted and even killed for the gospel, Jesus reveals himself as actively at work protecting that gospel. And eventually He will openly reveal himself as the ruler of those who oppose Him.

As the saints overcome the world system in Christ, they rule with Him over the kings of the earth who oppose them. Thus the saints themselves are called *"kings and priests"* (1:6).

We are kings and priests because Jesus *"loved us, and washed us from our sins in his own blood, and hath made us kings and priests"* (1:5). It was Jesus' own blood brought before the throne of God that has *"washed us from our sins."* It didn't just cover them up or do away with them for a season. Our sins were completely washed away, removed forever from the presence of God. Psalm 103 says, "As far as the east is from the west, so far hath he removed our transgressions from us" (verse 12).

Having accomplished that at the cross of Calvary, we can now stand before God without spot or blemish. We have a right to be in the presence of God. We did not earn it, nor do we deserve it. But, nevertheless, it is a right God grants to us. We are royalty in God's sight through the blood—kings and priests. *"To him be glory and dominion for ever and ever. Amen"* (1:6).

The priestly function to which we have fallen heir was prefigured in the Aaronic priesthood of the Old Covenant. There, a selective group of individuals ministered to, and in the service of, the Lord under the direction of a high priest. It was their job to wait upon the Lord in the tabernacle and later in the temple at Jerusalem. They offered up sacrifices to the Lord as God had commanded them to do. Their service was a labor of love to the Lord by His election.

So it is with the children of God walking in the New Covenant. We have a high priest, Jesus (Heb. 9:11-12), who has given us direction in the way to walk. We have been granted our position through the grace of God, by election (Rom. 11:5-6; 1 Thess. 1:4-5). Our service to God is a labor of love in which we, having become the temple or dwelling place of God (1 Cor. 3:16-17), offer ourselves a living sacrifice to God (Rom. 12:1) and offer sacrifices of praise to God for who He is (Heb. 13:15).

So much more could be said about our kingly and priestly function in Christ Jesus. These themes will continue to unfold as we press further into the Revelation.

There is so much more to Christianity than a salvation experience. God did not save us from our sins to have us fall back into them or live weak, defeated lives here on the face of this earth. We will spend an eternity of time in the presence of God as kings and priests unto Him. But that time is not all in the future. The prophecy says, *"he hath made us kings and priests"* (past tense), not "he will make us." Much of the blessing promised to the keeper of this prophecy begins right here at this basic premise of the Christian life.

A Preview of His Coming

In keeping with the idea that the Holy Spirit gets right to the point, look at verse 7. Here in the introductory portions of the text we find a quick preview of the second coming of Jesus, the One being revealed. *"Behold, he cometh with clouds; and every eye shall see him, and they also which pierced him: and all kindreds of the earth shall wail because of Him. Even so, Amen."* To this point we have but gotten the tips of our toes wet with the truth. With this verse, we dive in and get immersed in it. Let's first examine the cloud spoken of.

At Jesus' ascension, the writer of Acts records that "he was taken up; and a cloud received him out of their sight" (1:9). The confounded disciples, standing there in amazement, were told by two men in white apparel (probably angels), "Ye men of Galilee, why stand ye gazing up into

17

heaven? This same Jesus, which is taken up from you into heaven, shall so come in like manner as ye have seen him go into heaven" (1:11). Here, now, in the Revelation it says, *"Behold, he cometh with clouds."* Surely this is confirmation of God's Word, and yet there might be more to this simple statement than most observe.

The usual treatment of these companion Scriptures centers around the natural element of His ascension and return—a cloud. Indeed, viewing the natural application of these Scriptures, a cloud does seem to be the suggested medium for these events. But is there a spiritual application to be made as well?

The writer of Hebrews says, "Seeing we also are compassed about with so great a cloud of witnesses . . . let us run with patience the race that is set before us" (12:1). The idea being set forth is a great gallery of heavenly spectators, who are watching and encouraging those who are endeavoring to run the race of faith on earth. Hebrews 11 (the great faith chapter) carefully describes many who had already run the race on the face of this earth, a group who, in faith, had endured and now actually sat in the heavenly places.

Surely this is a heavenly cloud being spoken of. The figurative language of a cloud causes us to see these witnesses in the sky, observable only by looking up. They are above the level of the earth because they have passed from life on the earth to eternal life in the heavenly places. The important points are that they are people of faith (saints, if you will) and that they dwell in heaven. The reference made to them as a cloud is done so to see their heavenly position. They are a cloud of heavenly witnesses, people of faith such as Enoch, Noah, Abraham, Joseph, Moses, Stephen, John the Baptist and even the thief on the cross who repented in faith (Luke 23:43). They are the household of faith, that portion of the Church that has gone on to heaven (see Heb. 11:39-40,

18

The Amplified Bible).

Jesus was the first begotten of the dead. No one preceded him. But after His resurrection, Jesus began to assemble that heavenly cloud of witnesses, and He began with the Old Testament saints (Matt. 27:52-53). He even ministered the gospel to the spirits of those who were lost ("in prison"), scoffers and mockers such as those that moved in disbelief and disobedience in the days of Noah (1 Pet. 3:18-20). Even they which accepted Jesus of that number became part of the heavenly cloud. But most importantly, all after Jesus' ascension that would accept him as Lord and Savior would become part of that heavenly company, living a life of faith on earth and in heaven after their physical deaths. That comprised the cloud of witnesses mentioned in Hebrews 12.

Without diminishing the natural aspect of a cloud in Jesus' ascension and return, we might conclude that this spiritual cloud of witnesses, the Church, is indeed the cloud being referenced. It is interesting that at Jesus' ascension, it says He was received into a cloud (singular). At His return and after a period of grace on the earth, the Revelation says, *"he cometh with clouds"* (plural). The implication is that the size and number of that original cloud into which He was received had increased. Paul even tells the skeptical Thessalonians that, at the coming of Jesus, "we which are alive and remain shall be caught up together with them in the clouds" (1 Thess. 4:17).

To be sure, the symbolism of this cloud theme revolves around the Church. Jesus was received into the cloud to be in its midst (Rev. 2:1). He will also return with it, *"Behold, he cometh with clouds."*

The text continues, *"And every eye shall see him, and they also which pierced him: and all kindreds of the earth shall wail because of him. Even so, Amen."* Many authors have struggled to explain how all of this will happen. It is difficult to imagine every eye seeing Jesus at the same time. Some say it will be by television. Others say that he will position himself at one point in the sky for everyone on the earth to see as the earth rotates on its axis. I have a difficult time accepting either theory or ones like them.

The coming of Jesus at the appointed time will mark the end of all unrighteousness. Judgment will be carried out to complete the plan of God. The ungodly and rebellious will be cast into eternal destruction (2 Thess. 1:7-10). Those who are righteous in Christ will be rewarded for their faith. At this time of judgment, *"every eye shall see him."* God will allow everyone to see the One through whom salvation was so freely offered.

The Church will see Him. This group of people had the least trouble seeing Him in the first place. But even those saints who did have difficulty seeing Jesus will then behold Him. Heb. 9:28 is an interesting verse at this point, because it says, "Unto them that look for him shall he appear the second time without sin unto salvation." The mystery of all the ages will finally be revealed in His Church (see Col. 1:26-27).

Those that couldn't see Jesus, because they willed not to, will see Him then. Of particular mention are those that *"pierced him."* At first glance we might think that the reference is only to the Judaizers who rejected Jesus and crucified Him outside the city walls of Jerusalem, finalized with the piercing of a sword through His side. Jesus did come to the nation of Israel, and it rejected Him (John 1:11). It was this people who had not the eyes to see Him. In their midst, Jesus constantly sought those with eyes to see and ears to hear. But few would come. At His return, they will see Him.

We must not think, however, that the Judaizers were the only ones that refused to see Jesus and did, in fact, "pierce him." Scripture tells us that any who reject and walk away from Jesus "crucify to themselves the Son of God afresh, and put him to an open shame" (Heb. 6:6).

These also, as many as fit into this category, will see Jesus on that final day.

"All kindreds of the earth shall wail because of him." Why? Because they could have received Jesus and did not. They could have inherited the riches of the kingdom but will not. They could have spent eternity in the presence of God but will not. Instead, they will spend an eternity in a furnace of fire, in outer darkness where "there shall be wailing and gnashing of teeth" (Matt. 13:42). All of this could have been avoided if they had been willing to see Jesus. Now they see Him as a reminder of what they could have had.

We can rejoice as Christians that we will be a part of those who will spend eternity with Jesus Christ, who choose to see Jesus even now. He is Lord of all and can be seen "in the Spirit." He is alive now and for evermore. He lives in the midst of His Church and is available to those who have the eyes to see and the ears to hear by faith.

Proclamations of God's Majesty (1:8)

This passage (1:4-8), which indicates a message being sent to God's Church, represented in the seven churches of Asia, ends with God's majesty being proclaimed, *"I am Alpha and Omega, the beginning and the ending, saith the Lord, which is, and which was, and which is to come, the Almighty"* (1:8). This is the Lord speaking, and in it you can see Jesus.

Some of these very ascriptions will be seen representing Jesus when we examine the seven letters to the seven churches and as we see the rest of the Revelation. The Lord in Jesus Christ is the Alpha and Omega, the A to Z of all things. He is the Beginning (John 1:1) and the ending (Rev. 22:13). He is and was and is to come, the past, present and future. He is the Almighty.

We can see Him now if we seek Him. God says He is "a rewarder of them that diligently seek him" (Heb. 11:6).

21

To those He will reveal himself, as He did to Paul (cf. Gal. 1:15-16) and to John.

3
More of Jesus
(1:9-20)

The concluding remarks of the introductory passage, indicated in our Bibles as chapter 1 of the Revelation, contain what we might expect of a book which reveals Jesus—more of Jesus. Once again it unveils Him in the midst of His Church. He is seen there not just in the future. Neither is the focus on the past. He is seen in the midst of the Church past, present and future, as represented by the seven churches in Asia. The language to describe all of this becomes more symbolic at this point but not without explanation. Let's first examine John's situation when he received this great vision.

A Companion in Tribulation (1:9)

"I John, who also am your brother, and companion in tribulation, and in the kingdom and patience of Jesus Christ, was in the isle that is called Patmos, for the word of God, and for the testimony of Jesus Christ" (1:9). John was not on the isle of Patmos for the church Sunday school picnic. He did not go there specifically to write the book of the Revelation. He had not chosen Patmos as a place to see the sights. John was imprisoned there.

Patmos is a small, lonely little island in the Aegean Sea off the southwest coast of Asia Minor, which was used by the Roman government for what they considered to be the worst criminals. John's "crime" was not murder, theft, rape or any other civil one. He was a political prisoner of Rome, incarcerated because of his love for Jesus and his boldness to proclaim Him openly.

He lists the reasons the Roman government imprisoned

him there. The first was *"for the word of God."* This statement adds weight to the theory that this John was the Gospel writer and the author of the Epistles. He had proclaimed *"the word of God"* in written communication and by word of mouth. If this was the Gospel writer, many had read his account of the Word of God and had been influenced or even converted to Christianity as a result. As Christianity was viewed as a threat to the security of the Roman empire, it is easy to see how John could have become high on the list of public enemies and been carted away to Patmos to silence his proclamation of the Word of God.

But he was not only there for the Word of God, whether written or spoken. He was there *"for the testimony of Jesus Christ."* He had been testifying as a witness (Acts 1:8) to the change Jesus Christ had brought about in his life. He was testifying that Jesus is Lord. That might possibly have had greater influence than the written Word. To be sure, he was a prisoner of Rome because he dared to share his faith to the world.

He declares himself as a *"brother"* (probably meaning a brother in Christ) and a *"companion in tribulation."* He was in tribulation. The conditions and treatment at this colony on Patmos were probably difficult to endure. The same kinds of punishment and ill-treatment given to Jesus were most likely dished out to the political prisoners of that day as well. The Roman soldiers probably treated the Christians worst of all as they had caused them extra guard duty and responsibility. John's tribulation, as he was isolated from the rest of the body of Christ and treated like a common criminal, was real. He knew what it meant to take up his cross and follow Jesus.

But John said he was a *"companion"* in tribulation. That meant there must have been many others, not necessarily confined to Patmos, who were in tribulation for the Word of God and the testimony of Jesus. This raises some very important issues with respect to our understanding of the Revelation.

To begin with, the Church since the day of Pentecost has been in tribulation. Many commentators of the Revelation have emphasized only a futuristic aspect of the *"great tribulation"* mentioned in Rev. 7:14. The implication has been that only in the "end times" will the tribulation of Christians be "great." But is this really so?

Jesus said to the disciples, "In the world ye shall have tribulation: but be of good cheer; I have overcome the world" (John 16:33). Jesus said that tribulation was going to exist for them in the world. He also said, "I have chosen you out of the world, therefore the world hateth you" (John 15:19). It was inevitable. It was going to happen. It would probably take the form of verbal abuse, scorn, mocking, harassment, punishment, imprisonment and even death. Disciples of Jesus could expect any and all of these forms of tribulation (or persecution, if you will) to take place in their lives.

During the Sermon on the Mount discourse, Jesus told the vast crowd, "Blessed are ye, when men shall revile you, and persecute you, and shall say all manner of evil against you falsely, for my sake. Rejoice, and be exceeding glad: for great is your reward in heaven: for so persecuted they the prophets which were before you" (Matt. 5:11-12). He wasn't addressing that to just the end-time Christians. He was speaking to all who would follow Him, every disciple that would ever be.

Jesus was constantly preparing His followers to expect tribulation and persecution. History proves that Jesus' words were not idle. Countless Christians in the first centuries of the church were subjected to "great" tribulation, including death. For those Christians, there could be no greater tribulation than death. Nor were they the only ones to die for their faith. *Foxe's Book of Martyrs,*[1]

---

[1]John Foxe, *Foxe's Book of Martyrs*, written in the sixteenth century, now available in many editions.

one of the most comprehensive works ever done on the subject, relates the gory details of Christians being persecuted, tormented and being put to death for their faith down through the centuries in the life of the Church. There has always been and will always be tribulation for the saints of God who hold fast the testimony of Jesus Christ.

The idea that the "great tribulation" is strictly an end-times event is hard to conceive when you carefully weigh all the facts. There may be a time yet to come when the tribulation will increase for the Christians of the world. Indeed, it will surely increase whenever we get on fire for Jesus and are not ashamed to testify in His behalf. But tribulation is not limited to the future. Remember that the Revelation covers past, present and future. Tribulation will cover all three of those time frames until the day comes when all things are consummated in Christ Jesus and all evil has been purged.

The second misconception concerning tribulation in the book of the Revelation is that God will rapture or "snatch away" His Church out of the world before tribulation comes to the earth. This is an idea or theory which presupposes much, especially that the saints of God will not be able to endure it.

We have already seen that tribulation has been a fact in the life of the Church. There has been much tribulation in its history, and there will probably be much more. But the children of God have always been allowed to go through the tribulation, trials and tests of this life, to strengthen them in their faith. Biblical patterns show that God has always delivered them in the midst of their troubles.

The most striking scriptural example is God delivering the Israelites from the oppression of Egypt and placing them in the land of Canaan. The mighty hand of God came down hard on Egypt, because they would not release their evil grip on God's people. Ten plagues, most gruesome and just as terrible as the judgments mentioned in the Revelation, were placed on Egypt while the Israelites dwelt there in the land. God did not rapture His children while this judgment was being passed. He protected them and took them through it, even to the point of being spared from the very angel of death by the blood on the doorposts of their homes.

When they finally got to Canaan, the Israelites had to constantly engage the giants and enemies of the land who dwelt there and opposed their presence. They met a hostile welcoming committee that God repeatedly took out of their way. But He did not have to remove His children. He removed the enemy, the unrighteous.

This story is used frequently, as it should be, to parallel the work of Christ and the Church. The Church, as we'll see in chapter 4, is now the Israel of God. God will continue to provide, as He did in Egypt, for Israel, the household of faith, the Church of Jesus Christ. The judgment of the end times are not way out in the future. The earthquakes and disasters mentioned in the Revelation have been taking place and will probably increase in number. The kinds of judgments presented in the Revelation will, without doubt, come upon this earth. But God will keep His children. He doesn't have to remove them. In fact, He will probably remove the unrighteous and not the Church (cf. Isa. 13:9; Matt. 13:41-43).

God looks at the blood of Jesus Christ, covering us from harm, as He did the doorposts covered with blood in Egypt. He will protect us from the giants and enemies that oppose us as we walk the highway of faith.[2] But He doesn't have to remove us from the earth to do it. He will take us through it.

The word rapture exists nowhere in the Scriptures. It

[2]John Bunyan, *The Pilgrim's Progress* written in the seventeenth century, now available in many editions.

27

is a doctrine that was conceived in the nineteenth century[3] and propagated by those to whom it appealed. The Word is full of pattern and proof that God keeps His children through all tribulation.

Rapture doctrine is built principally upon 1 Thess. 4:13-18. Other Scriptures, such as 1 Cor. 15:52, are used as supporting material, but the passage to the Thessalonians is used the most. Verse 17 of that passage says, "Then we which are alive and remain shall be caught up together with them in the clouds, to meet the Lord in the air: and so shall we ever be with the Lord."

Make no mistake. God will translate the remaining saints into the complete spiritual realm at the coming or appearing of Jesus. The earthly creation which remains at His coming will be changed to match the spiritual nature of those already physically dead but with the Lord, clothed in their spiritual bodies. But that does not mean that God will remove them from tribulation, even the "great tribulation." He is going to take them through it.

John the Revelator was up to his chin in tribulation. Was he raptured? No! Polycarp, the great Christian of the first and second centuries, endured tremendous tribulation, to the point of death.[4] Was he raptured? No! The list of saints who found themselves in tribulation goes on and on, with none of them ever getting raptured. They endured the cross even to the death. Even in death, they were overcomers in Christ Jesus.

Tribulation is not just future. It is a normal part of the Christian's walk. Likewise, God will keep His children in the midst of their greatest troubles.

---

[3]Dave MacPherson, *Why I Believe the Church Will Pass Through the Tribulation* (Greenville, S.C.: Jewel Books, 1971), p. 8.
[4]John Foxe, *Foxe's Book of Martyrs* (New York: Pyramid Publications, Inc. 1968), p. 17ff.

Jesus in the Midst of the Church (1:10-20)

This chapter started out to show more of Jesus. We have looked at what the Scriptures say about tribulation, as that subject will again arise in later chapters. We now press on to see more of Jesus. John goes on to say, *"I was in the Spirit on the Lord's day"* (1:10). I believe this means Sunday, or the first day of the week. Much of the Christian community by the time of the Revelation had discontinued their sabbath observance of the Old Covenant and had met regularly on the first day of the week in celebration of Jesus' resurrection (John 20:1-10; Acts 20:7). That day was by now called the Lord's day.

John says that he was *"in the Spirit."* God did not physically take John away from Patmos but gave him the vision in the spiritual realm. Most likely he was worshiping God or communing with Him at the time. We, today, can be "in the Spirit," or "walking in the Spirit" (Gal. 5:16), as John was that day, by communing with God in worship and praise. We have already seen that, through Jesus, the way has been made for us to enter into the very presence of God. We don't have to be carried bodily into heaven for that to occur. Our experience of God's presence is a spiritual matter, a privilege of our heavenly citizenship and position in Christ Jesus (Eph. 2:4-6). God will reveal Jesus to us as we're "in the Spirit" and seeking "those things which are above" (Col. 3:1).

Notice that the first event in the vision did not consist of anything that John saw. The first thing that occurred was that John heard *"a great voice, as of a trumpet."* He did not say he heard a trumpet. He says that he heard a great voice that sounded like a trumpet. It must have been crisp and clear as that sound that only a trumpet can make.

The voice was surely that of God, identified as *"Alpha and Omega, the first and the last"* (1:11), terms with which we have become familiar. And though the Godhead is implied, we'll see that John saw Jesus when he looked (1:12).

The writer to the Hebrews explicitly identifies Jesus as the one through whom God has spoken in these last days (1:1-2). Before sending His Son, God had utilized many different kinds of messengers and vessels to proclaim His will, including angels, prophets and other chosen people of faith. Now Jesus would be that vessel. Through Him God would communciate with mankind.

Jesus is the Word of God made flesh. When we look upon him and "read" that Word "in the Spirit," we are instructed in God's will, seeing the absolute obedience He had toward the Father. In fact, saints who abide in Christ Jesus and His righteousness also reveal God's Word. This is confirmed by Paul to the Corinthians when he says that they were an "epistle [letter] written in our hearts, known and read of all men" (2 Cor. 3:2-3).

The Revelation now shows us another dimension through which God has chosen to reveal Jesus in these last days, the sound of His voice in our spirits. He speaks to us God's will. The instrument to which Jesus' voice is likened is a trumpet. Not only can He be seen, He can also be heard with clarity and distinction with the sound which comes from a trumpet.

Perhaps the trumpets which are sounded in Revelation 8-11 are actually the voice of Jesus proclaiming the love and judgment of God to all who will listen. We are examining a book written in signs and symbols. What better symbol could be used to represent the voice of Jesus speaking to the world, loudly and clearly, than that of a trumpet?

The whole key to seeing Jesus and hearing what He has to say comes down to this: do we have the eyes to see or the ears to hear? Jesus said to the perplexed multitude who had experienced the miracle of the bread and fishes, "Having eyes, see ye not? and having ears, hear ye not?"

(Mark 8:18). The same kind of challenge is issued forth in the Revelation, *"He that hath an ear, let him hear what the Spirit saith to the churches"* (2:7, 11, 17, 29; 3:6, 13, 22; 13:9). We must not only have our spiritual eyes open to Jesus but our ears open as well, perceiving spiritual truths as He trumpets it for all the world to hear. These spiritual senses are only activated if we truly seek after God. He will then reveal Jesus to us by sight and sound.

When John now *"turned to see the voice that spake,"* he *"saw seven golden candlesticks; And in the midst of the seven candlesticks one like unto the Son of man"* (verses 12-13). What John had heard and now saw was Jesus in the midst of the Church. An elaborate description of Jesus follows. We will examine this after we notice the seven stars in the hand of Jesus.

There can be no confusion about this symbolism, because Jesus explains to John what he is seeing. *"The mystery of the seven stars which thou sawest in my right hand, and the seven golden candlesticks. The seven stars are the angels of the seven churches: and the seven candlesticks which thou sawest are the seven churches"* (1:20).

The seven churches represent the whole Church. The seven candlesticks are symbolic of the Church holding the "light of the world." Actually, the original Greek more accurately denotes "lampstands," which would be indicative of a light holder fueled by oil. The Church is the light holder, or "lampstand," that shines forth the light of Jesus through the Holy Spirit, which is biblically synonymous with anointing or oil. Jesus is the Light. The Church is the holder of that Light. A candle would consume itself, but the light of Jesus will never go out.

Jesus stands in the middle of that Church yesterday, today and forever, giving it light. He loves it and is close to it. He speaks to it by His voice, shown here as seven stars, seven angels relaying the trumpet voice of Christ the Savior. That is what John saw.

The description we receive concerning Jesus shows us more of Jesus in a very colorful and imaginative way. It says He was *"clothed with a garment down to the foot, and girt about the paps with a golden girdle"* (1:13). His dress possibly reveals His functions as a priest and as a judge. That kind of dress would be appropriate in either capacity. He indeed was the instrument of judging sin at the cross of Calvary (Col. 2:13-15) and is, without a doubt, our High Priest in the area of redemption (Heb. 9:11-12) and intercession (Heb. 7:22-28). The golden girdle about his breast, or chest area, is significant of the fact that he was "tried by fire," purified like gold through obedience unto death, whereby He alone can be granted the authority as High Priest and Judge.

"His head and his hairs were white like wool, as white as snow; and his eyes were as a flame of fire" (1:14). The color white associated with Jesus' head and hair is suggestive of intense purity, without spot or blemish. A virgin bride usually wears white to signify her innocence and purity. The Bride of Jesus, for which He will return, will be white as snow, without spot or blemish in Him. His eyes were as a flame of fire but were not actually fire. John saw Jesus' look as penetrating and intense, seeing and perceiving all things, reflective of God's omniscience (all-knowing quality). This vision of the appearance of Jesus corresponds perfectly with the one Daniel had as recorded in Dan. 10:5-6.

"And his feet like unto fine brass, as if they burned in a furnace; and his voice as the sound of many waters" (1:15). Scripturally, brass speaks of strength and judgment, particularly when described as burned in a furnace (refined). These brass feet of Jesus represent a strong-standing Jesus bringing forth judgment. Theodore Epp points out that a "contrast to this is a portion of Romans 3 which tells us that the feet of men, that is natural men, 'are swift to shed blood: Destruction and misery are in

their ways' (vv. 15, 16)."[5]

His voice now described as the sound of many waters is not contradictory to the trumpet sound. It compliments that description by suggesting it was loud, dominant and overwhelming, as the roar of not just one but many waters (seas). Later in the Revelation, water is representative of *"peoples, and multitudes, and nations, and tongues"* (Rev. 17:15). In other words, the voice of Jesus could be viewed as speaking for and to all the people and nations of the world.

As previously noted, Jesus had seven stars in his right hand, which represent the seven angels used as message bearers to the churches of Asia, or the Church of all time. Please note the significance of a star representing an angel. We will see this symbolism used again in later chapters of the Revelation.

"And out of his mouth went a sharp twoedged sword" (1:16). This can mean only one thing—the Word of God. Heb. 4:12 confirms this by saying, "The word of God is quick, and powerful, and sharper than any twoedged sword, piercing even to the dividing asunder of soul and spirit, and of the joints and marrow, and is a discerner of the thoughts and intents of the heart." That is the work of this symbolic sword. It is not a real sword but one of words—the Word of God—seen again proceeding from the mouth of Jesus at His appearing (Rev. 19:15ff.; cf. Eph. 6:17).

"And his countenance was as the sun shineth in his strength" (1:16). This again portrays Jesus as the Light that shines on the world. Seen here in the midst of the

[5]Theodore H. Epp, *Practical Studies in Revelation*, vol. 1 (Lincoln, Neb.: Back to the Bible Broadcast, 1969), p. 56. Copyrighted material used by permission. (Note: There is much of Epp's work with which I do not agree. He is extremely futuristic and rigidly literal at places where the symbolism of the apocalypse should shine through. Nevertheless, I quote Epp here and in other places because he does have good insight with respect to some of the Revelation text.)

Church, he is the Light that illuminates every member of the Body. In the presence of Jesus, there is no need for other sources of light. He is truly the Son (Sun) of God (2 Cor. 4:6).

John must have been completely overwhelmed as he saw this vision of Jesus. He records, *"I fell at his feet as dead. And he laid his right hand upon me, saying unto me, Fear not: I am the first and the last: I am . . . alive for evermore. Amen; and have the keys of hell and of death"* (1:17-18).

Even in this brief encounter with John, more of the nature of Jesus is revealed. He is the One who calms our fears. He is completely identified with God who is love. "Perfect love casteth out fear" (1 John 4:18). Jesus reveals His love, in the midst of His majesty, to John. We are not to fear in the presence of Jesus. We are to be glad and joyous, freely expressing our praise to Him. Jesus is identified further with God as *"the first and the last,"* terminology synonymous with that used in verse 8 to describe the Father, *"the beginning and the ending."*

Jesus' resurrection and subsequent eternal life is mentioned, *"I am he that liveth, and was dead; and, behold, I am alive for evermore, Amen."* When we see Jesus, we must see Him as raised from the dead, having conquered death and now living forever at the right hand of God. When we completely identify ourselves with Jesus and abide in Him, we will see that He has "raised us up together, and made us sit together in heavenly places in Christ Jesus" (Eph. 2:6). The nature of Jesus and all that He has inherited belong to the Church (Rom. 8:16-17). We must not only see Jesus in the midst of the Church but ourselves in Him and He in us.

Jesus states also that He has *"the keys of hell and of death"* (1:18). These are probably on the same key chain with those of the kingdom (Matt. 16:19) and reveal the total authority that God has given Jesus Christ, His Son.

Jesus has been given control, through these symbolic keys, of our entrance to either life eternal (keys of the kingdom) or eternal destruction (keys of hell and death). In Jesus rests the authority to secure the locks of either that we choose. We can choose the kingdom or we can choose hell and death.

The remaining verses of Revelation 1 have already been covered. Verse 19 indicates the great time span to which the Revelation applies—past, present and future. In verse 20, Jesus tells John the meaning of the seven stars (angels) and the seven candlesticks or lampstands (the Church).

We have taken three chapters to explain the first chapter of the Revelation, because chapter 1 is so foundational. The principles and truths that we have uncovered here will carry throughout our examination of the remainder of the book. As we have laid the foundation of understanding here, less will be said when we find these principles and truths in subsequent chapters.

The next section of the Revelation to be examined contains the letters to the seven churches of Asia. But before we begin this section, we must first take a scriptural look at what the Church is.

4

The Household of Faith

So far we have seen that the emphasis of the Revelation is Jesus Christ. However, a secondary emphasis shows Jesus in the midst of the Church, often depicted in Scripture as the Body, or as the Bride of the Lamb. Since the rest of the Revelation will continue to reveal those themes, it is imperative, before we continue, that we understand the origin of the Church and who comprises it.

A most misunderstood facet of the Church is its identification as the Israel of the Bible. If we are ever to realize the blessing of the Revelation, we must understand that very point. So much of the text of the message is explicitly directed to Israel, or obviously implies Israel, and speaks of her in the sense of past, present and future.

The problem that Christians and students of the Bible are confronted with is that of seeing Israel as both a nation and the Church. The tendency has often been to see an Israel of the Old Testament (the nation or more precisely, the true believers within the nation, called "the remnant"—Rom. 9:6, 27; 11:5) and an Israel of the New Testament (the Church) as two separate entities, when actually they are one and the same (Rom. 11:17). Israel, as we'll see in this chapter, is a continuous line of people who love and serve God, having been chosen by God in His mercy and grace.

The word *Israel* in the Hebrew is a combination of two words which mean "he who rules with God." It is also the symbolic name given to Jacob and used typically to denote his posterity, all who would follow after God in faith. Israel is what I call "the household of faith." She will rule with God. She is comprised of people who walk in faith, chosen by God without respect to their nation, color, creed or any other qualification. "God is no respecter of persons" (Acts 10:34).

Israel actually begins with Abraham and continues in the line of Isaac, Jacob (Israel) and their seed—not the physical or natural seed of reproduction but a spiritual seed of faith. From Abraham's time forward the household of faith has been growing. Let's look at the Scriptures to see how all of this has developed.

A God of Covenants

To get the complete picture, we must go all the way back to Adam and Eve, back to the very beginning. God created them to have communion and fellowship with Him. The life that He breathed into them was eternal in nature. Scripture indicates that mankind was created as an immortal society. Mankind was a perfect creation of God, with whom He intended to maintain an intimate relationship.

Just as God had created mankind to be immortal, He also gave them a will. God wanted man to choose Him. He did not create robots who would praise and serve Him involuntarily. He wanted an obedient people who would praise and serve Him for who He is, making the step toward God on their own and not by force.

Unfortunately, it was in that free will that the separation between God and man began. We are all familiar with the plight of Adam and Eve. God had given them instructions and they did not obey. He had sought from them an obedience and love that would honor the Creator. They willed not to obey God. The origin of sin was theirs. The perfect creation became defiled in that it rejected its Creator's will. As a consequence, man spiritually died at that point, becoming subject to physical and eternal death.

God, who is holy and pure, could not allow sin to go unpunished in a universe so properly ordered and disciplined by His laws. Death was the punishment handed down. God did not love mankind any less. In fact, we all know that His great love eventually brought forth Jesus, the Savior. As a matter of fact, at the point of Adam and Eve's fall, God began the process of reconciling mankind to himself, as He clothed their nakedness with animal skins and promised them a Redeemer (Gen. 3:15, 21). The redemptive process that was culminated in the obedience of Jesus Christ at Calvary actually began thousands of years before.

God guaranteed His promise to Adam by establishing a covenant with mankind. A covenant is a contract. Viewed in today's terms, it was a legal document or agreement between God and man. The vessel with whom God chose to establish the contract was Abraham.

Genesis 17 records the event. One key sentence says, "I will establish my covenant between me and thee and thy seed after thee in their generations for an everlasting covenant, to be a God unto thee, and to thy seed after thee" (verse 7). Another says, "And ye shall circumcise the flesh of your foreskin; and it shall be a token of the covenant betwixt me and you" (verse 11).

The critical word is "everlasting." It was not going to be a short-term covenant. There would be no termination date. When you enter into a contract to buy a home, you usually agree to a price, a down payment and a date at which the contract is null and void if financing or other contingencies of the contract are not met. The contract has definite time boundaries. The covenant God presented to Abraham is everlasting, one which would never come to an end.

One might interject at this point that the Bible is clearly delineated by two covenants—an old and a new—represented by the Old Testament (or covenant) and the New

Testament respectively. The old covenant is that which was established at Mount Sinai when Moses was given the law on two tablets of stone, expressing God's intention for His children at that time (Exod. 19:1ff.). A better title for the Old Covenant would be the "law." Indeed that was what Moses brought down from the mount. The New Covenant, of course, is that which is established through Jesus Christ. The second covenant could be identified as one of "grace."

Neither the Old Covenant of law nor the New Covenant of grace is contradictory to the everlasting covenant God established with Abraham as recorded in Genesis 17. Although the covenant of grace replaced the covenant of the law, both were used by God as a method of carrying forth the everlasting covenant established with Abraham.

Hebrews 8 sheds some light on this matter. The writer to the Hebrews says, in essence, that the first covenant had faults and necessitated a second or better covenant, which would be mediated by Jesus. God did not institute a faulty covenant. The fault with the first covenant (or method) was man's inability to keep it. Paul confirms this when he tells the Romans that the law or first covenant served only to bring a "knowledge of sin" (Rom. 3:20). The covenant that was replaced was not the covenant of faith made with Abraham but the covenant of the "law" made through Moses. God used the law to show man his need for grace, which would be given in Jesus Christ. The salvation in Jesus comes by the same kind of faith exhibited in Abraham, the father of faith.

The second covenant, or that of grace, replaced the law. Hebrews instructs us that in this new covenant or method of the Eternal One, God would put the law on man's mind and heart. He would be a God to them and they would be His people. In this second covenant God says, "Their sins and their iniquities will I remember no more" (Heb. 8:13). He remembered them under the law, because the law highlighted the sin. In the second covenant, He forgets them, because they have been eradicated by the blood of Jesus. Both of these methods served the plan of God and supported the everlasting covenant of faith through Abraham.

Abraham's character as a man of faith was evidenced when he trusted God by offering to sacrifice his only Son in Moriah (Genesis 22). Knowing that God had promised to bless Abraham and multiply his seed after him and cause multitudes to be raised up through him, he trusted God in obedience by binding Isaac to the altar and raising the knife to slay him. God of course intervened and provided a sacrifice, as He would do with Jesus.

It is through faith that God has dealt with man. The ultimate faith would come in accepting Jesus Christ as Lord and Savior, in obedience and faith like that of Abraham. The reconciliation instituted first through Abraham and continued with the covenant of law at Mount Sinai would be culminated with the work of the cross, representative of the second covenant. They all contributed in bringing mankind to God by faith in His Son.

There is but one faith covenant. It is made up of sub-contracts, or covenant phases, if you will. Neither of these phases nullified the overall, everlasting covenant of God. We can see from this that God never intended to build two camps of followers, one called the nation of Israel (Old Covenant) and another the Church of Jesus Christ or spiritual Israel (New Covenant). Through both covenants it was His desire to raise up one camp of followers who would walk by faith. All believers comprise "the household of faith."

Believers within Israel the nation have been mistakenly separated from Israel the Church, when, in fact, they are members of the same spiritual Israel. Paul says that followers of God in faith outside the initial elect group of Judaizers (the nation of Israel) are "grafted in among them" to make one tree (the Church), with every branch drawing its nourishment and its vitality from the root, Jesus Christ (Rom. 11:17).

God is not divisive. He continues to work unity in all who would follow the path of righteousness. God has revealed that He is building one house (household) not made with hands, and comprised of those who accept Him in faith through Jesus Christ. That house, of which Jesus Christ is the cornerstone, is Israel.

The Seed of Abraham

The apostle Paul in his letter to the Romans explains these biblical principles concerning Israel and the everlasting covenant. Romans 4 should be read and compared to Genesis 17 where the initial covenant was established through Abraham.

Paul was a Jew by birth, and yet he perceived the spiritual truth concerning Israel. He wanted to see the people of his flesh saved by accepting Jesus Christ. He reveals the truth concerning the seed of Abraham and who would inherit the promises of God.

Genesis 17 has shown us that the covenant was given to Abraham and his seed who would follow after him through the generations. That "seed" was not simply those born of the flesh in the family of Abraham. Paul, though being of that Hebrew flesh, saw in the Spirit concerning that seed that it was not of the flesh.

Paul says, "For the promise, that he [Abraham] should be the heir of the world, was not to Abraham, or to his seed, through the law [or the receivers of the law, the Hebrew people alone], but through the righteousness of faith. For if they which are of the law be heirs, faith is made void, and the promise made of none effect: Because the law worketh wrath: for where no law is, there is no transgression. Therefore it is of faith, that it might be by grace; to the end the promise [the initial Abrahamic covenant] might be sure to all the seed; not to that only which is of the law, but to that also which is of the faith of Abraham; who is the father of us all" (Rom. 4:13-16).

The seed God referred to in Genesis 17 is revealed here in Romans 4. God was speaking of a people who walk in faith, particularly in the acceptance of Jesus Christ as Lord and Savior. The majority of the nation of Israel did not do this. John the Gospel writer says, "He came unto his own [Israel the nation], and his own received him not. But as many as received him, to them [people of faith] gave he the power to become the sons of God, even to them that believe on his name: Which were born, not of blood, nor of the will of the flesh, nor of the will of man, but of God" (John 1:11-13).

Paul crystalizes this by adding, "They which are the children of the flesh, these are not the children of God: but the children of the promise are counted for the seed" (Rom. 9:8).

The household of faith is comprised of all people who are born of the Spirit. "There is neither Jew nor Greek, there is neither bond nor free, there is neither male nor female: for ye are all one in Christ Jesus. And if ye be Christ's, then are ye Abraham's seed, and heirs according to the promise" (Gal. 3:28-29). God does not specially favor the nation of Israel. He favors spiritual Israel, the household of faith, within which there is no racial favoritism. God loves everyone equally in the Church of Jesus Christ and bestows His favor in abundance to all who are the seed of Abraham in faith.

All of the Scriptures which point to the future blessings of God on Israel refer to a larger body of people than that of national Israel (e.g., Ps. 115:12; Isa. 45:17; Joel 2:27). They refer to the faithful servants of God who come to Him in faith.

Revelation 12:17 says that Satan *"went to make war*

with the remnant of her seed, which keep the command-
ments of God, and have the testimony of Jesus Christ."
Note that the seed is described as those who *"keep the*
commandments of God and have the testimony of Jesus
Christ." Have the Jewish people of national Israel done
that? Not only have they rejected Jesus but they have
not kept the commandments of God. According to the
Scriptures, God is going to honor and favor the seed of
Abraham by faith, not by flesh.

The Use of Prefiguring

In order to understand the Church of Jesus Christ,
we must realize that God used the symbolism of the Old
Covenant to show what He was leading up to in Christ
Jesus. This technique is what I call prefiguring.

As I pondered the events of the Old Testament as a
young Christian, I had to ask myself the question, "Did
God fail in His attempt to raise up a chosen people of His
own in the nation of Israel?" It would seem that way on
the surface, considering that God had to allow the Israelites to be carried away into exile, only to return to their
land and never again be a victorious nation. But God did
not fail in His dealings with Israel. The people failed in
their attempt to live by the law.

God actually succeeded in accomplishing much through
the nation of Israel. He proved to the world that a Savior
was needed. Their weakness in obedience paved the way
for the Messiah to come and redeem a sinful world. That
Messiah, Jesus Christ, was born of Jewish descent, yet
was conceived by the Holy Spirit. In Him would the victorious Israel blossom forth.

God surely had this in His redemption plan from the
very beginning. The all-knowing God of the universe saw
a plan that would cause all people to be reconciled to
himself. Those people, should they choose God by accepting Jesus as Savior and Lord, would become part of a vast

43

multitude of saints who would be one with God, His very intention before man's sinful fall. What He accomplished in the nation of Israel was to prepare for the coming of Jesus upon this earth and to reveal the principles of the Church which would follow Jesus' death, resurrection and ascension. This was prefiguring. Jesus was the figure or focal point of the plan.

Other more biblical terms for prefiguring might be "example" or "shadow," as found in Heb. 8:4-5, "For if he were on earth, he should not be a priest, seeing that there are priests that offer gifts according to the law: Who serve unto the example and shadow of heavenly things." The priests of the tabernacle and temple in the Old Covenant were a shadow of our high priest, Jesus Christ, the substance that cast the shadow. Other good Scriptures that clarify the meaning of biblical "examples" are found in 1 Cor. 10:6-11 and Rom. 15:4.

A shadow is not the real thing. It is merely an image that is projected because of the real object. Your shadow cast upon the pavement as you walk in the sunlight is but a shape that has two dimensions. It has no substance and cannot be touched. But you are real, a three-dimensional being that causes the shadow to have form and to give anyone who sees it an idea or picture of what you look like.

Images produced in a shadow box are good examples. Someone with talent twists and contorts his fingers, hands and arms in all sorts of manners to produce images of animals on a light screen. The images produce the picture in our minds of what the creator is projecting. The images are not real, but the fingers, hands and arms that produce them are. So it is with Christ and the Church. The various aspects of the life of Israel the nation were but a shadow or image of the true household of faith, the Church. National Israel was used by God as an earthly shadow for heavenly things (Heb. 9:9; 10:1). That's what prefiguring is all about.

The depth of detail that God used in this prefiguring process is remarkable. Every last detail of the Old Testament in some way foretold a detail in the New Testament. The list is endless, and an entire volume could be dedicated to nothing but the description of the Old in relation to the New. We will give a few examples to illustrate the point here in hopes that it will create a desire in the reader to study the Scriptures for more detail and see just how God was setting up for the heavenly kingdom rule of Jesus Christ and His Church.

The tabernacle in the wilderness and later, in a more permanent fashion, the temple at Jerusalem were used to prefigure the ministry of Jesus Christ and the dwelling place of God.[1] That's the very reason so many details of the tabernacle are given in Exodus 25-31. God was using the tabernacle in the wilderness, fashioned in detail with human hands, as a shadow of the true tabernacle in the heavenly places fashioned in detail by God.

Of particular significance in the tabernacle and the temple was the Holy of Holies, the area in which God chose to dwell. The glory of God rested upon that place. As we have observed earlier, only the high priest could enter that room once a year. The Holy of Holies was prefiguring the heavenly tabernacle or abiding place of God. Jesus entered into the heavenly abiding place of God (Heb. 9:24) and appeared before God "to put away sin by the sacrifice of himself" (Heb. 9:26). Because of Jesus' sacrifice, we now have the right or privilege, through Jesus, to enter into the Holy of Holies in the heavenly places. The earthly tabernacle made with hands was the shadow, but the heavenly tabernacle or abiding place of God was the real thing. And through Jesus, we can now

---

[1] Two good volumes on this subject are B. Maureen Gaglardi, *The Path of the Just* (Burnaby, B.C., Canada: New West Press, 1963) and C.W. Slemming, *Made According to the Pattern* (London, England: Henry E. Walter, Ltd., 1938).

experience the real thing. "Having therefore, brethren, boldness to enter into the holiest by the blood of Jesus . . . Let us draw near" (Heb. 10:19, 22).

Understanding our position in the heavens is important, because in subsequent chapters of the Revelation we'll see a multitude of people before the throne of God, singing and praising Him. This worship is not just in the future or after a "rapture" while judgment is taking place on the earth. It is present as well as future, a worship by the saints of all time in the very presence of God through the Holy Spirit. Through that Spirit, we are continually in the heavenly places if we're in Christ Jesus. Paul indicates that truth in Eph. 2:6.

We indeed can worship God in the heavenly places now. Jesus said to the Samaritan woman at the well, "God is a Spirit: and they that worship him must worship him in spirit and in truth" (John 4:24). God cannot be really worshiped any other way. There is no need to interpret the worship scenes of Revelation as representing Christians worshiping God in the future in heaven, when they can do so now in spirit and in truth.

That's really what much of the Revelation is revealing. It is not showing a rekindled spark of the Old Covenant, with the nation of Israel getting special treatment. It is showing spiritual Israel, the Church of Jesus Christ, the household of faith in God's presence, "under the shadow of the Almighty" (Ps. 91:1). To try and understand the Revelation any other way causes frustration in justifying all the physical elements of the events which are related. National Israel always had God moving in their midst. But they prefigured spiritual Israel with God moving in her midst.

Much of the world, including some of the Church, still views the Jews as the peculiar people to whom God will show favor. There are "bless Israel" (the nation) campaigns, bumper stickers and movements. The nation, its cities and its people are put on a pedestal as "holy." In continuing our study of prefiguring, I want you to know who the real Jews are, who God really favors and considers holy. Those who are named as such in the Scriptures prefigured the spiritual Jew of the New Covenant, namely any saint of God who has accepted Christ Jesus.

Paul bears this out in Rom. 2:28-29, "For he is not a Jew, which is one outwardly; neither is that circumcision, which is outward in the flesh: But he is a Jew, which is one inwardly; and circumcision is that of the heart, in the spirit, and not in the letter; whose praise is not of men, but of God." Two things are revealed as being prefigured here, the real Jew and the sign of his authenticity, circumcision. Initially only the Jew of the flesh existed. The sign of his commitment to God was circumcision on the eighth day. Both he and his sign were shadows or types of the real thing.

The New Testament reveals that he is a Jew who is one inwardly, born of the Spirit and not of the flesh. The circumcision was prefiguring the sign of a saint's commitment to God through circumcision of the heart or, in other words, a spiritual change that would take place within. That is the real circumcision that counts in God's sight, and it relates to the Jew who is one inwardly. So, actually, each of us who has experienced spiritual circumcision is a Jew, one who "rules with God."

Paul, in his letter to the Colossians, picks up again on this theme when he says, "Beware lest any man spoil you through philosophy and vain deceit, after the tradition of men, after the rudiments of the world, and not after Christ. For in him dwelleth all the fulness of the Godhead bodily. And ye are complete in him, which is the head of all principality and power: In whom also ye are circumcised with the circumcision made without hands, in putting off the body of the sins of the flesh by the circumcision of Christ: Buried with him in baptism, wherein also ye are risen with him through the faith of the operation of God, who hath raised him from the dead. And you, being dead in your sins and the uncircumcision of your flesh, hath he quickened together with him, having forgiven you all trespasses" (Col. 2:8-13; cf. Phil. 3:3).

Those who place their emphasis on national Israel as God's chosen people are moving in the areas of "philosophy and vain deceit, after the tradition of men, after the rudiments of the world, and not after Christ." For we are "complete in him," having received "the circumcision of Christ" which changed our heart, causing us to be made alive, or "quickened together with him," as Paul says to the Colossians. The first circumcision, of the flesh, only prefigured that of the heart by Christ himself through "the operation of God."

A last area of prefiguring that we should be sensitive to is that of the city of Jerusalem and Mount Zion. Oh, the praises that are lavished upon Jerusalem in the Scriptures. "I was glad when they said unto me, Let us go into the house of the Lord. Our feet shall stand within thy gates, O Jerusalem. Jerusalem is builded as a city that is compact together: . . . Pray for the peace of Jerusalem: they shall prosper that love thee" (Ps. 122:1-3, 6). And another in Ps. 147:2, "The Lord doth build up Jerusalem: he gathereth together the outcasts of Israel."

Jerusalem, the city located in the Middle East, was chosen by God to be His city. After the wilderness journey of the Israelites when God dwelt in the portable tabernacle, God allowed David and Solomon to conceive and build a more permanent dwelling, a temple constructed in the city of Jerusalem. And there God took up His habitation. He chose to dwell there, and it became "holy" because of His presence.

What we must understand, however, is that the time came when the physical city of Jerusalem, like all the other prefigured objects, was replaced by a spiritual

48

counterpart, the New Jerusalem. Several times, Jerusalem was seiged and destroyed. Finally, in approximately A.D. 70, Jerusalem, along with the physical temple of God, was completely destroyed. Though the city has again revived through the centuries, the temple has never been rebuilt to house the presence of God, because He now dwells in us, the new temple of God (1 Pet. 2:5).

Jerusalem was favored by God because of His presence. When the Church of Jesus Christ became the temple of God, or the New Jerusalem, God shifted His favor to the real thing, the people who loved Him and became the household of faith through Jesus, His Son. All the Scripture that praises Jerusalem and speaks of her in present and future really speaks of New Jerusalem, which was prefigured by Jerusalem made with hands.

We really take on a major understanding of the Revelation when we look ahead to chapter 21. There we find John seeing a new heaven and earth. Coming down out of heaven from God is the holy city, new Jerusalem (21:1-2). And though it is described in elaborate detail in chapters 21 and 22, it is not an earthly city as we might envision, nor is it made with hands. What exactly is it, then?

Notice Rev. 21:9-10. One of the angels appears to John and says, *"Come hither, I will shew thee the bride, the Lamb's wife."* Now there can be no mistake as to who the bride represents throughout the New Testament. She represents the Church, with Jesus being the bridegroom. So what John is about to see is the Church in all her glory, the wife of Jesus, "the Lamb of God, which taketh away the sin of the world" (John 1:29).

Our passage in Rev. 21:10 continues by saying, *"And he carried me away in the Spirit to a great and high mountain."* Notice first that to see all the Church, John had to be *"in the Spirit."* It wasn't something he could necessarily perceive with his natural eyes. He had to see it through spiritual eyes, even though he could sense it and know it was coming down out of heaven from God. Notice secondly that the Church was on a *"great and high mountain."* This is where Mount Zion comes into focus. Jerusalem and Mount Zion are nearly synonymous in the Scriptures (Heb. 12:22). Mount Zion is one of the mountains or hills upon which the city of Jerusalem is built. Mount Zion just also happens to be the approximate location of the upper room where the Holy Spirit fell on the day of Pentecost, which is really the beginning of the Church. Described as being "on a mountain great and high," the Church is clearly seen as a spiritual entity. It is the bride, the wife of the Lamb, sitting in heavenly places, empowered by the great Holy Spirit of God (Eph. 2:6).

And that is what John saw, *"that great city, the holy Jerusalem, descending out of heaven from God."* John may have been seeing her in the future, completely spotless and without blemish but he was seeing her as a spiritual creation of the heavenly places. If we are in Christ Jesus, we are already part of the New Jerusalem. It may not be finished in its entirety. There may be others in the years ahead who have yet to become part of it. There may be more finishing work to be done by the Holy Spirit in our lives. But it exists, and we can be part of it in Christ Jesus.

We have really only covered a fraction of the prefiguring that exists between the Old and New Covenants. But I think you can see how God has used examples and shadows to make known His will for the world. As we continue our study of the Revelation, more of this prefiguring will be brought out. Enough has been covered now to move on.

The Real Israel

The real Israel is not an earthly nation. The Scriptures show us otherwise (1 Pet. 2:9-10). It is a heavenly creation. Jesus said, "My kingdom is not of this world" (John 18:36). It does not conform to the world nor condone its ways. And when we become part of the kingdom by joining ourselves to the Church, the New Jerusalem, through the blood of Jesus Christ, we are heavenly citizens. "Now therefore ye are no more strangers and foreigners, but fellow-citizens with the saints, and of the household of God; And are built upon the foundation of the apostles and prophets, Jesus Christ himself being the chief corner-stone; In whom all the building fitly framed together groweth unto a holy temple in the Lord: In whom ye also are builded together for a habitation of God through the Spirit" (Eph. 2:19-22). We truly are part of the household of faith.

All of the Old Covenant and Israel the nation have pre-figured the New Covenant and spiritual Israel, the king-dom of God, a kingdom not made with hands. Spiritual Israel is referred to all through the Bible, and it is spiri-tual Israel that is in view in the book of Revelation. We must see this truth if we are to fully comprehend this great vision given John.

Keeping all these things in mind, we want to go on now and examine the messages sent to the Church of Jesus Christ as symbolized by the seven churches of Asia.

5

To the Church in Ephesus

(2:1-7)

Chapters 2 and 3 of the Revelation contain messages to the seven churches in Asia. As demonstrated earlier, these seven churches most likely represent the character and nature of the Church universal, seven representing completeness or perfection. Each of the seven has its strong and weak points. Together they present a composite of the Church in the past, at the present and in the future.

Jesus has already been seen standing in the midst of the Church. In his right hand were seven stars (1:16), representing seven angels, one for each church to which a message was going to be sent. There is an indication here that possibly each local assembly of the universal Church has a ministering angel, one through whom Jesus communicates the Father's will. John is even instructed to write what follows *"unto the angel of the church."* To reemphasize an earlier point, angels are used by God as "ministering spirits, sent forth to minister for them who shall be heirs of salvation" (Heb. 1:14). Applying that Scripture to its fullest, each heir of salvation, or saint of God, perhaps has a ministering angel assigned to him. In any case, Jesus sends messages to the churches, through angels, to impart instruction and guidance.

Some have theorized that the seven churches might represent a chronology of the Church from the time of Pentecost through to the second coming of Jesus. One such theory would divide the time as such:

Ephesus—the apostolic or early Church
Smyrna—the Church in persecution

Pergamos—the corrupted Church (the beginning of apostasy and falling away)

Thyatira—the "Dark Age" Church (A.D. 500 to 1500)

Sardis—the Protestant Church (post-Reformation)

Philadelphia—the Church in revival (late nineteenth century, early twentieth century)

Laodicea—the Church just before the "rapture" and the "tribulation" (cold and lifeless)

Advocates of this theory have felt that the Church could, at any point in history, identify where it was along this time line to determine how close the second coming of Jesus was. However, the Church has always had persecution and tribulation, which simply cannot be relegated to one narrow time frame of its history. Apostasy and falling away are also not hallmarks of one specific era and have happened to some degree or another in all stages of the Church (the writer to the Hebrews specifically addresses the subjects of apostasy and falling away, which occurred in the first century). The Church has had its "dark ages" and its times of revival and reformation, some greater than others. But these characteristics apply to the Church past, present and future.

Not only can these messages be accepted at the universal Church level but can be applied, just as easily, at the local church level and to individual saints. There may be specific strengths or weaknesses in these Asian churches which apply to your local assembly. They might also be very personal for each of us. A good example would be whether we have left our *"first love"* (2:4). That could apply to the universal Church, a local assembly or any believer.

As we address these messages, let us first examine ourselves to see if there might be a change that God wants to make in us or in our local church. The first church to be addressed is Ephesus. Before we take a look, however, note that each message has a common outline.

	Ephesus	Smyrna	Pergamos
Reference	2:1-7	2:8-11	2:12-17
Descriptions of Jesus	who holdeth the 7 stars in his right hand, who walketh in the midst of the 7 golden candlesticks	the first and the last, who was dead and is alive	he that has the sharp two-edged sword (Word)
Commendations	works, labor, patience, rejection of evil—trial of false apostles—not fainted—hate the deeds of Nicolaitans	tribulation, poverty (though rich)—blasphemy of those of Satan	holding fast my name—didn't deny faith
Admonishment	left your first love		some hold the teachings of the Nicolaitans and Balaam
Exhortation	remember fallen state—repent and do the first works	fear not suffering—be faithful to receive the crown of life	repent
Promise to overcomers	eat of the tree of life (22:2)	shall not be hurt of the second death (20:14)	give the hidden manna—white stone with new name

54

Church of Jesus Christ

Revelation 2-3

Thyatira	Sardis	Philadelphia	Laodicea
2:18-29	3:1-6	3:7-13	3:14-22
eyes like a flame of fire, feet like fine brass	has the 7 Spirits and the 7 stars	holy, true, has the key of David	Amen, the faithful and true witness, beginning of creation
works, love, faith, ministry, patience and increased works	some have not defiled garments	works—little strength—kept my word, didn't deny my name	
permit activities of false prophetess and teacher (Jezebel)	no works perfected		lukewarm, self-righteous
hold fast till I come	remember the word, keep it and repent	hold fast to what you have	try me—open the door to me
authority over the nations	arrayed in white garments—name not blotted out of book of life—confess name before Father	pillar in temple—be with Him forever—write names on Him	sit with me at throne

A Basic Pattern

God, throughout the Scriptures, establishes patterns for us to see His will. In chapters 2 and 3 we see a very basic one (see the diagram entitled "Messages for the Church of Jesus Christ"). The angel of the church is sent a message starting with a description of Jesus. Every one of the seven letters tells some facet of our Lord Jesus, confirming again the purpose of the entire book, which reveals Him.

This is followed by a commendation for those things which the church was doing well. The love of God is evident in this. Before admonishing and exhorting, the Lord commends them, to build their faith and courage. The apostle Paul did that many times in the letters he sent to the New Testament churches. He would always give them a good word before moving on to "doctrine . . . reproof . . . correction and instruction in righteousness" (2 Tim. 3:16). That is a good pattern for us to develop in our relationship to other believers, as well.

Following the commendation comes a rebuke or admonishment for some area in which they were weak or lacking. These admonishments are given gently yet directly. Next would follow a word of exhortation or encouragement. God deals with the Church as we should with one another, "speaking the truth in love" (Eph. 4:15).

Lastly in our pattern comes a promise to that church of a blessing from God if they will be overcomers in Christ Jesus. These are not actually new promises but reinforce the promises of the Word already given in the Old Covenant, in the Word made flesh (Jesus) and in the New Covenant.

This pattern is consistent throughout the seven letters, with the exception that one receives no commendation (Laodicea) while two receive no admonishment (Smyrna and Philadelphia). Through this chapter and the succeeding six chapters we will examine each of the seven churches, following that basic pattern. Let's begin now with Ephesus and remember that what the message contains applies to that local assembly then, to the universal Church of all time, to our local assemblies today and personally to us.

Descriptions of Jesus (2:1)

"Unto the angel of the church of Ephesus write: These things saith he that holdeth the seven stars in his right hand, who walketh in the midst of the seven golden candlesticks" (2:1).

These descriptions reflect what we've already learned about Jesus. He is in communication with His bride through angels, which are represented as stars in His right hand.

He is also in the midst of His Church. Jesus told the disciples, "Where two or three are gathered together in my name, there am I in the midst of them" (Matt. 18:20). This refers to the spiritual presence of Jesus by the Holy Spirit, which is manifested when saints assemble themselves together. The Holy Spirit dwells in every believer, but when two or more assemble, Jesus manifests himself in their midst by the Holy Spirit. This might take the form of just knowing and sensing His presence or through the exercising of the gifts of the Holy Spirit to edify or build up the Church. These descriptions confirm that wonderful fact.

Commendation (2:2-3, 6)

"I know thy works, and thy labour, and thy patience, and how thou canst not bear them which are evil: and thou hast tried them which say they are apostles, and are not, and hast found them liars: And hast borne, and hast patience, and for my name's sake hast laboured, and hast not fainted" (2:2-3).

Jesus commends them in several areas. First for their

works and labor. They evidently had been a church that put its faith into action, probably in the form of winning other people to the Lord, feeding the hungry, clothing the poor and ministering to the widows and homeless. As noted by this commendation, God is pleased when the Church and each of its members reaches out in some way to a needy world. Our works cannot save us (Eph. 2:8-9), but that is not an excuse to remain idle. We must express our faith in works (James 2:17), performing them all unto the Lord. This church was doing that.

They are also patted on the back for their patience. Several areas concerning patience come to mind. They might have been patient with one another in day-to-day relationships, patient in the gospel work of spreading the news of Jesus Christ and patient concerning the second coming of Jesus, about which other assemblies had become restless (the Thessalonians, for example). Patience is one aspect of the fruit of the Spirit, and Ephesus is commended for it.

One reason that patience in a believer or assembly of believers is pleasing to the Lord is that it indicates more of the nature of Jesus in that vessel. God is pleased to see the flesh crucified and the Spirit allowed to manifest itself in us as it did in Jesus.

The church at Ephesus also scored high in the area of rejecting evil. They would have nothing to do with evil, as was commanded by the apostles. Paul specifically told the Thessalonians, "abstain from all appearance of evil" (1 Thess. 5:22). That meant evil and sinful practices or anything that even looked like or had the appearance of being evil or sinful.

Individuals within the church who are involved in homosexuality, adultery, slander and other sinful practices must be confronted, as Paul instructed the Corinthians (1 Cor. 5:1-5). Sin that is not dealt with ruins the lives of the individuals involved. Furthermore, open sin stains the spotless nature of a church, washed white as snow by the blood of Jesus, and it must be purged from its midst. Nothing specific is spelled out concerning the rejection of evil at Ephesus, but indications are that they kept order and discipline in their midst with respect to sin. And God was pleased with that.

Closely connected to the Ephesians' rejection of evil was their good quality of "testing the spirits" in the area of discerning false apostles, *"Thou hast tried them which say they are apostles, and are not, and hast found them liars"* (2:2). Most New Testament exhortation along these lines centers on false prophets and teachers. Here we find a warning against false apostles.

An apostle is someone who is "sent forth" (as the Greek word indicates) with the power and authority of God. The apostolic ministry, particularly in the first century, was carried on by individuals who were chosen of God to spread the gospel message and establish local assemblies to strengthen the Church. Not all who came into town proclaiming to be such were apostles. Not all who come along today claiming to have a particular ministry are really called to that ministry, whether it be prophecy, teaching or apostleship. The Body of Christ is to discern what is true and what is false.

Warning after warning is given to us to beware of false ministries coming into our midst (Matt. 7:15; Phil. 3:2; 2 Pet. 3:17). You can tell them by their fruit (Matt. 7:20), by whether they proclaim Jesus as Lord (1 Cor. 12:3) and by discerning their message by the power of the Holy Spirit (1 Cor. 12:10). The church at Ephesus had been careful in doing that.

Jesus also says to them, *"and hast borne, and hast patience, and for my name's sake hast laboured, and hast not fainted"* (2:3). In other words, they hadn't given up, hadn't gotten discouraged over little things or thrown in the towel when trouble struck. Churches constantly face situations which test their spiritual strength and endurance. Individual believers experience the same thing. Satan always opposes the proclamation of the gospel. The Ephesians continued to labor, *"for my name's sake."*

One further commendation comes in verse 6, *"But this thou hast, that thou hatest the deeds of the Nicolaitans, which I also hate."* We do not have accurate records from history as to who these Nicolaitans were. Martin says they were "a sect or party of evil influence in early Christianity . . . although we cannot be certain, it appears that the Nicolaitans held that it was lawful 'to eat things sacrificed to idols and to commit fornication.' "[1]

Epp probably has the right idea when he says, "The best explanation lies in the meaning of the word Nicolaitans itself. It comes from *nikao* which means 'to conquer' and *laos* which means 'people.' It is from *laos* that we get our word laity. If this word is used symbolically in this passage, then it has reference to the earliest form or idea of what we call a priestly order or clergy which later on in church history divided people, who had an equal standing in the churches, into priests and laity or clergy and laity."[2] According to that explanation, the word Nicolaitans might have meant those who ruled (or conquered) the people.

The probable reason for the Ephesians hating their works was that the concept of clergy-laity interposed a human element through which people would have to go in order to have fellowship or access to God. Jesus had died on the cross to take all the barriers away. After Calvary, we no longer had a "wall of partition" (Eph. 2:14)

---

[1]William C. Martin, *The Layman's Bible Encyclopedia* (Nashville, Tenn.: The South-Western Publishing Co., 1964), p. 566.
[2]Theodore H. Epp, *Practical Studies in Revelation*, Vol. 1 (Lincoln, Neb.: Back to the Bible Broadcast, 1969), pp. 87-88. Copyrighted material used by permission.

between us and God. There was no need for priest or clergy to intercede on our behalf, because we have but one high priest, Jesus, who "liveth to make intercession" (Heb. 7:25) for us.

Any order or level of humanity that sets itself up as a mediating force between man and God fits into this deception of Nicolaitanism. God has ordained authority figures in the life of local churches. Ephesians 4 relates the various gifts given to diverse individuals in the church to feed the sheep and tend the flock. Among them are pastors and teachers. But these are ordained of God to guide and prompt, counsel and exhort in the Word of God, that all may be equipped "for the work of the ministry" (Eph. 4:12).

None of the church leadership as identified in the New Testament is above the other members of the flock. None are spiritually elevated higher. Their office and authority is God-granted. God is no respecter of persons. He looks upon us equally. Anything in the life of the Church that goes against God's will in this area should be removed. And evidently the Ephesians did remove those who exalted themselves over the people.

Admonishment (2:4)

One admonishment is given to the church at Ephesus, *"I have somewhat against thee, because thou hast left thy first love"* (2:4). They weren't being told that they had lost their love for God and His kingdom altogether. But they were being told that their love was not as fervent and sincere as it was when they first believed and first began assembling in the name of Jesus.

Exhortation (2:5)

The subsequent exhortation to Ephesus is this, *"Remember therefore from whence thou art fallen, and repent, and do the first works; or else I will come unto thee quickly, and will remove thy candlestick out of his place, except thou repent"*(2:5). These are very serious words. In restoring their first love, God first asks them to remember from where they had fallen. He didn't tell them to live in the past. Rather, they were to remember their original fervency and compare it with their present laxness. If they were to ever again experience their first love, they would have to see the need for repentance and come before God with a sorrowful heart. Many Christians are not willing to do that. Because of pride they are unwilling to admit their need for a fresh touch by Jesus. They are not willing to die to self when they've been instructed in the Word to do it daily.

This exhortation shows God's great love for us. He is drawing us to himself. He is desirous of a close relationship full of love. When that isn't happening, God would have us reflect, repent and respond by doing the first works. "If we confess our sin, he is faithful and just to forgive us our sins, and to cleanse us from all unrighteousness" (1 John 1:9).

If our love for God isn't what it used to be, we should just reflect for a moment. We always think that it is God who has left us when, in fact, it is we who have ignored God. If we repent and do the first works, our love will be as it was at the beginning.

If we don't do that, the consequences are spelled out for us (herein lies the very serious warning we find in this exhortation), *"I will come unto thee quickly, and will remove thy candlestick out of his place."* God will remove the anointing of His Spirit in our lives and, in the worst cases, remove His very presence altogether. That can happen to a local church, and it can happen to an individual believer.

The candlestick or lampstand that shines for Jesus is bright and beautiful. But if that vessel is producing little or no light and becomes a poor reflection of the power of

God, the source of the true light—the Holy Spirit—is removed for a season, until there is repentance.

It is because of God's great love that He purges sin from the midst of His Church. He must keep His Word, which cannot fail. That Word has proclaimed a Church that is without spot or blemish. The Church is made up of "sinners saved by grace." But through Jesus, in whom we are complete (Col. 2:10) and washed clean by His blood (Rev. 1:5), we stand before God white as snow, without any spot or blemish. The Church or individual believer that drifts away from God and their first love, however, has left that covering and cleansing and must be removed from the midst of those who choose to love God with all their heart.

It is a terrible thing to have experienced God and then to have His Spirit removed. It can be avoided by walking with the Lord each day with a committed and loving heart, one that will open itself to God in repentance, when necessary, to keep a solid relationship with Him. God is in the midst of His Church, and He is going to keep it pure through the blood of Jesus. Repent and do the first works.

Promise to Overcomers (2:7)

The promise given to us through this local church is this, *"To him that overcometh will I give to eat of the tree of life, which is in the midst of the paradise of God"* (2:7). This being the first promise, we should understand what it means to be an overcomer.

Jesus said, "In the world ye shall have tribulation: but be of good cheer; I have overcome the world" (John 16:33). Jesus is the overcomer. He overcame sin and death by obedience to the Father. He was telling His disciples, including you and me, that there would be difficult times for us as Christians, but that our comfort would come in knowing that He had already overcome every difficulty on the cross. If we will but abide in Jesus Christ, we are overcomers. Revelation 12:11 says, *"They overcame him [Satan] by the blood of the Lamb, and by the word of their testimony."*

Each of the seven churches of Asia is given a promise for overcoming in Christ Jesus. This first promise provides for our sustenance and wholeness through Jesus. Jesus is *"the tree of life"* (Rev. 22:2). He is the vine; we are the branches. As such, our life can only come in the vine, the trunk, the root. Abiding in that vine, we can eat of that tree and be filled. As we overcome through tribulation and persecution, we can feast more and more on Jesus, relying on Him to provide our life.

He is the tree of life and the focal point of this Revelation. He stands *"in the midst of the paradise of God,"* right in the very presence of God. Adam and Eve had access to the tree of life (Gen. 2:9). But instead of choosing it, they chose to disobey God and eat of the tree of the knowledge of good and evil (Gen. 3:6). If we can yield our lives to Jesus to the point of overcoming tribulation as we face it, He will make us whole and complete in the paradise, or presence, of God.

Every promise that follows bears a similar blessing. They are ours if we overcome in Jesus.

6
To the Church in Smyrna
(2:8-11)

The Spirit of God has a short and direct message to the church at Smyrna. This is one of the two churches that does not receive admonishment, which means that their walk with the Lord must have been sincere and strong. Some of the things shared with Smyrna confirm this.

Descriptions of Jesus (2:8)
The description of Jesus given in 2:8, *"the first and the last, which was dead, and is alive,"* parallels very closely the one given in 1:17-18. Jesus is the first and the last of all things because "in him dwelleth all the fullness of the Godhead bodily" (Col. 2:9). One with the Father, Jesus is the Everlasting, the Ancient of Days, in whom all things begin and end.

There is nothing mystical about these descriptions, which are attributes of God. Jesus was and is God come in the flesh. Jesus was God manifested in our midst. He was always with God. In fact, He was involved in creating the world. This is so clear in Gen. 1:26 when, prior to creating man, God said "let us [plural] make man in our image." Jesus was there because he is part of the Godhead, the Trinity, the Creator of the universe.

His resurrection is also mentioned again, *"which was dead and is alive."* Death at the cross could not swallow up Jesus, the Everlasting. Neither can it swallow us up if we live in Him (1 Cor. 15:54-57).

Commendation (2:9)
Some of the same good characteristics that were found

in Ephesus are found here. God says to them, *"I know thy works"* (2:9). They had evidently been working in and for the glorious kingdom of God. Their *"tribulation"* was also recognized. How comforting it is to know that God sees the tribulation we face and is there to keep us through it. He personally sees our most feeble efforts to perform His will and appreciates our acts of obedience.

Another characteristic which God noted was their *"poverty."* They were not affluent in things to eat and drink, clothes to wear and homes to live in. But still they were rich—*"(but thou art rich)"*—in the things of the kingdom.

We can have little or nothing when it comes to earthly possessions and yet be wealthy in heavenly treasure. Jesus had taught not to lay up earthly treasure, which can rust or corrupt and thieves can steal, but to lay up treasures in heaven, which cannot be damaged or stolen by anyone (Matt. 6:19-21). Apparently, that was the practice of this church. They were seeking first the kingdom of God and had the right priorities with respect to earthly things.

In concluding the commendation, the Spirit of God says, *"and I know the blasphemy of them which say they are Jews, and are not, but are the synagogue of Satan"* (2:9). There were those in Smyrna who claimed to be Jews, the chosen of God, but did not meet God's qualifications. Paul wrote in Rom. 2:28-29, "For he is not a Jew, which is one outwardly . . . but he is a Jew, which is one inwardly." Some may have known of this writing of Paul and were attempting to become "inward" Jews without accepting Jesus Christ as the Messiah. They were attempting to become Jews in the flesh, when it could really only happen in the Spirit. Because of this, God says they are the synagogue (assembly) of Satan. (For further discussion, see chapter 4, "The Household of Faith," and the comments on Rev. 3:9.)

There is only one way to be part of the family of God, a real Jew of the household of faith, a dweller in the kingdom of God, and that is through Jesus Christ. Anyone trying to enter another way is a "thief and a robber" (John 10:1). Without Jesus, one is still aligned with unrighteousness and sin, of which Satan is the ringleader. In Christ Jesus all sin is put away. Until that is done with a sincere heart commitment, Jesus will tell them as he did the scribes and Pharisees, "Ye are of your father the devil, and the lusts of your father ye will do" (John 8:44).

The commendation is evident in the fact that God knew the real children of God at Smyrna and wanted them to know that He saw the blasphemy of those who claimed to be part of them when really they were still sold out to Satan. Not all those who attend church services are born again or are real Jews grafted into the tree of faith. God looks upon the hearts of all who gather to worship and knows who is sincere and who belongs to Him.

Exhortation (2:10)

With no admonishment for this assembly, the Spirit moves right into exhortation or encouragement, *"Fear none of those things which thou shalt suffer: behold, the devil shall cast some of you into prison, that ye may be tried; and ye shall have tribulation ten days: be thou faithful unto death, and I will give thee a crown of life"* (2:10).

Because of their faithful witness for Christ, some at Smyrna would be imprisoned, actually placed in jail for their faith. But this message of exhortation can be applied by all Christians who, at some time or another, face tribulation, suffering or trials for their faith which place them behind bars in a figurative way.

Sometimes we are imprisoned by the enemy (Satan) through the trials where our faith is put to the test. Satan tries to "corner us" and "box us in" with the temptations of lust, greed, envy and the like, which are all outside the

67

spectrum of the Christian life. Submission to them can restrict and bind us to the point of spiritual imprisonment, which can be far worse than physical detention.

Certainly some at Smyrna did go to prison for their faith. Someday perhaps we will, too. But we need to understand the broader scope of this exhortation. Satan is out to test our faith.

"Fear none of those things," says the Lord. God allows us to go through the attacks of Satan for the building of our faith. Job went through severe afflictions and came out the victor. So did Paul and Peter and John. And so will you; don't fear these things!

Tribulation will come to each of us. *"Ye shall have tribulation ten days."* The use of the number ten is symbolic, indicative of a short period of time. We cannot be imprisoned by the enemy for long.

The number ten, as many Bible numerologists will agree, is suggestive of divine order. Two examples would be the ten commandments and the ten plagues in Egypt. All who are in Christ Jesus will have their "ten days" (which actually may be twenty or thirty) in the molding and shaping of their lives, as God conforms them to the image of His Son. Tribulation is part of the package.

There is nothing to fear. In fact, a promise is given to those who remain faithful even unto death, *"I will give thee a crown of life."* This crown is not something to be physically worn on our heads. It is not referring to eternal life in the future. The crown refers to the ruling and reigning of saints with Jesus Christ, the King of kings.

Crowns have always been symbolic of royalty and rule. The crown that Jesus wore first was one of thorns, so obviously indicative of His suffering and death. Having conquered death, Jesus was crowned with all power and authority and made to sit on the right hand of God to rule and reign in the heavenly places. When we die to self and abide in Christ, we too rule and reign with Him (Eph. 2:6), particularly as a result of suffering with Him. Paul tells Timothy, "If we suffer, we shall also reign with him: if we deny him, he also will deny us" (2 Tim. 2:12).

We need not fear tribulation; it is a divinely ordered part of the Christian walk that crowns us with life in Christ. Our troubles are merely to teach us to rule and reign with Him, now and through eternity.

Promise to Overcomers (2:11)

The closing of the message to Smyrna provides another promise, *"He that overcometh shall not be hurt of the second death"* (2:11). This is an obvious parallel with Rev. 20:14-15. We shall cover this more fully when we get to that point. Let it suffice to say that if we are overcomers in Christ Jesus and persevere to the end, we will not be placed in the company of those whose end is death and hell. Ours is life eternal in Jesus!

7

To the Church in Pergamos

(2:12-17)

Pergamos is the third church of Asia that receives a message. Although there are some good comments about this assembly, there are some very serious problems mentioned, problems which have been evident in one form or another in the life of the universal Church throughout the centuries, and particularly in our day. Some of their problems were a result of their location, but most of them were a result of failure to reject sin.

Before examining these problems, we have the opportunity to review another description of Jesus and the commendation that Pergamos receives.

Descriptions of Jesus (2:12)

"These things saith he which hath the sharp sword with two edges" (2:12). Already mentioned in Rev. 1:16, this sharp sword with two edges is the Word of God. It is God's will spoken to mankind. It is proceeding out of the mouth of Jesus, through whom God has spoken in these last days (Heb. 1:1-2).

The sword is referenced again in the exhortation to Pergamos (2:16) and later at the return or appearance of Jesus (19:15). He alone is worthy to bear the sword. It brings judgment against sin and justice to the entire creation. Elevated to His place of authority, Jesus is the only one given the right by God to slay with it, not in the physical realm but in a spiritual sense. The sword of the Spirit, the Word of God, is wielded by Jesus in cutting off sin and separating righteousness from unrighteousness.

In our conversation as Christians we often refer to the

Word of God as the sword. I've heard some categorize large study Bibles, smaller reading editions and pocket-sized testaments as machetes, butcher knives and pen-knives respectively. Though this is a cute analogy of the use of the sword, the Word of God, it presents an image that we are out to kill or seriously maim with it, when we really do not have the authority or right to do either.

We are told by Jesus to proclaim the gospel to all the world, that good news, the Word of God. We are to share it and bear witness to the Word, but we are not to execute people with it. Jesus is the one who will execute judgment, because He is the Word of God. "Vengeance is mine: I will repay, saith the Lord" (Rom. 12:19). He will make right the injustices of the world with both sides of that sharp sword. If we will be faithful in sharing the Word, Jesus will do the cutting and trimming by the Holy Spirit.

Commendations (2:13)

"I know thy works," says the Lord, a good characteristic that we've seen in each church so far. God knows our works, whether they are good or bad. He knew the works of this assembly, and they must have been commendable.

"I know thy works, and where thou dwellest, even where Satan's seat is" (2:13). Pergamos must have been a challenging place to be a Christian. We know from history that it was a place of idol worship, a center for all sorts of erotic spiritual blasphemy. Epp says, "Some of the things worshipped were nature, medicine and science. Significantly enough the symbol of their worship was the serpent. It is no wonder our Lord designated Pergamos as the place 'Where Satan's seat is.' "[1] Though all this Satanic activity was going on about them, the church at Pergamos had held fast the name of the Lord and had not

---

[1]Theodore H. Epp, *Practical Studies in Revelation*, vol. 1 (Lincoln, Neb.: Back to the Bible Broadcast, 1969), p. 99. Copyrighted material used by permission.

denied His faith, *"even in those days wherein Antipas was my faithful martyr, who was slain among you, where Satan dwelleth."*

Antipas was obviously a Christian at Pergamos who had been slain by the Satan worshipers. But his death did not cause the church to retreat or draw back. The Lord wants a loyal people, and Pergamos had remained loyal in the face of the worst kind of trouble—death.

Although Pergamos is specifically called *"Satan's throne,"* Old Slewfoot makes his abode wherever he is given a home. He and his demon entourage make camp in the places God is rejected. Many at Pergamos had done that, but the little band of faithful Christians continued to shine the light of Jesus.

Much of the world today could be classified as "Pergamos." We have the same kind of challenge facing us today that Pergamos did then. While many around us are worshiping the dollar, the stock market, their assets, their sports team or their job, God is calling for His people to remain faithful, to hold fast His name and not to deny their faith in Him. It is not an easy task but one quite attainable in Christ Jesus.

Admonishments (2:14-15)

Having encouraged them for their faithful stand, the Lord points out a few things which spotted their record. *"Thou hast there them that hold the doctrine of Balaam, who taught Balac to cast a stumblingblock before the children of Israel, to eat things sacrificed unto idols, and to commit fornication"* (2:14).

It is important to see that this admonishment is not directed to those holding the doctrine of Balaam. They were probably few in number but nevertheless present. The rebuke is directed to those in the church who allowed it to go on unchecked.

The doctrine of Balaam is recorded in the Old Testament (Numbers 22-25) and is very central to all apostasy and falling away from God. Balaam was a diviner who was employed by Balak, the king of Moab, to curse the children of Israel as they passed through Moab on their way to Canaan. Balak was afraid of the Israelites. His intentions were to break their unity and strength before they could get settled anywhere close to Moab and cause Balak problems.

Balaam, though, had heard of the Israelites and their powerful God. The word was out about this people who had been delivered from the iron hand of Pharaoh in Egypt, a people who had been given an eternal promise of being a great nation. With that knowledge, Balaam tried in vain to curse them but then wised up and blessed them, to the disgust of Balak.

Balaam could not curse Israel whom God had blessed, and he knew it. So instead of trying to curse them or destroy them quickly, Balaam sought to destroy their strength by causing them gradually to turn away from the security they had in their powerful God (Num. 31:16). His plan would be accomplished by inducing the Moabites to mingle with the Israelites, intermarrying and breaking them down by diluting their attitudes and commitments to God.

The doctrine of Balaam is simply this: since the blessing of God is on Israel, they can only be destroyed by causing them to sin. Balaam was used as a vessel for Satan's activity and destructive work, by infiltrating the lines and destroying from within.

The admonishment to Pergamos mentions some of the things they had allowed to take place, *"to eat things sacrificed to idols, and to commit fornication."* These were probably the first of many sinful practices which would follow, and the Lord wanted it purged before it went any further. These things *"cast a stumblingblock before the children of Israel"* and would have the same effect on

Pergamos were it not stopped.

The doctrine of Balaam and the sin found at Pergamos has continued to make its way into the life of Israel, the Church, all through history. Satan is always out to pollute and defile the children of God, as he did in Moab and later in Pergamos.

Pergamos is also scolded for having those in their midst who heeded the doctrine of the Nicolaitans (2:15), a subject we have already discussed (2:6). This problem, coupled with that of the doctrine of Balaam, was good cause for the exhortation which follows.

Exhortation (2:16)

"Repent; or else I will come unto thee quickly, and will fight against them with the sword of my mouth" (2:16). The instruction here is extremely similar to that given Ephesus—repent. God was pointing out that their sin could only be dealt with by repentance. If they heeded the exhortation by repenting, they could expect the forgiveness God has promised (1 John 1:9). If they refused to heed the warning, God would have no alternative but to deal with them in correction.

The exhortation warns, *"I will come unto thee quickly."* The Lord wasn't speaking of the second coming of Jesus. He was saying that God would move quickly to bring judgment to them and make right, in short order, the sin that tarnished their white robes.

Ephesus was told that their candlestick would be removed. Pergamos is similarly told that God would *"fight against them with the sword of my mouth."* In other words, He was going to use the Word of God, that sharp two-edged sword, in executing judgment upon their sin. Just exactly how that would all transpire is not told. We see, however, that God would do it quickly and that He would use the Word.

God will discipline us, because He loves us. God moves

quickly to ensure that those children of His who remain faithful are kept from the evil influences of those who fall into sin without repentance.

We will see more of God's judgment in chapter 19 of the Revelation. Judgment always comes by the Word of God through Jesus, God's instrument of justice and judgment.

Promise to Overcomers (2:17)

"He that hath an ear, let him hear what the Spirit saith unto the churches; To him that overcometh will I give to eat of the hidden manna, and will give him a white stone, and in the stone a new name written, which no man knoweth saving he that receiveth it" (2:17).

This twofold promise begins by providing *"hidden manna"* to overcomers. Manna was the breadlike substance provided by God in the wilderness for the children of Israel. It provided sustenance and life to them. The *"hidden manna"* referred to here symbolizes the sustenance and life in the Spirit provided by God to all who come to Him through Jesus.

Jesus called himself the bread of life (John 10:35). The manna in the Old Testament prefigured Jesus. When we partake of Jesus, we shall not hunger or thirst, and we will be overcomers. Conversely, when we are overcomers in this life, God gives us more of Jesus, or of His Spirit, upon which we can feed spiritually.

The manna is called *"hidden"* because it would not be readily visible to the world or to Christians who were so conformed to the world that they were no longer overcomers. The deep and rich spiritual things of God are promised and given to those who seek God and His kingdom with a whole heart. To those who ignore the Creator, the manna, or spiritual life in Christ, is indeed hidden.

The White stone is a second part of this promise for overcomers. Epp explains, "This is a rather obscure reference in our day but it was well known in John's day.

When a man was tried in a court of law and found innocent, he was given a white stone which signified two things. First of all, it was a stone of acquittal and at the same time it was a stone of approval. We will receive full approval of our Lord if we let Him live His holy life in us.

"It was to this fact that Paul made reference when he said in 2 Cor. 5:9, 'Wherefore we labour, that, whether present or absent, we may be accepted of him.' This is not a reference to the initial phase of our salvation, but rather His approval or 'well done.' We must all appear before the Judgment Seat of Christ to have our works as believers evaluated. The deeds done in the body must be considered as to whether they have been good or bad. God rewards us for those that He approves (1 Cor. 3:13-15).

"An added truth concerning the white stone is that there is a new name written in it which no man knows except the person who receives it. It is a secret perhaps kept in anticipation of a later revealing. It might even be something of the designation of our new character in Christ."[2]

Indeed we are new creatures in Christ Jesus. As biblical names are often significant of that person's nature, the name written in that stone will reflect the change made in us by the divine nature of God. Just as Jacob (supplanter) became Israel (prince with God), our name will be synonymous with all that Jesus is, because we abide in Him.

---

[2]Epp, *Practical Studies in Revelation*, vol. 1, pp. 206-7. Copyrighted material used by permission.

8

To the Church in Thyatira
(2:18-29)

The fourth church, Thyatira, like Pergamos, receives a good report accompanied by a strong warning to some who were defiling the work of the Holy Spirit in their midst.

Descriptions of Jesus (2:18)

If there had ever been any doubt as to whom these descriptions applied, it is erased at this point. Jesus is clearly identified as *"the Son of God."* To Him alone can these marvelous attributes apply, *"eyes like unto a flame of fire, and his feet are like fine brass"* (2:18). These characteristics have already been discussed in the comments concerning Rev. 1:13-16. To reiterate, His eyes are seen as flames of fire—penetrating and intense—suggesting omniscience as well as illumination.

His feet of fine brass reflect the judgment He brings. The adjective *"fine"* suggests brass that has been refined, or purified, as indeed Jesus was in obedience to death. Brass feet also indicate strong footing. We are given a picture of the strength of a pure and holy Judge whose vision is bright and searching and fair.

The intent of these descriptions is not for us to formulate pictures in our minds from which we might be tempted to create images to use in worship. Neither are they given to frighten us or create an illusion of overwhelming horror to bring about obeisance. They are given that we might understand the divine nature placed in Jesus.

Commendations (2:19)

The commendations given Thyatira are similar to

77

those given Ephesus, Smyrna and Pergamos. The Lord could see their good works, the charity or love they had in their hearts, the attitude of servanthood which they exhibited, the faith in which they moved and the patience they had in their Christian walk.

This is the only church of the seven to which the Lord says twice, *"I know thy works"* (2:19). With all of the exemplary qualities listed, their works must have been great for the Lord to commend them twice. Not only are their works praised but they are said to be better than they were at the beginning, *"and the last to be more than the first."* This last phrase could well apply to all their qualities but certainly applies to their works.

This is consistent with one of the themes that dominate the seven letters. God is pleased by those who increase in ardor and intensity for spiritual things, who want to move on instead of remaining stationary.

This extra praise may have been given not only for what they did but also how they did it. Their charity, or love, must have been the motivating factor for their good works. They did the works out of love and not out of a sense of obligation or desire for self-esteem.

Admonishment (2:20-21)

All was not well at Thyatira, even though they received much praise. Sin had crept into the assembly. The Lord says to them, *"Thou sufferest that woman Jezebel, which calleth herself a prophetess, to teach and to seduce my servants to commit fornication, and to eat things sacrificed unto idols"* (2:20).

As with the other churches, we cannot be sure of the exact circumstance there nor of the particulars of the situation. We can be sure that someone there, whom the Lord calls Jezebel, was causing the people to sin. Taken in a literal sense, there could have been a self-proclaimed prophetess there by that name. On the other hand, the

Lord may have been speaking of some sinful woman, man or group of people, using the symbolic title *"Jezebel."*

The reference to Jezebel may very well refer to the nature of the woman in the Old Testament (1 Kings 16:29-33). Jezebel was the foreign wife of Ahab, the terribly backslidden king of Israel. Ahab was, at that time, already a casualty of Balaam's doctrine that we saw in Rev. 2:14. He disobeyed the Lord, allowing himself to be persuaded and enticed by foreign people who came into Israel's midst and weakened their faith. One of them, Jezebel, he married. Ahab was so influenced by her evil ways that he forsook God and followed after the nonexistent god Baal.

The same thing was happening to some at Thyatira. Their *"Jezebel"* was enticing them to *"commit fornication"* (sexual relationships by unmarried people) and *"to eat things sacrificed unto idols"* (an act which aligned them with paganism and the occult). Seen in a direct physical sense, these acts were fleshly sin and were assuredly abominable in the sight of God. The sins of Jezebel, however, can be spiritual as well. "Jezebel" can represent any person or movement which causes the people of God to commit spiritual fornication against God.

In Jesus Christ we are married to the God of the universe. We are joined in a righteous relationship, a pure and holy wedlock established in love. We are one in body, soul and spirit, after which the relationship between a husband and wife is patterned. When we choose to walk away from our God and His great love to indulge in the occult, Satan worship or any other sort of spiritual blasphemy not associated with the one true God, we have committed spiritual fornication against Him. This intercourse with perverted spiritual ritual is as great as sin, if not worse, than the physical act of fornication and adultery. It is a direct rejection of our union with God.

The prophet Hosea tried to relate this to the people of

Israel over 700 years before the birth of Christ. Using Hosea's tragic marital experiences as the motivating force of his prophecies, the Lord spoke through him to Israel as a people who had "gone a whoring from thy god" (Hos. 9:1), who had committed "whoredom . . . because they have left off to take heed to the Lord" (Hos. 4:10).

The whole point of this admonishment to the church in Thyatira, the Church in general and to every saint is one of highlighting the spiritual infidelity in which we can be involved if we leave the love of God for "lovers" of this world. The admonishment is directed toward the faithful few at Thyatira who allowed this to continue in their midst.

The love of God is seen when He says, *"I gave her space to repent of her fornication"* (2:21). The Lord in His mercy always does this in an attempt to make us faithful servants. Unfortunately, the Jezebel of Thyatira had not repented, and her just reward is noted.

Exhortation (2:22-25)

"Behold I will cast her into a bed, and them that commit adultery with her into great tribulation, except they repent of their deeds" (2:22). The symbolic language at this point is clear. The harlot enticing the saints is being judged. She is *"cast into a bed"* or, in the words of Paul, was given up to "uncleanness through the lusts of their own hearts . . . unto vile affections . . . over to a reprobate mind" (Rom. 1:24, 26, 28). God would allow them to indulge in these sinful things together, if they so chose, but not in the presence of His saints. God casts them *"into a bed"* in the house of iniquity so that their sin is not causing disastrous effects in the house of God. All the while He is willing to forgive if they will repent.

"I will kill her children with death; and all the churches shall know that I am he which searcheth the reins and hearts: and I will give unto every one of you according to

your works" (2:23). God knows what we think and what our motivations are. He promises here to reward every one according to his works. The Jezebels, her followers and their children (others caused to sin by them) are doomed to death and destruction, with a great deal of misery on the way. To those who remain faithful He promises life.

"But unto you I say, and unto the rest in Thyatira, as many as have not this doctrine, and which have not known the depths of Satan, as they speak; I will put upon you none other burden" (2:24). The Lord is promising to support the faithful. *"That which ye have already hold fast till I come"* (2:25).

The unfaithful in Thyatira would have a great burden, a very heavy weight caused by the curse of sin. But for the faithful that would hold fast, He would add no further burden. Why? Because through Christ Jesus and His redemptive act on Calvary, both the curse and the burden were removed (Gal. 3:13; 2 Cor. 5:21).

Promises to Overcomers (2:26-28)

Several promises are given to overcomers. First, overcomers are promised *"power over the nations: and he shall rule them with a rod of iron; as the vessels of a potter shall they be broken to shivers: even as I received of my Father"* (2:26-27). This is a direct reference to the privilege of ruling and reigning with Christ Jesus for all saints who abide in Him.

As heirs and joint-heirs with Jesus, we have the same rights and privileges as the very Son of God. In the obvious scriptural reference, the Lord has decreed, "Thou art my Son; this day have I begotten thee. Ask of me, and I shall give thee the heathen for thine inheritance, and the uttermost parts of the earth for thy possession. Thou shalt break them with a rod of iron; thou shalt dash them in pieces like a potter's vessel" (Ps. 2:7-9). In this passage, God is speaking to Jesus. In our Revelation passage, the Spirit of God is speaking to each of us.

This is a very important theme, one which has different interpretations with respect to timing. Most agree that the saints of God will rule and reign with Christ on the earth. Many, however, only see this in the future. Of that number, most would say this applies to the "millennium," a select one-thousand year period of earthly rule by Christ. But in the spirit of past, present and future already established for this book of Revelation, this time of earthly rule should not be confined to the future.

Paul told the Ephesians that we (the saints) have already been made to "sit together in heavenly places in Christ Jesus" (2:6). Moreover, the Lord has revealed that the enemies of Jesus Christ (or of righteousness) are being made His footstool with the very reign of Jesus in their midst (Ps. 110:1-2; Heb. 1:13; 10:13). If we are ruling and reigning with Jesus, as denoted by these Scriptures, and all power and authority has been given to us as it was to Jesus (Mark 16:15-18; John 14:12), then that reign has been in effect since Calvary. Our reign is not just future. It is now and forevermore, though it will be all the more glorious at the appearing of Jesus, when all evil will have been purged from the earth. That's what the Spirit of God reveals in Rev. 5:10, that we are *"kings and priests: and we shall reign on the earth."*

We are not the conquered; we are the conquerors (Rom. 8:37)! We are not defeated; Satan and his followers are (Col. 2:15)!

The second promise to overcomers says, *"I will give him the morning star"* (2:28). This refers to Jesus. He is the *"bright and morning star"* (Rev. 22:16). As early in the Scriptures as the book of Numbers we see Jesus prophesied as such, "There shall come a Star out of Jacob, and a Scepter shall rise out of Israel" (Num. 24:17).

Jesus is called a *"morning"* star because those which

shine at that time usher in the great light of the sun. Supporting this, Peter says, "Take heed, as unto a light that shineth in a dark place, until the day dawn, and the day star [Jesus] arise in your hearts" (2 Pet. 1:19).

When we overcome in Christ Jesus, we are promised more of Him. He is the Light (John 1:9) and will continue to provide the illumination which keeps us out of darkness (sin and death). All that God asks of us is to be overcomers in Him.

9

To the Church in Sardis
(3:1-6)

Beginning with the third chapter of the Revelation
we find our fifth church, Sardis. To this fellowship of
believers the Lord has little to say in the way of compliments. The reasons will be made clear when we see the
admonishments and exhortations. Suffice it to say that
for the Lord not to open with commendations as He has
with the first four churches, this one must have been in
terrible shape spiritually, an unenviable position for any
local church or individual believer.

Descriptions of Jesus (3:1)

The descriptions given of Jesus tie together His one-
ness with the Holy Spirit and the Spirit's faithfulness in
ministering to the Body of Christ through His angels, *"he
that hath the seven Spirits of God, and the seven stars"* (3:1).

We have already seen that the seven Spirits mentioned
really describe the spiritual completeness of the Holy
Spirit of God. Though there is one Spirit, He has many
facets and manifestations, even as God is one yet three in
nature and being.

The seven stars have been identified as the angels of
the seven churches. Their ministry and function appears
to be that of communicating God's Word and blessing to
those churches. They are mentioned here in the descriptions of Jesus possibly to highlight the lordship and authority of Jesus over all the creation. They minister to us
for Him (Heb. 1:14).

Jesus, the subject of the Revelation, is the focal point
in the Church. Moving in the Holy Spirit of God through

the many ways He can be manifested, Jesus, the Head, directs the activities of the Body, calling upon those ministering spirits, the angels, to perform a work on behalf of his saints. Only Jesus has the authority to do that.

Commendations (3:4)

This assembly receives no commendation as did the other churches. The message being given to them starts right out with admonishment and exhortation.

Right in the middle of the message to Sardis, however, we find a personal commendation to a very faithful few, *"Thou hast a few names even in Sardis which have not defiled their garments; and they shall walk with me in white: for they are worthy"* (3:4).

The initial inference made in this statement is that the majority of the saints there had defiled their garments, or fallen into a life of sin. At the other churches the majority had remained faithful, with only a few reprimanded for their apostasy and slothfulness. In Sardis, however, most had fallen away.

The Lord always has, as seen here, a faithful remnant, a people who won't compromise the Word and conform to the world. Even at their worst, the nation of Israel in the Old Testament had a remnant (Isa. 10:20-23). The organized or institutional church has had a remnant throughout the years. This remnant is the true Church, washed clean in the blood of the Lamb. The Lord has a remnant today and will in the future. Together, all these faithful comprise Israel, the Church.

There were only a few faithful ones at Sardis, but the Lord graciously acknowledges them. He knows the heart of every man, woman and child. This remnant at Sardis, like all the faithful of Israel, had not *"defiled their garments,"* a term used in the Scriptures to denote character or nature. Their garments, or character, were not soiled with the sin and depravity of fallen man. These pure garments indicate the new nature of Jesus Christ, which clothes us in righteousness. The children of God in their union with Jesus Christ are described in Rev. 19:8 as the bride of the Lamb, *"And to her was granted that she should be arrayed in fine linen, clean and white: for the fine linen is the righteousness of saints."*

Those at Sardis and the faithful of all time will never be forgotten or ignored by God. They are ever before Him in Christ Jesus, clothed in the white, pure, clean linen which is the righteousness of saints (and of Christ). Only they shall *"walk with me in white: for they are worthy."*

This is the brief commendation for a few names in Sardis. All the rest that God has to say to this church is not good at all.

Admonishment (3:1)

It appears that the message to this church begins like all the rest, *"I know thy works"* (3:1). This has been used as the opening phrase in commending all the churches in their strong areas. However, Sardis is not commended, as this phrase is qualified and used to begin admonishment, *"I know thy works, that thou hast a name that thou livest, and art dead."*

The assembly at Sardis was a church in name only. Any life that they may have had at one time had diminished to the point where the Lord says they are dead. For any local church, which teaches and moves in spiritual matters, to be dead means that church is void of the Spirit that gives life.

Consider the human body as an analogy. The human body needs up to ten pints or more of blood circulating through it to remain alive. The heart pumps that blood supply to every inch of the body. The blood is life itself, as it carries oxygen and nutrients needed to sustain growth and stability. Drain the blood out of that body and it is dead.

The Holy Spirit is the life-giving supply of the Church. It flows in the Church and brings life to every member of the Body. It carries what is necessary to sustain growth and stability. Take away the Spirit and there is no life; the Body is dead.

So it is with any local church that endeavors to live without flowing in the Spirit in the areas of praise, worship, guidance and so forth. It can be dead spiritually even though the name "church" is on the sign in front of the meeting place, and even though to the world's standards the church is successful in the areas of attendance and offering. *"Thou hast a name that thou livest, and art dead."*

The word *church* comes from the Greek *ekklesia*, meaning the "called-out" (from the world). God is raising up and building a Church with "lively stones" (1 Pet. 2:5), building material that will ensure a living body. His Church will have no dead stones in it. It will be a spiritual house, not only in name but in action. To that end, the Spirit of God prompts Sardis to examine themselves.

Exhortation (3:2-3)

The Lord moves quickly to several exhortations which address their situation. He first says, *"Be watchful, and strengthen the things which remain, that are ready to die: for I have not found thy works perfect before God"* (3:2).

The assembly at Sardis was to concentrate on strengthening and building the body that still remained there, even though it was close to being dead. Some must have had a little life left in them, and God says, *"strengthen the things which remain."*

The question of quantity (the number of people in a fellowship) versus quality (the spiritual sincerity and fervor of that group) has always been a problem. In this exhortation given Sardis, the Lord seems to be stressing quality. If those who are serious about the Lord can be strengthened and made to hold fast, concentrating on spiritual growth instead of numerical increase, new converts will be drawn into their midst through the love of Jesus Christ, not through programs which exclude the salvation message of rebirth, commitment and service.

"Be watchful," the Lord tells Sardis. Don't be lulled into a trance by the world. *"Remember therefore how thou hast received and heard, and hold fast, and repent"* (3:3). Turn away from your stupor. God is always ready to forgive and reestablish those who will come to Him. Otherwise *"he will come on thee as a thief, and thou shalt not know what hour I will come upon thee."*

God is not speaking of the second coming of Jesus Christ. He is relaying the same type of message delivered to Ephesus (*"remove thy candlestick"*) and Pergamos (*"fight against them with the sword of my mouth"*). He will come to that church and surprise them as a thief does when he breaks in, except that God will not steal or remove valuable earthly things. He will judge them by His Word and remove things of the Spirit, tearing down the dilapidated house built on hypocritical sand and move on to other vessels who choose to be faithful and be built up as a strong house upon the rock of Jesus Christ.

Promises to Overcomers (3:5)

"He that overcometh, the same shall be clothed in white raiment; and I will not blot out his name out of the book of life, but I will confess his name before my Father, and before his angels" (3:5). Three important promises are made here. The first has already been mentioned. Overcomers in Christ Jesus shall be clothed in white raiment. They are clothed in the beauty and purity of Christ. Any sin which may have caused them to be impure, spotted or blemished before the Lord is cleansed by the blood of Jesus (Rev. 1:5).

The second promise is for the overcomer, *"I will not blot*

out his name out of the book of life." It is written there and will remain for the overcomer. But what about those who do not overcome? The implication is that anyone not overcoming in Christ can have their name blotted out or removed from the book of life. Some believe this book of life contains the names of all people and that the blotting out will take place at the Great White Throne Judgment described in Rev. 20:11-15. It seems more likely, however, that no one has their name inscribed in the book of life unless they have been born again and made alive in Christ, for we are dead through our trespasses without Him (Eph. 2:1). We are told later in the Revelation that *whosoever was not found written in the book of life was cast into the lake of fire"* (20:15). The main point, however, is this: Be an overcomer in Christ and you'll not have to be concerned about having your name blotted out of the book of life.

The third promise ties into the second and describes what the Lord Jesus does for us as overcomers, *"I will confess his name before my Father, and before his angels."* Christ is our intermediator and intercessor to the Father. He confesses a knowledge of us to God the Father when we overcome by sharing our testimony. If we consistently deny him, he also denies us before the Father, saying, "I never knew you: depart from me, ye that work iniquity" (Matt. 7:23). But we have the wonderful promise of his acceptance, approval and recognition as overcomers.

10
To the Church in Philadelphia
(3:7-13)

Three things are said of Jesus to the church in Philadelphia. The first shows us that Jesus is *"holy."* He is God and deserves this most divine attribute.

Webster gives three meanings of the word holy, which help us understand this description of Jesus. First, to be holy means "belonging to, or coming from God; consecrated; sacred." Jesus is holy because God, in His fullness, is holy (consecrated, sacred). Jesus was the manifested presence of God, descended from heaven to make way for our salvation. He, in the completeness of the Godhead, is called "holy" (Rev. 4:8; 15:4).

To be holy also means to be "spiritually perfect or pure; untainted by evil or sin; sinless; saintly." This describes our Lord Jesus. He was "tempted like as we are, yet without sin" (Heb. 4:15). He was the "Lamb of God which taketh away the sin of the world" (John 1:29). For these reasons He is the only one worthy to break the seven seals beginning in Revelation 6.

Lastly, holy means "regarded with or deserving deep respect, awe, reverence, or adoration." Jesus receives this reverence in His exalted position at the right hand of God the Father. This is best seen in Rev. 5:12-13, where the entire creation ascribes praise and majesty to *"him that sitteth upon the throne, and unto the Lamb."* These three meanings all emphasize and clarify the holiness of Jesus.

Secondly, Jesus is described as *"true."* He is absolute, the standard of perfection, in contrast to a world full of changing and shifting values. In construction, the builder uses a measure that is true and accurate, producing a structure with the same qualities. The Lord God, the Master Builder, has chosen His Son to be the true measure for building the house of God. By His pattern and example, each stone (member of the household of God) is put in place.

Jesus is further described to the church in Philadelphia as *"he that hath the key of David, he that openeth, and no man shutteth; and shutteth, and no man openeth"* (3:7). The prophet Isaiah had already said this of Jesus hundreds of years before (22:22). Both references speak of the power and authority given Jesus.

To illustrate this power and authority, consider the jailer, or turnkey. That individual has a great deal of responsibility and utilizes the power and authority invested in him through the use or disuse of the keys to the cell blocks. He can literally detain or keep behind bars those individuals in his care. Likewise he has the keys to open the door and grant freedom at the appointed time.

Jesus is the spiritual turnkey for the kingdom of God. He has the *"key of David,"* a reference made to denote his lineage and position of rule. The key of David is on the same key chain with the *"keys of hell and death"* (1:18). In a spiritual sense, then, Jesus grants freedom to enter the kingdom through the appointed act of Calvary or can refuse entrance to any individual who tries to come in another way.

We are dead spiritually before rebirth in Christ. We are locked up in the "jail of sin" and can only be granted freedom through Jesus, who holds the keys. Once He opens the door to the kingdom for us, it cannot be shut on us. Conversely, if He shuts the door on us, no man can open it for us. The key of David is not a mysterious object. It is a symbolic reference to kingdom rights granted Jesus by our heavenly Father. I can think of none other who I'd want to handle those keys!

These descriptions of Jesus continue to reveal the importance for each of us to commit ourselves fully to Him. If we are to know God and be obedient to His will, a total submission to Jesus must take place.

Commendations (3:8-10)

This is the second of only two churches which do not receive admonishment. This fellowship's obedience to the will of God can be seen in the kind remarks the Lord makes about them. He knew their works, like all the rest. As nothing is said to indicate they were lacking in any way, we can only assume they practiced good works full of the love and justice of God.

Because of their faithfulness the Lord says, *"I have set before thee an open door, and no man can shut it"* (3:8). This is a testimony to the divine ordering and direction which God brings about in the lives of those who will follow Him. There are no "closed doors" of promise or opportunity for the children of God. The Spirit of God is ever before us opening doors and "blazing the trail" in our spiritual walk.

The Spirit goes on to say that Philadelphia had a *"little strength, and hast kept my word, and has not denied my name"* (3:8). Philadelphia moved more on the strength of the Holy Spirit than on their own strength, described as *"little."* When we attempt to live and act in our own strength, which is little, the works and results are little. But when we trust in the strength of the Lord and let Him provide our energy, the results reflect power.

The Lord would have us to move in His strength and in His timing. When we do, nothing will get in the way, for He has opened the doors before us. Nothing will slow us down or hinder the progress, because He has provided the strength. Most importantly, and as a result of moving in His strength, He will be glorified and not us.

In the midst of these glorious commendations to the

church in Philadelphia we find two encouraging promises before the Lord moves on to exhortation. First, the Lord says, *"Behold, I will make them of the synagogue of Satan, which say they are Jews, and are not, but do lie; behold, I will make them to come and worship before thy feet, and to know that I have loved thee"* (3:9).

Many of the Hebrew people, descended from Abraham in the flesh, claimed to be the real Jews. Yet without accepting Jesus, the only access to God the Father, the Lord sees them as the synagogue, or "gathering," of Satan. At one point in His ministry, Jesus even said to those who would not open their hearts to God, "Ye are of your father the devil" (John 8:44). That's how they could be called *"the synagogue of Satan."*

The real Jew is the one fashioned "inwardly" (Rom. 2:28-29), having made a heart confession of sin and profession of Jesus as Lord. The real Jew is not of the flesh, revealed outwardly in a physical circumcision, but is one who has been circumcised inwardly in the heart through faith (Gal. 5:6; Eph. 2:11-13; Col. 2:8-11). There were many who claimed to be Jews without any of these inner operations.

God tells Philadelphia that they would see a time when all these false Jews (all unbelievers aligned with the devil and unrighteousness) would worship before their feet and know the love that He had for the true Jew. This may very well be a reference to the Great White Throne Judgment of Revelation 20, where the spiritually dead unbelievers are brought before the Lord before being cast into the lake of fire. These unbelievers will be making obeisance to God, maybe for the only time in eternity. They will not be worshiping the saints but rather the Lord God, around whom the saints are gathered. Thus would they be worshiping at the saints' feet.

This phrase could also be referring to a time when many of the synagogue of Satan would be converted and become true Jews, entering into spiritual worship of God with the other saints. But whether it would be either of these interpretations or another, the saints of Philadelphia and all the universe will see the day when the scoffers, mockers and rejecters of God's Word will "change their tune" and see the great love God has for His children.

The second promise says, *"Because thou hast kept the word of my patience, I also will keep thee from the hour of temptation, which shall come upon all the world, to try them that dwell upon the earth"* (3:10). Many of those who believe that the church will be "raptured" or snatched away from the earth before the return of Jesus Christ use this verse as supporting Scripture for their doctrine. In the Lord's Prayer, however, Jesus says, "Lead us not into temptation, but deliver us from evil" (Matt. 6:13). He knew fully well that Christians of all time would face temptation and even tribulation. The temptation alluded to in Rev. 3:10 is not just a short period of time which many would relate to the great tribulation named in Rev. 7:14. It is the temptation and trial faced by the Church of all ages, and God is perfectly able to keep the saints from it without removing them from the face of the earth altogether. Jesus in John 17:15 uses the same Greek words of Rev. 3:10 in praying that God would "keep" His disciples "from" temptation, after He prayed specifically that God would *not* take the Christians out of the world.

Exhortation (3:11)

"Behold I come quickly: hold that fast which thou hast, that no man take thy crown" (3:11). Here is a promise that God would manifest himself in their presence quickly. Actually the truer meaning would be "suddenly." This could refer to the sudden appearance of Jesus at His second coming. Or, since there is no admonishment for them, this may imply that Jesus' manifested presence would

come quickly because of their advanced spiritual state. Because He would come quickly to them, they were to hold fast to that which they had attained spiritually, allowing no man to take their crown.

The exhortation was for those at Philadelphia not to lose their position of ruling with Christ, through compromise with the world. Although they had grown to varying levels of maturity in the Lord, they could throw it all away to earthly pleasure and worldly fame (cf. John 15:5-7; Phil. 3:16).

Promises to Overcomers (3:12)

The promises given to overcomers here are glorious. *"Him that overcometh will I make a pillar in the temple of God, and he shall go no more out: and I will write upon him the name of my God, and the name of the city of my God, which is new Jerusalem, which cometh down out of heaven from my God: and I will write upon him my new name"* (3:12).

Let us understand first that God is building a house, a spiritual creation not made with hands. Moses built a temporary house for the Lord in the wilderness, which the Scriptures call the tabernacle. Later, David and Solomon built a more permanent house for the Lord in the temple at Jerusalem. But God, through Jesus Christ, is building an eternal house, with Jesus as the cornerstone and the saints as the structure. "Ye also, as lively stones, are built up a spiritual house, an holy priesthood. . . . Wherefore also it is contained in the scripture, Behold I lay in Sion a chief corner stone, elect, precious: and he that believeth on him shall not be confounded" (1 Pet. 2:5-6).

The spiritual house Peter referred to is the temple of God mentioned here in the letter to Philadelphia, as well as in many other places in the Bible. It is called by many names, but all mean the same thing—the Church (called out) of Jesus Christ. The house of God, the household of faith, the temple of God and the new Jerusalem are all synonymous terms. It is the heavenly structure made possible by God's grace and the obedience of His Son.

If we are overcomers in Jesus, we become pillars in that structure. From the moment of spiritual birth we are destined to be part of the house or temple of God. Yet when we overcome and hold fast, we become pillars in the temple, a part of the structure which is permanent, helping the other "lively stones" remain in place.

As a pillar, *"he shall go no more out."* Overcomers find themselves so much a firm part of the temple of God that they can no longer be removed. They will be in the presence of God forever.

The name of God, the name *"new Jerusalem"* and the name (or character) of Jesus himself will be written upon them. They are identified completely with God, having been given a right standing with Him that cannot be taken away.

This is the triumphant Church of Jesus Christ, in which we must see ourselves as a vital part. It is described in detail in Revelation 21 and 22, and it is revealed throughout the entire book. It is coming down out of heaven from God, even as Jesus did. It is seen through spiritual eyes by those who walk in the Spirit and seek a deeper relationship with the Lord God.

This temple of God is for all who will respond to the call of God. The more we grow in spiritual truth, the more we'll realize its existence, purpose, eternal destiny and just exactly what part we play in it. Overcomers will serve as *"pillars"* therein and have the name of Jesus written upon them.

11

To the Church in Laodicea

(3:14-22)

Laodicea is the last of the seven churches of Asia to which the Spirit of God speaks. It is a very serious and stern word with which God confronts them. The life of this fellowship and that of its members must have been spiritually impotent at the time. The fact that they receive absolutely no commendation is an indicator of their weak spiritual state.

The Lord speaks firmly and directly to this weakness, at the same time endeavoring to draw them into His perfect will. The text of this letter, coupled with that of the other churches, rounds out the overall message God has in Revelation for His Church.

Descriptions of Jesus (3:14)

Three things are said of Jesus in verse 14. First, He is called the *"Amen"* a unique description not encountered to this point. To be called *"Amen"* meant that He was established. He was, as He had always been and will be, a part of the unchanging God of the universe.

The word amen is often sung on the end of hymns, and it comes out of our mouths occasionally without our knowing the meaning. The word means "so be it" or "it is so." The amen corners of many an old church would resound with "amen" (so be it) at the proclamation of some great truth. Even today, the word amen is often spoken in agreement to something that has been said. Jesus is the *"Amen"* of spiritual wisdom and truth. In the past, present and future He is the expression of God's absolute standards. Until we lose our life in him, we are not established in anything permanent or of lasting value.

Jesus is also called *"the faithful and true witness,"* as He was in chapter 1. He has always witnessed to the God of creation. He is God come in the flesh, Immanuel, God with us. His life pointed people to God. As such He was a true witness.

Because when He was on earth He took every possible opportunity to witness to the love and majesty of God, He was the faithful witness as well. Many situations in His short ministry could have been occasions for Him to receive glory and honor. Instead, He chose to witness to his Father.

At the end of His earthly stay, Jesus witnessed to God's great love by giving His own life, that many after Him could be without sin and live. He is a faithful and true witness.

Finally, Jesus is said to be *"the beginning of the creation of God,"* a description given earlier in Revelation 1. This is not saying that Jesus was the first being created—for He was not created (1:8)—but that He is the originator of every creation. He and the Father are one. The beginning of all things is found in Him.

Specifically, the creation of God of which Jesus is the beginning may very well refer to the Body of Christ, the Church. In uniting the Old and New Testament saints, Jesus is said to have "abolished in his flesh the enmity, even the law of commandments contained in ordinances; for to make in himself of twain one new man [the household of faith, the Church], so making peace" (Eph. 2:15). Jesus is the beginning of this new creation of God, being the firstborn from the dead (Rev. 1:5; Rom. 8:29; Col. 1:15-18).

Jesus has been revealed to the seven churches in fourteen descriptive ways, which give us a good picture of God himself. These descriptions are grouped by church in the diagram on pages 55 and 56.

Admonishment (3:15-17)

With no commendation, the message turns directly to rebuke. *"I know thy works, that thou art neither cold nor hot: I would thou wert cold or hot. So then because thou art lukewarm, and neither cold nor hot, I will spue thee out of my mouth"* (3:15-16).

God's spiritual thermometer for the Laodiceans read *"lukewarm,"* a temperature which was totally displeasing to the Lord. It indicated such things as apathy about the Word of God and compromise with the world or, as Sardis, Christians in name only. The Lord is more grieved with a church or an individual who is lukewarm than one who is spiritually cold. Why?

The answer revolves around the source of the heat. Spiritually hot Christians are that way because of the vast measure of the Holy Spirit allowed to flow in and through them. They are not just filled once but continue to receive more of the Spirit as they use the measure already given them. They will continue to be spiritually hot as long as they consume that measure and take on more. A wood stove is a good analogy. When plenty of fuel (wood) is placed in the stove, a hot fire results. It remains hot because the fuel is consumed and more is put in.

In contrast, spiritually cold churches or individuals have little or no Spirit flowing in and through them. In all likelihood, they might have never received any portion of the Holy Spirit, through ignorance or choice. Though this displeases God, it is still not as tragic as a lukewarm church or individual. Why? Because the potential of them receiving the Spirit through repentance and seeking God still exists. Their stove is still empty. Heat-producing fuel has never been allowed to ignite within them, but the grace of God will graciously kindle it should they open up to its warmth.

The lukewarm church or individual displeases God so because they have once had the hot fire of the Spirit and, through apathy, indifference and neglect, have lost their heat. In other words, they have turned away from the things of the Spirit, where once they were hot and knew the good things of the Lord. The cold group has never had the "hot" experience, which could yet become a reality for them.

We must depart from our analogy at this point because, for all practical purposes, a half-lit stove is easier to rekindle and make hot than one with no fire at all. But the Scriptures indicate that if at one time the fire of the Spirit existed and was allowed to become lukewarm, it is harder to rekindle than if no fire existed at all.

This principle is illustrated in 2 Pet. 2:20-22, "If after they have escaped the pollutions of the world through the knowledge of the Lord and Saviour Jesus Christ, they are again entangled therein, and overcome, the latter end is worse with them than the beginning. For it had been better for them not to have known the way of righteousness [cold], than, after they have known it [hot], to turn from the holy commandment delivered unto them [lukewarm]." Also compare Heb. 6:4-6.

Many or all in Laodicea were lukewarm. God is seeking a people who want to be hot for Jesus Christ. There is no middle ground or in-between temperature that will do. The cold still have half a chance to become hot and remain that way. But the lukewarm are scripturally pronounced to be in great danger.

To remain hot, God's people must continually receive the Spirit. One dose just will not do. The stove does not remain hot unless refilled. Our filling and refilling comes in worship, praise, prayer and fellowship. All of these contribute to the generation of spiritual heat and, through the consuming process, necessitate the addition of more Spirit. The Christian life should demonstrate a continual infilling of that Spirit.

Referring to the lukewarm, God will *"spue thee out"* of His mouth. That means that He will, in a very real way, vomit the lukewarm Christian from His inner being. We cannot abide in the Lord except we be hot.

A second admonishment to the Laodiceans says, *"Because thou sayest, I am rich, and increased with goods, and have need of nothing; and knowest not that thou art wretched, and miserable, and poor, and blind, and naked"* (3:17).

At the root of the Laodiceans' lukewarmness was an attitude of pride and self-sufficiency. They had become so enamored with earthly things that they could say, *"I have need of nothing."* Underlying that statement, they were saying, "We don't even need God, we're doing just fine."

But the Lord has something different to say about all this, *"knowest not that thou art wretched, and miserable, and poor, and blind, and naked."* The Laodiceans thought they were rich. The Lord says they are poor. In fact, they had become so arrogant and puffed up that God proclaims them to be wretched (distressed) and miserable (unhappy) and blind (spiritually) and naked (walking in sin and shame with no covering).

Exhortation (3:18-20)

The first exhortation given this faltering fellowship picks up on their self-sufficient attitude and gives the solution for becoming wealthy and complete in God's sight. *"I counsel thee to buy of me gold tried in the fire, that thou mayest be rich; and white raiment, that thou mayest be clothed, and that the shame of thy nakedness do not appear; and anoint thine eyes with eyesalve, that thou mayest see"* (3:18).

There is a type of *"gold"* that God counsels us to buy—spiritual gold. Earthly gold is valuable. In 1979, it reached a record price of over $700 an ounce and will

101

probably go much higher in the years ahead. But spiritual gold is priceless. Its value is beyond compare.

This gold of the spiritual realm is the vast richness of knowing Christ and becoming like Him. God's gold is having Jesus Christ in our lives and being conformed to His image. That is the only way we can become rich in the Lord.

The Lord wants to make us wealthy in Christ. All that God has granted Jesus He grants to us. The gold that God offers is gold of the highest quality. It is gold refined in the fire. Even though there were no impurities in Jesus, the trials, tribulations and suffering He went through caused Him to be the highest quality gold that we can have in our lives.

The Lord also says to buy of me *white raiment, that thou mayest be clothed, and that the shame of thy nakedness do not appear"* (3:18). The white raiment, or garment, that we can wear is the righteousness of Jesus Christ. Without it, the shame of our nakedness is exposed, even as it was originally in the garden of Eden. We put on this white raiment when we repent and are born anew. Then we continue to have our garments washed by the blood of Jesus, that we may always have "clothing" to wear.

The Lord further exhorts this lukewarm fellowship to *"anoint thine eyes with eyesalve, that thou mayest see."* Without the Spirit of Jesus Christ in us, we are spiritually blind. We cannot perceive the richness of the Word or ever hope to understand the will of God. But Jesus through the Holy Spirit provides this *"eyesalve"* to restore sight and perception.

Every aspect of the Laodiceans' condition is addressed in this exhortation. Their spiritual poverty can be replaced by the golden character of Jesus. Their spiritual nakedness can be covered by the garments of Christ's righteousness. Their spiritual blindness can be healed by the Holy Spirit, who gives sight. This exhortation stands as an eternal promise for all who would buy from the Lord the precious spiritual commodities listed. We are sufficient in the Lord.

To continue the exhortation, the Lord says, *"As many as I love, I rebuke and chasten: be zealous therefore, and repent"* (3:19). If God hadn't loved them, He would never have taken the time to point out their sin. But He loves us all and constantly chastens us to draw us to himself (cf. Heb. 12:6; Prov. 3:12). The Laodiceans had much of which to repent, but the Lord was ready to forgive. He was ready to make them rich and provide for their every need.

The Lord's compassion is evident in the last part of this exhortation, *"Behold, I stand at the door, and knock: if any man hear my voice, and open the door, I will come in to him, and will sup with him, and he with me"* (3:20). In a symbolic way, the Lord is saying, "I want to commune with you." He is ever standing at the door of man's heart and, when opened in repentance and commitment, He comes in and abides in them. That did not and could not happen under the Old Covenant of law (John 14:17). But with the advent of Jesus, all this has changed. The presence of God with which to sup, or commune, is now available to us.

We don't have to wait until heaven. In essence, heaven has come down to us in Christ Jesus. He says that if we open the door, He will come in. You cannot get any closer to God than that, the omnipotent Spirit of God dwelling within your mortal body.

The Laodiceans were spiritually low, yet God was ready to open the door to them again. All He asked was for them to be zealous and repent. That is what He invites all to do. To the obedient, He reveals Himself in a very real way.

Promise to Overcomers (3:21)
The closing promise to the overcomers in Christ Jesus

says, *"to him that overcometh will I grant to sit with me in my throne, even as I also overcame, and am set down with my Father in his throne"* (3:21). Paul, by the Spirit, had told the Ephesians that He "hath raised us up together, and made us sit together in heavenly places in Christ Jesus" (Eph. 2:6). The more we overcome in Christ, the more we'll see ourselves reigning in the heavenly realm. God has made all this possible through Calvary.

12

In the Presence of God

(4:1-11)

The Revelation of Jesus Christ continues in a slightly different setting in chapter 4. John had just finished observing Jesus in the midst of the Church on earth through the seven representative Asian churches. What he sees next is in the heavenly or spiritual realm. Indeed, the remainder of the Revelation is in this setting. Like the first three chapters, the remainder of the Revelation also covers the present, past and future aspects of God's plan (not just the future).

At this point in the Revelation some have assumed that the "rapture" or "catching away" of the Church from the earth has taken place, because many saints are seen in the heavenly places. However, if such a momentous event as that were going to happen before all the events of Revelation 4 through 22, surely God would reveal it and describe it to us, either literally or in signs and symbols as He has in the rest of the vision. But no rapture or similar event is described at all. The only thing that has changed in the Revelation of Jesus Christ at this point is the setting. We are seeing the Church in the heavenly places, its rightful place of citizenship now and forever (Eph. 2:6; Heb. 12:22).

Now many of the events from this point forward will be future. Some of them had taken place before John received the vision (particularly chapter 12). Most of the events that occurred after John received the vision were future for John but are present and past for us. The unfolding of Church history and the progression of God's eternal plan has not been standing still since John was on the isle of Patmos. Things have been happening ever since that day and continue to happen in our time.

This large section of the book beginning with chapter 4 is definitely prophetic, yet it does not abandon the focus on Jesus and His relationship to the Church. If you have that as your expectation, you will receive the blessing which the book promises (1:3).

After These Things (4:1)

The King James Version begins chapter 4 by saying, *"After this."* The question might be "after what?" After the events which were described in chapters 2 and 3. The American Standard Version translates "after these things," clarifying that John is about to describe what he saw next in the vision.

This transitional phrase is used to change the scene and not to suggest chronology as some suppose. *"After this,"* or "after these things," does not refer to what was going to happen next in the history of the Church. Neither does it suggest that the Church, since it is seen in the heavenly places, has been "raptured" into the next "dispensation" or age. It simply means next in the sequence of events of the vision given to John.

A Door Opened in Heaven (4:1)

"After this [the events of chapters 2 and 3] *I looked, and, behold, a door was opened in heaven."* Remember that John was *"in the Spirit on the Lord's day"* (1:10) and thereby was perceiving spiritual reality through spiritual eyes and ears. This door was probably shown to him to represent symbolically a "passageway" from earth to heaven. A door provides access into another room or area. This particular entrance led into the heavenly plane. It provided a way for John to see heavenly things.

Jesus himself is the door opened in and to heaven. Jesus said, "I am the way" (John 14:6) and even "I am the door" (John 10:9), alluding to the fact that we must enter into the kingdom through Him. He is our entrance and access to the Father and all other spiritual reality. If we are ever to see the heavenly realm, it will only happen by coming through Him and being united with Him (Eph. 2:6).

The Voice As of a Trumpet (4:1)
The symbolism of the door is further clarified when we find next that *"the first voice which I heard was as it were of a trumpet talking with me."* John sees the door and hears a trumpetlike voice. This voice, as of a trumpet, is the same one which John heard in Rev. 1:10. It is that of Jesus Christ.

Jesus taught that "my sheep hear my voice, and I know them, and they follow me" (John 10:27). Jesus speaks and His disciples follow. Jesus provides the way or "door" and His disciples enter in. We have an audio and a visual encouragement in Jesus Christ to experience the heavenly realm, that plane of life with God the Father which was given to and forfeited by Adam. Jesus restores that privilege and has become the door opened in heaven to communion with God. With His voice He beckons us to enter in.

Come Up Hither (4:1)
With this voice as of a trumpet, Jesus says to John, *"Come up hither."* All three words are very important. Let's examine each one.

Jesus definitely says, *"Come."* He said it all through His earthly ministry and continues to say it to all who will hear His voice and follow. He is saying come unto me. Come unto the perfect way of my Father. Come be with us where we are.

To John He provides specific direction, *"Come up."* We automatically perceive that to experience the heavenly realm we must go *"up"* somewhere. Now the real question at this point is "Where is up?" Is it in the atmosphere or peripheral space close to the earth? Is it so many miles or light-years away from the earth and, if so, in what direction? The universe is a vast place, which exists in every direction from the earth. Where is God? Where is heaven? How can we get up to it? For some, a comprehension of heaven revolves around the illustrative description in Revelation 21 and 22. They deem this heavenly "city" to be somewhere in a far corner of the universe, in a galaxy or solar system not visible to the naked eye or other sophisticated equipment. It is to this faraway "heaven" that many see themselves being transported, or "raptured," before the awful doomsday, end-time events which are prophesied for this earth.

Actually, heaven is not as far away as one might suppose. Heaven is where God is. Jeremiah the prophet said of God, "Am I a God at hand, saith the Lord, and not a God afar off? Can any hide himself in secret places that I shall not see him? saith the Lord. Do not I fill heaven and earth? saith the Lord" (Jer. 23:23-24). God occupies all the universe, filling heaven and earth. He is omnipresent, existent in all places at the same time. Heaven is therefore not necessarily space. It is in the presence of God, a spiritual location not identifiable in earthly or celestial terms.

Heaven is a spiritual plane above the sinful platitude of the world. It is very real. That is why John was told by Jesus to *"come up hither."* Every man, through the inherited consequences of Adam's disobedience, crawls in the dust of the earth with the devil until he takes on new life in Jesus Christ. Then, in the Spirit, he can move "up" to and taste heavenly things.

As spiritual as John was, he had to be invited "up" to fully perceive the heavenly plane. And that brings us to our third word. Jesus said, *"Come up hither* [here]."

108

Where was that? It was above the level of development in Christ that John was at that time. To get to heaven to see this vision John had to be *"in the spirit"* (4:2). The Revelation says nothing about John being whisked away across space and time to be with God in the heavenlies. It simply says, *"immediately I was in the spirit"* and he saw heaven.

We proceed toward the heavenly places by moving upward in spiritual development until that day we become like Jesus. "We all, with open face beholding as in a glass the glory of the Lord, are changed into the same image from glory to glory, even as by the Spirit of the Lord" (2 Cor. 3:18). In the Spirit over a period of time (though John's heavenly experience happened immediately for him to receive the vision) God changes us from "glory to glory," or from one level of glory (honor, praise, worship) to another. Through that process, we are becoming like Him, and we will be fully like Him at His appearing (1 John 3:2). This transformation is an upward progression to the heavenly realm.

Things Which Must Be Hereafter (4:1)

One further subject remains before we examine what John saw in the heavenly place. The voice of Jesus said, *"Come up hither, and I will show thee things which must be hereafter."* Jesus didn't say *in* the hereafter (or the afterlife). He said *hereafter*, meaning "after these things." Marshall's interlinear Greek-English New Testament translates this phrase, "I will show thee things which it behoves to occur after these things." After what things? The things described earlier in the vision.

Most of what John was about to see would be happening from his time forward. He was going to receive a prophetic vision for the Church and what it could expect from that time on. It's important to understand this. What John saw and recorded were progressive events culminating in the appearing of Jesus Christ in Revelation 19.

These events, however, were given to John in segments, some being retold, reviewed and revealed in different ways. They are not a chronology. They are a mosaic given by the Holy Spirit and crafted together in a symbolic fashion to reveal Jesus Christ and His relationship to the Church from John's day on Patmos through eternity.

The Heavenly Throne (4:2-9)

What did John see as he was caught up immediately in the Spirit? He saw that *"a throne was set in heaven, and one sat on the throne"* (4:2). What he saw was the manifested presence of God in heaven. Scripture after Scripture testifies to this vision of God on the throne (Ps. 11:4; Isa. 6:1; Matt. 5:34; Heb. 12:2). His position on the throne indicates His universal reign. The throne was *"set,"* His authority permanent. He is the Ancient of days, the Almighty, the Everlasting, forever the Ruler of all creation.

John sees Him as one. As we'll see, he actually viewed the Father, Son and Spirit. But the Word indicates that they are one (1 John 5:7), as John was privileged to behold.

How could John see God, when he wrote elsewhere that "no man hath seen God at any time" (John 1:18)? John went on, however, to say that "the only begotten Son [the focal point of our revelation], which is in the bosom of the Father, he hath declared him." John spoke those words in his beautiful Gospel message, intending for us to see that God could not be seen except we view him through Christ Jesus, our access to the Father. Even Moses, who was given a brief glimpse of the glory of God, did not see his face but only his "back parts" (Exod. 33:19-23).

With every obstacle taken out of the way by Jesus, we can now behold Him in the Spirit. John did that day and begins to describe the glory of God by saying, *"And he that sat was to look upon like a jasper and a sardine stone: and there was a rainbow round about the throne, in sight like unto an emerald"* (4:3).

This seems to be an unusual way to describe God—like jasper and a sardine stone. Our earthly minds force us to imagine something more majestic and lofty, like an immense manly figure sitting on a thousand-mile-high throne among the stars of heaven. But John must have been overwhelmed by what he saw, the eternal Creator-Spirit of the ages, and therefore described God the best way he could.

The glory of God was *"like a jasper and a sardine stone,"* brilliantly colored gems. The jasper described by John was probably deep green, while the sardine stone, or sand, was a brilliant orange-red. In this colorful and sparkling way, the God of the universe is described.

"There was a rainbow round about the throne, in sight like unto an emerald," John continues. Aside from its color of beautiful transparent green (emerald), the rainbow John saw is highly significant. After the flood subsided, God promised mankind through Noah that he would never again flood the earth (Gen. 9:1-17). As an everlasting token of His unfailing word, God set a bow in the cloud. It was to serve as a reminder that He would never again destroy all flesh. The rainbow round about the throne symbolizes the eternal covenant of grace through Jesus Christ. As God looks upon us who are in Christ Jesus, He sees His righteousness (that of Jesus) and therefore cannot destroy us because of our past sin. Jesus is our "bow" and protection.

"Out of the throne proceeded lightnings and thunderings and voices" (4:5), highly reminiscent of God's visitation to the children of Israel at Mount Sinai (Exodus 19). His presence is always accompanied with a great display of power. He is omnipotent and magnificent to behold. All who have ever experienced any measure of God's manifested presence have experienced this awesome show of might and overwhelming glory. Some have seen the lightning and heard the thunder and voices. Others have

simply been unable to stand in His presence, physically impotent in the explosion of the dynamic spiritual presence of God.

The One sitting on the throne is God the Father. John also saw the Holy Spirit, *"And there were seven lamps of fire burning before the throne, which are the seven Spirits of God"* (4:5). These seven Spirits, which John already mentioned in Rev. 1:4 as part of the salutation, represent the totality of the Holy Spirit. These Spirits are before the throne, enveloping the Father and illuminating His glory.

Also *"before the throne there was a sea of glass like unto crystal"* (4:6). This "sea" is surely the overflow of the *"river of water of life, clear as crystal"* described in Rev. 22:1. Proceeding from God, and more specifically from the Holy Spirit, this river of life forms an immense volume. The water from this river and this sea can be in us and cause life. "Out of his belly shall flow rivers of living water," Jesus said (John 7:38). With the enormous capacity of a sea, we can easily reckon that there is a vast supply with no end from which we can partake. This crystal-like "sea" was before the throne, suggesting we must get in that sea, immersing ourselves fully, to arrive at the very throne of God in heaven.

So far we have seen the Father and the Spirit. The last dimension of the Trinity is now revealed in four beasts, or creatures. *"In the midst of the throne, and round about the throne, were four beasts full of eyes before and behind. And the first beast was like a lion, and the second beast like a calf, and the third beast had a face as a man, and the fourth beast was like a flying eagle. And the four beasts had each of them six wings about him; and they were full of eyes within: and they rest not day and night, saying, Holy, holy, holy, Lord God Almighty, which was, and is, and is to come"* (4:6-8).

The four beasts are not Jesus himself. He will be seen

in Revelation 5. These beasts do, however, reveal the nature and character of Jesus, the Son of God, the third part of the Trinity.

It may seem a strange thought that *"beasts"* reveal Jesus. A look at the original language is helpful. The Greek word *zōon*, from which "beast" is translated, simply means "a live thing." The living things seen by John are not ugly or grotesque, in the contemporary connotation of "beasts," but are rather created things of God with a specific purpose. What God creates is beautiful, for He seems to have given them the purpose of revealing Jesus.

Notice that they are both *"in the midst"* and *"round about the throne."* They are all over this heavenly scene, defying our finite sense of objective reality. They each have *"six wings,"* providing them mobility in all of space. They are *"full of eyes before and behind"* and *"within."* Nothing escapes their sight. These descriptions, common to all four creatures, symbolize the omnipresence and omniscience of God granted to Jesus.

"The first beast was like a lion." A parallel to this creature's description of Jesus is found in Rev. 5:5 when Jesus is called the *"Lion of the tribe of Juda."* The lion is strong and recognized by other animals as "king of the beasts." Jesus is our strength. He is the King of kings and Lord of lords.

The second beast is *"like a calf."* Whereas the first showed forth Jesus' strength, the second beast portrays His sacrifice to take away sin. Though ultimately the Lamb of God is used to signify this sacrifice, calves were also used to atone for sin (Leviticus 9).

The third beast *"had a face as a man,"* as indeed Jesus had become to do the will of the Father. Called the "Son of man," Jesus was the "word . . . made flesh" (John 1:14). He was both God (divine) and man (flesh). He became a man to suffer obediently and to endure the trials and temptations we face (Heb. 4:15). He subsequently became

113

the only perfect sacrifice that could atone for our sin once and forever (Heb. 9:12ff.).

The last of the four beasts was *"like a flying eagle."* The eagle symbolizes Jesus' victory over sin. "They that wait upon the Lord shall renew their strength; they shall mount up with wings as eagles" (Isa. 40:31). Jesus waited upon the Lord as an obedient Son and received this promise. We too, in Christ, can mount up with wings as eagles. He carries us up on those eagle's wings into the heavenly realm (Rev. 12:14).

In Ezekiel 1 is given a description of four creatures almost identical to those of Revelation 4. Apparently, Ezekiel and John saw the same four creatures which reveal Jesus.

What we have examined in the heavenly throne room to this point has been the glory and majesty of God in the Father, Son and Holy Spirit. They, being one, fill the heavens and the earth (Jer. 23:24). God, in all these manifestations, sits on the unmovable throne of heaven above the earthly plane. Now we shall discuss what else John saw in the presence of God round about the throne.

The Twenty-Four Elders (4:4, 10)

John continues his description of the heavenly scene with a comment on the twenty-four elders. He has already referred to these elders in verse 4 when he said, *"Round about the throne were four and twenty seats: and upon the seats I saw four and twenty elders sitting, clothed in white raiment; and they had on their heads crowns of gold"* (4:4).

A reminder may be in order here that this vision was sent and signified by the angel of Jesus Christ (Rev. 1:1). It was given in signs and symbols. This is crucial to remember as we consider the twenty-four elders. They are on twenty-four *"seats,"* or thrones. The Greek word *thronos* means a stately seat or throne. Twenty-four elders seated on twenty-four heavenly thrones. What does this mean for us?

There is a wide variety of opinion as to the meaning of the twenty-four elders. One of the more popular interpretations is that twelve of them are the sons of Jacob (Israel) while the other twelve are the original disciples of Jesus. This would represent twelve Old Testament saints (or elders) and twelve New Testament saints, all elevated to special positions of authority and privilege in the presence of God.

Elders are identified in the Scriptures as the shepherds of the body of Christ. They are the God-appointed tenders of the flock. They are to be examples to the saints (Heb. 13:7; 1 Pet. 5:3). Paul instructed Titus to "ordain elders in every city" (Titus 1:5). Elders in the biblical sense, whose strong Christian character is described in 1 Tim. 3:1-7 and Titus 1:6-9, are truly representative of the Church.

Whether or not the twenty-four elders of the Revelation represent the twelve Old Testament patriarchs and the twelve New Testament apostles, all twenty-four clearly represent the household of faith described in chapter 4 of this book. Indeed, John may have been shown the Church round the throne of God through the symbolism of twenty-four elders representing the people of faith of all time.

The elders are not twenty-four individuals, such as Judah, Benjamin, Asher, Naphtali, Matthew, James, John, Peter, etc. These individuals are not placed in the heavenly realm with any greater degree of honor than any other person of faith throughout all history. "God is no respecter of persons" (Acts 10:34) and will not play favorites. The twenty-four represent the Church of all time.

The elders were seated on thrones in heaven with God just as Jesus said all "overcomers" would in Rev. 3:21, *"To him that overcometh will I grant to sit with me in my throne, even as I also overcame, and am set down with my Father in his throne."* They also were clothed in white raiment, a truth promised the overcomers in Rev. 3:5, *"He that overcometh, the same shall be clothed in white raiment."* Finally, *"they had on their heads crowns of gold."* Crowns of life were promised the faithful in Rev. 2:10. Can there be any doubt that these are the triumphant saints, the overcomers in Christ Jesus?

Most will agree to this point. Identifying when they are seated *"round about the throne"* is the bone of contention. Is it only in the future or has it started already in the Spirit? Jesus told John that he was going to see *"things which must be hereafter"* (from this point forward). And that's what John saw when he was immediately in the Spirit. He temporarily left the earthly plane to see the Church in the Spirit. It was around the throne of God. Some of that Church, including John, were still on the earth in the flesh, but they were one with the saints in the Spirit who had gone on before them.

If there was going to be some great event which carried the Church from earth to heaven in the future before this heavenly vision which John now saw, why is it not mentioned here or, for that matter, anywhere in the Revelation? The answer is that there is none. We in Christ are already seated in the heavenly places (Eph. 2:6). Any time we are in the Spirit worshiping and praising God, we are there by the Spirit, tasting the inheritance which someday will become permanent. The twenty-four elders represent our present position in the heavenlies as kings and priests.

Heavenly Worship (4:9-11)

The Church in the presence of God is worshiping and praising God, *"who liveth for ever and ever."*

As the four beasts worship by giving *"glory and honour and thanks"* (4:9), the Church does the same. They *"cast their crowns before the throne"* as an acknowledgment of God, the Lifegiver. The crown of life they are privileged to wear is laid at the Lord's feet in humility and adoration.

The redeemed say to the Lord, *"Thou art worthy, O Lord, to receive glory and honour and power: for thou hast created all things, and for thy pleasure they are and were created."* This ascription of praise is an example of the kind of heavenly worship we should give the Godhead. It expresses the glory and honor and power that God has and deserves. It is the kind of worship of which the Church must be a part now and forever.

Our heavenly Father is searching and seeking for those who are not ashamed nor hesitant to invest the time to worship Him as He should be worshiped. Jesus said to the Samaritan woman at the well, "The hour cometh, when ye shall neither in this mountain, nor yet at Jerusalem, worship the Father. Ye worship ye know not what: we know what we worship: for salvation is of the Jews. But the hour cometh, and now is, when the true worshippers shall worship the Father in spirit and in truth: for the Father seeketh such to worship him. God is a Spirit: and they that worship him must worship him in spirit and in truth" (John 4:21-24).

This heavenly worship scene should be happening now. The saints, whether on earth or in heaven, should be praising Him always. "Rejoice in the Lord alway: and again I say, Rejoice" (Phil. 4:4). "Rejoice evermore. Pray without ceasing. In every thing give thanks: for this is the will of God in Christ Jesus concerning you. Quench not the Spirit" (1 Thess. 5:16-19). "Praise ye the Lord. Praise God in his sanctuary: praise him in the firmament of his power. . . . Let every thing that hath breath praise the Lord. Praise ye the Lord" (Ps. 150:1, 6).

An inability to worship God in spirit and in truth is a sign of noncommittal. It speaks of an unwillingness to die to self and do what is pleasing to God. Worship pleases Him! He has desired communion with man ever since He created him. This worship and praise which we see through John's vision is that into which we must enter.

God is seeking praisers, those who will prostrate themselves in His presence to magnify His name. He is worthy and deserves our worship. If we receive nothing else from this chapter, we should receive this—be open, in the Spirit, to worship God as we see here in the Revelation. Worship will be easy if we allow ourselves to be filled with the Holy Spirit. Void of that liberating Spirit, our worship will be mere ritual and tradition.

13

The Only One Worthy

(5:1-14)

Revelation 5 is a continuation of chapter 4. The chapter division inserted here in no way breaks the trend of thought. The scene is heaven. The Church is seen there in the presence of God the Father, Son and Spirit, with Jesus being the central focus. Though the sealed book and its content will serve to add deeper meaning to the entire revelation, Jesus must be the real focus. He is the one being revealed.

As we continue to see the Revelation, our attention is not to be absorbed solely by the events of the sealed book. We should continue to see past the symbols to the only one who is worthy to open the book—Jesus.

The Sealed Book (5:1)

"And I saw in the right hand of him that sat on the throne a book written within and on the backside, sealed with seven seals" (5:1). God had in His hand a sealed book. The seven seals are indicative of its content being perfect and complete, spiritual qualities associated with that number.

The fact that the book was sealed meant that its content was established. It was written and was not to be changed, though it was about to be revealed. The sealing process has always been done to secure a matter and make it established. When Daniel was placed in the lion's den, King Nebuchadnezzar had a great stone placed over the mouth of the den and then sealed it with his own seal "that the purpose might not be changed concerning Daniel" (Dan. 6:16-17). In the same way, God had sealed this book with seven complete seals to signify that

119

nothing in it could be changed. God had established it, and it would come to pass.

It is most certain that the events which were written in the book and about to be revealed were decided by the Lord and ordered long before this time when John saw it, before the foundations of the world were laid. The events revealed in Revelation 6 through 16 comprise the divine redemption plan, a series of God-ordained happenings which would redeem mankind from sin and place it again in the proper relationship to God, the Creator.

Whether or not the book was real is insignificant. John saw the book and its events *"in the spirit,"* in the heavenly realm. As with other aspects of the vision, it was given to clarify the events of the revelation and to underscore their importance.

This is not the *"book of life"* (Rev. 20:12), or the *"Lamb's book of life"* (Rev. 21:27). That book contains the names of those who are redeemed by Jesus, the Lamb of God. This sealed book, about to be opened, contains the circumstances of redemption, portrayed in a highly symbolic way for those who have spiritual eyes to see them.

Daniel had a similar vision, which God said to "shut up" and "seal" until the "time of the end" (Dan. 12:9). Though the essence of John's vision had already been made known to Daniel and all the Old Testament saints through the prefiguring and prophetic process, the real message of redemption would not come to full fruition until the coming of Jesus and the establishment of the Church.

This vision of John's and particularly the events of the sealed book, were going to happen from Jesus' time forward and could not therefore be fully proclaimed until the Church had been firmly established. These events are "end times" events. We have been in the "end times" since the first advent of the Lord Jesus (1 John 2:18). The *"things which shall be hereafter"* (1:19) have been occurring since the days of John ("from this time forward"), and they will continue to occur until Christ's second advent. If we can understand this point, the seals, trumpets and vials will make more sense to us.

A Search for the "Worthy" (5:2-4)

"And I saw a strong angel proclaiming with a loud voice, Who is worthy to open the book, and to loose the seals thereof? And no man in heaven, nor in earth, neither under the earth, was able to open the book, neither to look thereon. And I wept much, because no man was found worthy to open and to read the book, neither to look thereon" (5:2-4).

What a fix! John had been elevated to the heavenly realm by the Holy Spirit for the express purpose of seeing the events and circumstances recorded in the sealed book. Yet when the strong angel comes forward with a booming voice seeking someone worthy to open the book and break the seals, no one could initially be found.

The King James Version says no "man," but a more faithful rendering would be no "one" (man, woman or any created thing). No one in heaven or earth could be found worthy to perform the task. Whether they be saints in the earth or saints already in heaven, not one could open the book, nor even look at it.

Perhaps some tried to open the book and were completely unable to do so as they approached the glory of God and realized their complete unworthiness to do it. The glory of the book was so great that it was impossible for man even to look at the book *"in the right hand of him that sat on the throne"* (5:1).

This must have been discouraging for John, who surely had great anticipation of what was to transpire. So saddened was John that he *"wept much."* He was burdened that no one, in all the creation, could be found *"who is worthy to open the book, and to loose the seals thereof"* (5:2).

121

The Worthiness of Jesus (5:5-7)

John was comforted to find that there was, after all, One who could open the book. But only one in all the universe was able to come forth. John writes, *"And one of the elders saith unto me, Weep not: behold the Lion of the tribe of Juda, the Root of David, hath prevailed to open the book, and to loose the seven seals thereof. And I beheld, and, lo, in the midst of the throne and of the four beasts, and in the midst of the elders, stood a Lamb as it had been slain, having seven horns and seven eyes, which are the seven Spirits of God sent forth into all the earth. And he came and took the book out of the right hand of him that sat upon the throne"* (5:5-7).

Before we discuss the worthiness of Jesus, we should note the position from which Jesus emerges in this scene. He was *"in the midst of the throne and of the four beasts"* (5:6). In other words, he was "one" with God. He wasn't even seen until He came forth from the midst of the heavenly throne. He was seated there, exalted at the right hand of God the Father (Eph. 1:20-23), yet He did not overshadow the Father. Jesus has been manifested to us as part of the Trinity, and we should not forget that He is God. He, the Father and the Spirit are One.

Not only was Jesus in the midst of the throne and the four beasts, He was also in the midst of the twenty-four elders, or the Church, as we have already determined. He was seen in the midst of that Church on earth in Rev. 1:13 and here in the midst of the Church in the heavenly places. Being omnipresent, through spiritual principles we do not understand, Jesus is always with His Church, the Bride. The final wedding feast and celebration to which the Church looks forward will be held when Jesus has gathered "together in one all things in Christ, both which are in heaven, and which are on earth; even in him" (Eph. 1:10).

Jesus, the Lamb of God, was worthy enough to initiate

what God wanted to reveal. He was worthy for one chief reason. Jesus had been totally obedient to the Father, not just in going to the cross of Calvary but also in doing His will upon the face of the earth. He came to live a sinless, perfect life while facing all the temptations we do. That, for Jesus, might have been the heaviest cross of all to bear.

We could reason that it was easy for Jesus to live a perfect life before God, because He was God come in the flesh. But despite his deity, he was human. He felt and sensed what every human does, including temptation. The writer of Hebrews says, "In the days of his flesh, when he had offered up prayers and supplications with strong crying and tears unto Him that was able to save him from death, and was heard in that he feared; Though he were a Son, yet learned he obedience by the things which he suffered, And being made perfect, he became the author of eternal salvation unto all them that obey him" (Heb. 5:7-9).

"Strong crying and tears" doesn't sound like Jesus had it easy, does it? "In the days of his flesh" He learned "obedience by the things which he suffered," though he were a Son. God was so extremely pleased with Jesus, His Son, because He was showing mankind the way to be united with God by being obedient, not fulfilling the lusts of the flesh but drawing close to the Father. And because of this, Jesus is worthy in God's sight. He takes the sealed book from the hand of God so that it may be opened and presented to mankind.

In order for us to fully understand the worthiness of Jesus to open the book, let us consider an Old Testament parallel. It is the principle of the "kinsman-redeemer," which Theodore Epp so clearly relates.

The law of redemption in the Old Testament was very simple, yet profound. When property had been sold by one family (or if it had been confiscated or lost through death or other means), a scroll was prepared and on the inside of this scroll were written all the necessary details of what was required to purchase back the property. The scroll was then sealed. On the outside of the scroll were listed details telling what was involved internally, whether property or some other item, and the scroll was then placed in the hands of the priest.

When a near kinsman decided to buy back the property, he could check the outside of the sealed document to see if he qualified. Evidently the names of the family were mentioned there, and he could see if he qualified as a near kinsman. If he did, he could claim the scroll from the priest and tear it open and redeem the property.

There were three conditions that absolutely had to be met in order to qualify as a kinsman-redeemer. First, he had to be a near relative. Second, he had to be willing to act. Third, he had to be able to pay the price of redemption.

In the story of Ruth and Boaz, we find the finest biblical illustration of this law of redemption and the kinsman-redeemer. In the Book of Ruth we read that Elimelech, his wife, Naomi, and his family left Bethlehem in the land of Canaan because of a famine. They left all they had and went to the country of Moab.

But the time came when Ruth [whom one of Elimelech's sons had married in Moab] and Naomi returned [Elimelech and both his sons had died in Moab] and faced the problem of how to get the property back. A kinsman-redeemer had to be found and Boaz was that man. Boaz offered to do his part as the kinsman-redeemer, but he admitted to Ruth that there was a nearer kinsman than he. The other kinsman refused to purchase back the property because it could nullify his own inheritance. So we see that even though he qualified as a near kinsman and was apparently able to pay the price of redemption, he was not willing to act. This permitted Boaz to play the part of the kinsman-redeemer because he was not only a near relative and able to pay the price, but also willing to act.

In Revelation 5, then, the search is on to find a kinsman-redeemer who can and will redeem the earth on the conditions in the book. Adam lost the possession through sin and forfeited his right to be ruler of all the earth. Satan now holds claim to the earth by reason of Adam's sin, but Satan is only a usurper of the throne.

Nevertheless, the Word of God says that the whole world "lieth in wickedness (in the evil one)" (1 John 5:19). But when Jesus died on the cross and propitiated (satisfied) the Heavenly Father for the sins of the world, He also passed judgment on Satan (1 John 2:2; 3:8). . . . Jesus Christ is presented in Revelation 5:5 as the One who "hath prevailed to open the book, and to loose the seven seals thereof." Through His sacrifice on the cross, Christ has provided redemption for the world. He has paid the price to redeem man from sin and to prepare him for heaven. . . since Jesus Christ is entirely God, as well as entirely man, He is fully able to pay the price of redemption. Not only was He a near relative and able to pay the price of redemption, but He was also willing to act. He was willing to be the "Lamb of God, which taketh away the sin of the world" (John 1:29).[1]

Jesus in all these ways is worthy to open the book. Likewise, he is worthy to receive praise.

Jubilation in Heaven (5:8-14)

"And when he had taken the book, the four beasts and four and twenty elders fell down before the Lamb, having every one of them harps, and golden vials full of odours, which are the prayers of saints. And they sung a new song, saying, Thou art worthy to take the book, and to open the seals thereof: for thou wast slain, and hast redeemed us to God by thy blood out of every kindred, and tongue, and people, and nation; And hast made us unto our God kings and priests: and we shall reign on the earth. And I beheld, and I heard the voice of many angels round about the throne and the beasts and the elders: and the number of them was ten thousand times ten thousand, and thousands of thousands; Saying with a loud voice, Worthy is the Lamb that was slain to receive power, and riches, and wisdom, and strength, and honour, and glory, and blessing. And every creature which is in heaven, and on the earth, and under the earth and such as are in the sea, and all that are in them, heard I saying, Blessing, and honour, and glory, and power, be unto him that sitteth upon the throne, and unto the Lamb for ever and ever. And the four beasts said, Amen. And the four and twenty elders fell down and worshipped him that liveth for ever and ever" (5:8-14).

The immediate response made by all who observed Jesus' worthiness was one of jubilation and praise. And rightly so. In Jesus, we have much about which to rejoice. The four creatures and the elders, i.e., the Church, fall down before Jesus (the Lamb) and sing a new song. It

---

[1]Theodore Epp, *Practical Studies in Revelation*, Vol. 2 (Lincoln, Neb.: Back to the Bible Broadcast, 1969), pp. 35-37. Copyrighted material used by permission.

should be noted that each one in the Church had a harp (an instrument of praise) and golden vials full of odors (specifically identified as the *"prayers of saints"*—5:8). These definitely symbolize two key ministries of every saint—to worship God and to pray.

As they worship, they sing a new song to the Lord, especially to the Lamb. To say the song was new meant that it had not been sung before. Moses and the children of Israel sang a similar song of praise and worship which declared their jubilation in being set free from the bondage of Egypt (Exodus 15). The song now being sung declared the creation's jubilation in being freed from the bondage of sin (which Egypt prefigured). The old song of Moses prefigured the new song of the Church. This has been the new song of deliverance since Jesus' earthly ministry and will continue to be forever.

It is a simple song declaring a profound message of love and redemption. Jesus was *"worthy to take the book, and to open the seals thereof"* (5:9), reason enough to be jubilant. But Jesus had also been *"slain"* and had *"redeemed us to God"* by his *"blood"* (5:9). He was the perfect, one-time sacrifice who, having atoned for the sins of the world, became the "firstborn among many brethren" (Rom. 8:29). He had been raised from the dead to become the "head of the body, the church" (Col. 1:18). Many brethren would be raised to newness of life because of His obedience to God. For this He is greatly adored.

We must also see the origin of this great Church of which Jesus is the Head, *"out of every kindred* [family], *and tongue, and people, and nation"* (5:9). It was not fashioned exclusively from the Hebrew race. It was established out of all peoples of the earth regardless of their family background, what language they spoke or what nation they represented. The Church of Jesus Christ, which began officially on the day of Pentecost, is comprised of a diverse lot, saints from the four corners of the earth, "fitly joined together and compacted [put together closely] by that which every joint supplieth" (Eph. 4:16).

This Church is the one John saw praising the Lord Jesus and our heavenly Father. The Church has been singing this new song ever since that glorious day. Why? Because Jesus has made us *"kings and priests"* (5:10) unto our God (cf. 1:6). We who are Christians rule with Jesus as kings. We are overcomers and conquerors in Him. We reign above the sin of man and of earth. In concert with our kingly function as joint-heirs with Jesus (Rom. 8:17), we are also priests to God, presenting ourselves "a living sacrifice, holy, acceptable unto God, which is your reasonable service" (Rom. 12:1). We are kings and priests, *"and we shall reign on the earth"* (5:10).

Further rejoicing is observed by John as he sees angels join in heavenly praise with the beasts and the Church. The number of this assembly is stated to be 100,000,000 (*"ten thousand times ten thousand"*) plus millions (*"thousands of thousands"*) more (5:11). It is a vast company which ascribes praise to the Lord Jesus, saying, *"worthy is the Lamb that was slain to receive power, and riches, and wisdom, and strength, and honour, and glory, and blessing"* (5:12).

In one last expansion of this praise, John sees every creature worshiping the Godhead and saying, *"Blessing, and honour, and glory, and power, be unto him that sitteth upon the throne* [Father], *and unto the Lamb* [Jesus] *for ever and ever"* (5:13). To this the four creatures say, *"Amen"* (so be it), as the worship of the Church continues on into eternity (5:14). This complete worship by all created things, with the Church at the center, is given to Jesus, the worthy Lamb. He reveals God, reestablishes

God's communion with man and is worthy to receive all the praise for His work.

What follows in Revelation 6 through 16 is the redemption plan of God, revealed through the symbolism of the seals, trumpets and vials.

14

The First Six Seals

(6:1-17)

In this chapter we want to examine the first six seals and the events which transpire as they are broken by Jesus. Our understanding of these seals will be limited, however, if we do not see them in the larger context of the seals, trumpets and vials.

As Jesus breaks the first seal (6:1), a complete series of events, of which the seals are the first segment, begins to unfold before our spiritual eyes. The seals are but the "tip of the iceberg" in this redemption plan, which actually covers Revelation 6 through 19. This long section is the heart of the revelation of Jesus Christ. Revelation 1 introduced us to Jesus and the message of this book. Chapters 2 and 3 were a composite message to the Church on earth. Chapters 4 and 5 shifted the setting to the heavenly or spiritual realm in which the Church really operates and prepared us for the main message of the book.

The redemption plan which is written in the seven-sealed book and described in the following chapters covers the time span from Jesus' first coming until His return. The angel has told John, *"I will shew thee things which must be hereafter"* (4:1). The *"hereafter"* includes all of the intervening centuries through our day and until the coming again of Jesus.

The seals cover the entire spectrum of the redemption plan from the first advent of Jesus, pictured on a white horse bringing forth God's Word (6:2), to the second advent of Jesus described in Rev. 19:11, where he is seen on the same white horse. The seals (6:1-17; 8:1) are the major outline headings of the redemption story, while the trumpets (8:7-9:21; 11:15) and vials (16:2-17) provide more specific details on the events leading up to and including the second coming of Jesus. In addition to the trumpets and vials, other descriptive chapters and passages (7; 10; 11:1-14; 12-15) supplement, review and reiterate the message of the seals, trumpets and vials to make it complete and understandable. Just prior to the second coming of Revelation 19 we are provided two chapters (17 and 18) which give us key definitions of symbolic figures and happenings which were already given in preceding chapters, e.g., the seven heads (17:9) defines 13:1. Together, all this information tells the complete story.

The diagram entitled "Seals, Trumpets and Vials" should help to clarify and establish in our minds the outline of this story. The first six seals are opened and their events described. As the seventh seal is broken, it gives way to the sounding of the trumpets, which reveal God's judgment. With the sounding of the seventh trumpet, the seven vials of wrath are poured out. The events described by the trumpets and the vials happen as a result of the seventh seal being broken and occur during that time span. So the seals delineate the story outline while the trumpets and vials are but subheadings under the last major topic, the second coming of Jesus, represented by the seventh seal and culminated in Revelation 19.

The events of the seals, trumpets and vials do not carry us away from the main subject of the entire book, which is the revelation of Jesus. Please refer to the diagram entitled "Revelation on Jesus in the Seals, Trumpets and Vials." The seals show Jesus as Priest, the focus of our redemption plan, who appears at the conclusion of the events of the last seal. But this last seal includes the seven trumpets which show the judgment of God upon flesh. These seven trumpets show Jesus as King. The last trumpet includes the seven vials of God's wrath upon sin and

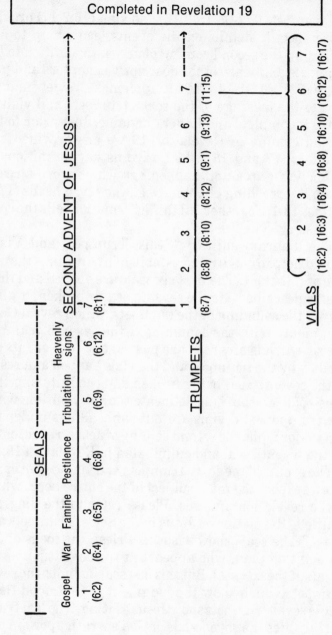

Seals, Trumpets and Vials

Completed in Revelation 19

SEALS

Gospel	War	Famine	Pestilence	Tribulation	Heavenly signs
1	2	3	4	5	6
(6:2)	(6:4)	(6:5)	(6:8)	(6:9)	(6:12)

SECOND ADVENT OF JESUS

TRUMPETS

| 7 | 1 | 2 | 3 | 4 | 5 | 6 | 7 |
| (8:1) | (8:7) | (8:8) | (8:10) | (8:12) | (9:1) | (9:13) | (11:15) |

VIALS

| 1 | 2 | 3 | 4 | 5 | 6 | 7 |
| (16:2) | (16:3) | (16:4) | (16:8) | (16:10) | (16:12) | (16:17) |

132

Revelation of Jesus in the Seals, Trumpets and Vials

Seals
(Show Christ as *Priest*)

1. White horse—6:2 (JESUS)
2. Red horse—6:4 (FLESH)
3. Black horse—6:5 (WORLD)
4. Pale horse—6:8 (DEVIL)
5. The Old Testament Faithfuls—6:9
6. Sun, moon, stars—6:12 (upheaval)

Trumpets
(Show Christ as *King*)

1. Hail, fire, blood—8:7 (cast upon earth)
2. Great mountain—8:8 (cast into sea)
3. Satan . . . . Wormwood—8:10 (bitter waters)
4. Sun, moon, stars—8:12 (partially darkened)
5. Opening bottomless pit—9:1 (darkness)
6. Fire, smoke, brimstone—9:13 (torment)

Vials
(Show Christ as *Judge*)

1. Poured upon earth—16:2
2. Poured upon sea—16:3
3. Rivers and fountains of waters—16:4
4. Sun—16:8
5. Seat (throne) of the Beast (darkness)—16:10
6. Upon the Euphrates—16:12 (three unclean spirits)

These calamities are visited on the world and the nations at large. What are the people of God doing during this time?

| 144,000 Sealed—Ch. 7 | Eat The Little Book—Ch.10 | Watch and Keep Garments—16:15 |

---

7. Silence in heaven—8:1 (half-hour)

7. Great voices—11:15 (rejoicing)

7. It is done—16:17 (finished)

The events of the seals tell the redemption story. The seventh seal includes the trumpets.

The trumpets reveal God's judgment upon *flesh*. The seventh trumpet includes the vials.

The vials show God's wrath poured out upon sin and unrepentant mankind.

133

unrepentant mankind and shows Jesus as Judge.

You may occasionally wish to refer back to the two diagrams to put the story back into focus. In the process of studying all the events and their details, it is very easy to lose sight of Jesus, who is being revealed. Even through all the cosmic and cataclysmic happenings of the vision, it is Jesus who is seated at the right hand of the Father and given "authority to execute judgment . . . because he is the Son of man" (John 5:27).

The Story-Thread of the Redemption

We often tend to view God's redemption of mankind in terms of the cross only. Indeed the cross was the place that the blood was shed by Jesus to "redeem us from all iniquity, and purify unto himself a peculiar people" (Titus 2:14). But the results of the work of the cross would take centuries to be applied in the lives of those who would respond to the call of Christ. And the completion of the redemption plan will occur when the bride is ready, as described in Revelation 21 and 22. It is during that complete chronology that the seven seals events occur.

There is nothing new about the text of the seals message. Like the rest of Scripture, it has been confirmed in other parts of the Word. In a brief study of Revelation, James McConkey[1] provides the essential clue to our understanding of John's vision, particularly the seals.

Jesus Christ did tell before this very same story of the End of the age and of His Coming again. And He told it to His same servant John. For on the Mount of Olives years before Christ sat and told to John and three other disciples the same story, in great brevity and simplicity, which He told in all its fulness and richness years

---

[1]James H. McConkey, *The Book of Revelation* (Pittsburgh, Pa.: Silver Publishing Co., 1921).

later to John alone upon the isle of Patmos.

Here, then, is an open secret. The Olivet story of Christ's Second Advent is the clue to the Book of Revelation. It is in a nut-shell what the Revelation is in full. It is the Master's pencil-sketch of which Revelation is the complete painting. The key to the story which Christ tells from heaven is this story which Christ told on earth years before. The twenty-fourth (24th) chapter of Matthew is the seed of New Testament prophecy, of which Revelation is the full-blown flower. Let us turn therefore to the ABC or Story-Thread of Matthew Twenty-Four. You remember the story. His disciples had been showing Him the great temple. They had pointed out to Him its lofty pinnacles, its rich adornments, its massive stones. And then the Lord turns to them and quietly says: "there shall not be left here one stone upon another, that shall not be thrown down." Doubtless they were amazed, and perplexed. I can fancy them saying one to another, "tomorrow we will go up to the Mount of Olives with Him. There we will sit at His feet and hold sweet communion as is our wont. Let us ask Him then what He means by this strange remark." So when they had come to the Mount and the Master was seated, they say,

> "Tell us when shall these things be?
> And what shall be the sign of Thy coming
> and of the end of the age?"

Note that they asked of Him a double question. There is a line of cleavage between the first clause and the second. First, "when shall these things be?" And by "these things" they meant the downfall of Jerusalem, and the overthrow of the temple of which He had just spoken, a disaster which was to take place in less than a half century from that time. Second, they asked Him, "what shall be the sign of Thy coming, and of the End of the Age?" a dual event which has not yet taken place, and which is separated from the first named catastrophe by almost two thousand years of time. Thus His answer covers events separated by a gap of many centuries simply because their question refers to both. The same line of cleavage in the disciples' interrogation appears therefore in Christ's answer. It cuts that answer sharply in twain between the fourteenth and fifteenth verses of this chapter. The first fourteen verses have to do with the first clause of their inquiry, "when shall these things be?" The remainder of the chapter is His reply to the second clause, "what shall be the sign of thy coming and of the end of the age?"

McConkey lays it out very neatly for us by paralleling the events of Matthew 24 (the thumbnail sketch) with those of the Revelation seals. The following diagram illustrates this comparison. Note that the events of the first four seals are general signs which occur during the life of the Church. They are not in the future, nor are they after any "rapture." Jesus said, "these things must come to pass, but the end is not yet" (Matt. 24:6). There would come wars, rumors of wars, famine, pestilences, earthquakes and the proclamation of the gospel. "And then shall the end come" (Matt. 24:14) but not before.

These things have been happening since the Church began. We see and hear of them in the news constantly. They are general signs of the times. The spreading of the gospel, war, famine and pestilences have always been and will continue to be until the Lord brings them to an end in the fullness of time. The Church is quite familiar

Matthew 24—Revelation Comparison

Matthew 24 Text			Revelation Text		Seal #
Gospel	(v. 14)	General signs	Gospel	(6:1-2)	1
War	(v. 6)		War	(6:3-4)	2
Famine	(v. 7)		Famine	(6:5-6)	3
Pestilence	(v. 7)		Pestilence	(6:7-8)	4
Tribulation	(vv. 15-28)	Special signs	Tribulation	(6:9-11)	5
Heavenly signs	(v. 29)		Heavenly signs	(6:12-17)	6
Second advent	(vv. 30-31)		Second advent	(8:1-19:21)	7

with them.

The fifth, sixth and seventh seals compare directly to tribulation, heavenly signs and the second advent happenings of Matthew 24. Whereas the first four seals were general signs of the times, these last three are special signs related to Jesus' coming. But, again, these events happen throughout the history of the Church, not in the future only. They may accelerate and be specifically evident to those on earth at Jesus' coming, but they are in progress even now.

There will be tribulation that will be difficult even for the Church to endure (Matt. 24:22). Then, "immediately after the tribulation of those days" (Matt. 24:29) heavenly signs and wonders will proclaim His advent. Finally He "shall gather together his elect from the four winds" (Matt. 24:31) at His coming. These Matthew 24 occurrences correspond precisely to the Revelation seals. Let's look at each one separately.

One: The White Horse (6:1-2)

"When the Lamb opened one of the seals, . . . I saw, and behold a white horse: and he that sat on him had a bow; and a crown was given unto him: and he went forth conquering, and to conquer" (6:1-2). The opening of the first seal reveals a rider on a white horse. The symbolic description gives us the clues we need to properly identify him. It is Jesus.

The white horse alone begins the clarification. Everything we have seen to this point concerning the color white has been associated with Jesus and the righteousness for which He stands, e.g., white raiment. It is little wonder that, in an event described by signs and symbols, Jesus would be portrayed on a white horse. This will be in direct contrast to the next three riders seen on red, black and pale horses.

"He that sat on him had a bow." Is this a "bow and arrow" type of bow, for the purpose of shedding blood? I think not. The Greek word for bow in this text is *toxon*, which is used in no other place in the New Testament. It translates "bow" but actually comes from the base Greek word *tiktō*, which means "to produce (from seed, as a mother or a plant), to bear, be born, bring forth, be delivered, be in travail." What else can this bow represent but the Word of God, which so accurately aligns itself with our definition? (See Jer. 1:11-12 for a similar "play on words.") Jesus said, "The words that I speak unto you, they are spirit, and they are life" (John 6:63). He also told the disciples in a parable that "the seed is the word of God" (Luke 8:11), identifying it as that which brings forth or bears life. The white horse rider of Revelation 19 has a sharp sword going from his mouth, in contrast to the bow seen with the white horse rider of the first seal. But both are weapons which pierce and cut asunder, in a symbolic way, the toughest skin and hardest hearts with the gospel message of life, that word which brings forth life as a seed.

Jesus is revealed here at the beginning of the redemption story. He is the *"beginning and the ending"* (1:8), the "author and finisher of our faith." He is shown bringing forth God's Word, the New Covenant of grace. He is going forth, by the Spirit of God, conquering and to conquer with the intent to save and foster life, not destroy it.

Although some Bible scholars call this rider the antichrist, the symbolism strongly points toward Jesus. He is even given a crown to wear, as surely the forces of Satan would not be. This is Jesus, the Word of God made flesh, proclaiming peace and life. He is the "firstborn among many brethren" to bring forth and proclaim the good news, the gospel message. And today it is going forth stronger and louder than ever through the Church, which is utilizing every given means to proclaim the gospel, such as television, radio and the printed media, as well as by word of mouth.

Our Matthew 24 parallel says that "this gospel of the kingdom shall be preached in all the world . . . and then shall the end come" (24:14). Taken in conjunction with the first seal, this tells us that the unfolding of this event will transpire in the life of the Church. Jesus brought the Word (He was the Word), and His Church will continue to proclaim it.

Two: The Red Horse (6:3-4)

"And when he had opened the second seal. . . . there went out another horse that was red: and power was given to him that sat thereon to take peace from the earth, and that they should kill one another: and there was given unto him a great sword" (6:3-4). This rider appears extremely different than the first. Though the white horse rider was a conqueror, this one is a killer.

The red horse upon which he is seen is descriptive of blood or bloodshed. He is given a great sword, symbolizing his ability to invoke it. His mission bears this out in that he was granted to destroy peace and cause men to kill one another. Who or what can this rider represent? Could he possibly be an agent of the Lord with such a dastardly objective? I believe not. But this rider, who is out to stir up war between the people of the world and strip it of peace, is permitted by God to carry on his activities.

The message is clear. *"Power was given to him . . . to take peace."* He or whoever he represents did not have the power to do this unless someone would grant it to him. The Lord is surely the only One who could grant such authority and power. We just learned that God *"created all things"* (4:11). So this must be a creation of God permitted to take peace from the earth and incite the earthly inhabitants to kill one another.

God did not create them specifically to do this. He has always been a Lifegiver and One to restore instead of destroy. Even in the Great Flood His purpose was to restore mankind to its original state. A force of spiritual beings (represented by the red horse rider), probably fallen angels, are allowed by God to cause this worldly agitation as part of His redemption plan. Humans are not God's only creation. He created angels long before us. And some of them rebelled long before us as well. It is that company of fallen angels, demonic spirits if you will, that God utilizes to accomplish His purposes.

God's purpose in permitting this ungodlike action seems at least twofold. First, the warlike atmosphere and unrest would serve to be a continual sign of earth's plight without Jesus and the kingdom He ushered in. Our Matthew 24 parallel says, "Ye shall hear of wars and rumors of wars. . . . For nation shall rise against nation, and kingdom against kingdom" (Matt. 24:6-7). This is clearly a sign to the earth, a general sign prophesied by Jesus, which indicates the breaking down of all earthly things (like the original temple), that heavenly or spiritual things may be built up in their place (like the Church).

Secondly, the wars and rumors of wars would have a tendency to cause mankind to choose between war and peace, earth and heaven, evil or righteousness, Satan or God. The Lord must have known that many more would choose the way of righteousness in the face of turmoil. This is true of the next four seals as well. God has the power to grant these things, and He can use them to His good.

Wars and rumors of wars are not simply for the future. It is a general sign for the Church age, one not designed by God but tolerated by Him in the growth and maturing of His Church through the centuries.

Three: The Black Horse (6:5-6)

"And when he had opened the third seal, I heard the third beast say, Come and see. And I beheld, and lo a black horse; and he that sat on him had a pair of balances in his hand. And I heard a voice in the midst of the four beasts say, A measure of wheat for a penny, and three measures of barley for a penny; and see thou hurt not the oil and the wine" (6:5-6). The first horse was white, signifying the righteousness of God. The second was red because of the war and bloodshed it represented. This horse is black and can only depict one thing—darkness or despair.

The kind of gloom this illustrates is revealed in what else John saw and heard. This time the rider had a pair of balances in his hand, the kind with which one might measure food. In fact, that is just what is spoken of—wheat, barley, oil and wine, the very basic staples of life, particularly in that day. The despair enters in when it is announced that it will take a *"penny"* (6:6) to purchase one measure of wheat or three measures of barley.

A penny's worth at the time of John's writing was valued at a full day's wages. It would take a full day's wages to buy one measure of wheat (approximately one quart) or three measures of barley (three meals' worth). When conditions are that serious, a famine is generally in progress.

This is distinctly confirmed if we go back to our Matthew passage. Not only would the general signs of the times include the gospel going forth and war, but it would include famine at various places on earth, "And there shall be famines . . . in divers places" (Matt. 24:7). Many of the affluent countries of the world have never experienced famine. But it is real to many parts of the world, particularly in places where the Lord God is shunned for the worship of false gods, cattle, images and the like.

The rider on the black horse is symbolic of worldwide famines. This seems to be a companion woe with that of war (the red horse) and that of pestilences (the pale horse yet to come). Again it would appear that God has permitted it to be so with the express purpose of drawing people to himself. Jesus told Satan, "Man shall not live by bread alone, but by every word of God" (Luke 4:4, from Deut. 8:3). In another place He said, "I am the living bread which came down from heaven: if any man eat of this bread, he shall live for ever" (John 6:51). To have physical life we must eat. But Jesus promised eternal life if we would partake of Him. Often it isn't until our stomaches are empty, and we are faced with the prospect of paying a day's wages to fill them, that we think of God, the Creator-Provider. It may be for that very purpose that this general sign is given and permitted by God.

The voice in the midst of the four beasts was careful to specify, *"and see thou hurt not the oil and the wine."* Here we are given assurance that God will provide for the saints even in the midst of famine. Though unbelievers may someday find themselves without provisions, God's people will always be cared for.

The rider of the black horse may also signify the famine of the Word of God in the world. Hosea spoke for the Lord to Israel, "My people are destroyed for lack of knowledge"

(Hos. 4:6). This black horse may very well also portray the hardship of a world which will not feed upon the knowledge of God, nor will they even hear it (cf. Amos 8:11). Whether you consider this spiritual aspect or see it fully in the natural realm, famine has been and is reality in the world. It is a sign of the end times with which the Church is acquainted.

Four: The Pale Horse (6:7-8)

"And when he had opened the fourth seal, I heard the voice of the fourth beast say, Come and see. And I looked, and behold a pale horse: and his name that sat on him was Death, and Hell followed with him. And power was given unto them over the fourth part of the earth, to kill with sword, and with hunger, and with death, and with the beasts of the earth" (6:7-8).

This is the last horse John saw, even though there are three more seals. This horse is pale, literally pale green. Upon this ghastly looking horse is a rider with the name Death, an implication of what would happen to many upon the earth. Death was also followed by Hell, the subsequent step for all who have not received salvation.

The message is highly visible. One-fourth of the earth's inhabitants would die and perish in hell. They would be destroyed by the sword (representing war and vicious crime), hunger (famine), the beasts of the earth (of which many are man-killers) and other forms of death. Jesus supplemented this account by describing in Matthew 24 "pestilences, and earthquakes" (24:7).

These kinds of tragedies have always been with us. Whether earthquakes, disease, disasters or other catastrophes, many have perished from the face of the earth. If statistics could have been kept on these throughout history they probably would total one-fourth of the population. Here, as with the red horse rider of war, *"power was given unto them"* to do it. Only God holds that kind of power, and it fits into His divine redemption arrangement. The God of love and mercy in His wisdom knows best what actions must be taken to turn men to himself, the source of life.

Five: The Faithful Souls (6:9-11)

"And when he had opened the fifth seal, I saw under the altar the souls of them that were slain for the word of God, and for the testimony which they held; and they cried with a loud voice, saying, How long, O Lord, holy and true, dost thou not judge and avenge our blood on them that dwell on the earth? And white robes were given unto every one of them; and it was said unto them, that they should rest yet for a little season, until their fellow servants also and their brethren, that should be killed as they were, should be fulfilled" (6:9-11).

When the fifth seal is opened, John beholds *"the souls of them that were slain for the word of God, and for the testimony which they held"* (6:9). First, let's consider where John saw them. He saw them under the altar. This altar in the heavenly realm signified the sacrifice that they had made for the Word of God and testifying for Jesus. This specifically implies those physically martyred for the faith. Yet it includes all of the saints who have gone on before us, those who have physically died and fully apprehended the heavenly realm in the Spirit.

In order for us to be born into the kingdom of God, we must die to the old man and be *"slain,"* if you will, for the Word of God. Paul told the Romans, quoting Ps. 44:22, "For thy sake we are killed all the day long; we are accounted as sheep for the slaughter" (Rom. 8:36). The "sword of the Spirit, which is the word of God" (Eph. 6:17) must pierce us through and slay us (the old man) before we can live (the new man). Therefore this assemblage of souls in heaven under the symbolic altar of sacrifice represents both those who have been martyred for Jesus' sake

144

(here we see the Matthew 24 parallel of tribulation) and those who have given themselves as a "living sacrifice . . . unto God" (Rom. 12:1). Tribulation has been a reality for the Church. From the first apostles to the disciples of modern day, many have given their lives for the gospel's sake. Persecution and tribulation for the faith have swelled that number of souls under the heavenly altar.

Secondly, and very importantly, they are alive and in the presence of God. The souls of believers are not asleep or still laying in the ground awaiting a resurrection. They are with God. With the death of the physical body, we are immediately in heaven. Jesus told the thief on the cross, "To day shalt thou be with me in paradise" (Luke 23:43). All Christians who have ceased to live on the earth are eternally alive and with God.

So alive and in touch with God are they that they ask, *"How long, O Lord, holy and true, dost thou not judge and avenge our blood on them that dwell on the earth?"* (6:10). They were ready for God to invoke judgment and wrath, which we shall see when we get to the trumpets and vials. The Lord gives them white robes to wear, confirmation of His promise in Rev. 3:5 to the overcomers. He then tells them to rest *"until their fellow servants also and their brethren, that should be killed as they were, should be fulfilled"* (6:11). This is just another way of saying to be patient until all those who should become part of the universal Church do so in the fullness of time and grace.

This is a picture of the faithful souls in the Lord waiting for judgment and the completion of the Church. From the death of the very first convert of Christianity until today, this has been the scene in heaven. We are not the only ones who get impatient with the grace of God. "The whole creation groaneth and travaileth in pain together until now. And not only they, but ourselves also, which have the firstfruits of the Spirit, even we ourselves groan within ourselves, waiting for the adoption, to wit, the redemption of our body" (Rom. 8:22-23). The fifth seal is not so much an event in time as it is a truth about the Church waiting to be completed and made ready.

Six: Great Upheaval (6:12-17)

"And I beheld when he had opened the sixth seal, and, lo, there was a great earthquake; and the sun became black as sackcloth of hair, and the moon became as blood; And the stars of heaven fell unto the earth, even as a fig tree casteth her untimely figs, when she is shaken of a mighty wind. And the heaven departed as a scroll when it is rolled together; and every mountain and island were moved out of their places. And the kings of the earth, and the great men, and the rich men, and the chief captains, and the mighty men, and every bondman, and every free man, hid themselves in the dens and in the rocks of the mountains; And said to the mountains and rocks, Fall on us, and hide us from the face of him that sitteth on the throne, and from the wrath of the Lamb: For the great day of his wrath is come; and who shall be able to stand?" (6:12-17).

With the opening of the sixth seal, John observed great upheaval both in the heavens and upon earth. We see events such as a great earthquake moving mountains and islands, the sun and moon being affected, stars falling from heaven to earth and the heaven being *"departed as a scroll when it is rolled together"* (6:14).

These seem to find their counterpart in Matt. 24:29, "Immediately after the tribulation of those days shall the sun be darkened, and the moon shall not give her light, and the stars shall fall from heaven, and the powers of the heavens shall be shaken." This corresponds exactly to our text and precedes the second coming. These are great heavenly signs which cause sinful mankind to hide and cry for the mountains and rocks to fall on them.

As with the first five seals, these events relate to current history. They could no doubt occur in the natural

146

realm prior to the second coming but are more likely spiritual happenings made known through heavy symbolism. They compliment the wars, pestilences, tribulation and death already described and, in a real sense, underscore God's everlasting intention to "shake" the heavens and the earth until unrighteousness exists no longer.

Hebrews 12:26-29 should be read as balancing Scripture. Verse 26 describes the great upheaval, "Yet once more I shake not the earth only, but also heaven." The purpose of God's "shaking" is to remove those things which are "made" (such as the incomplete works and sinful practices of men) in order that the things which cannot be shaken (the kingdom of God, the saints of the universal Church and their works in Christ) may remain. That is what the sixth seal portrays.

The combination of the first six seals tells of the dynamic events which God has ordained in His redemption plan to save the righteous in Christ Jesus. Looking upon these seals with a spiritual eye, it is obvious that all of them are in operation to some degree or another. The events of the first six seals are happening now, even though they will intensify just before the second coming of Christ. The events of the seventh seal occur with the return of Jesus. We will examine them directly.

Before moving to the "trumpets" of the seventh seal in Revelation 8, let us consider the thought-provoking seventh chapter of the Revelation.

15
The Redeemed
(7:1-17)

This chapter of the Revelation, though temporarily breaking the immediate thread of the seals and trumpets, adds great meaning to the situation being prophesied. It is given to us at the conclusion of the six seals and just prior to the opening of the seventh, which reveals the second coming.

The second coming is signaled by the trumpets (judgment) and vials (wrath). As the seventh chapter opens, we begin to apprehend the impending fury as we see four angels *"holding the four winds of the earth, that the wind should not blow on the earth, nor on the sea, nor on any tree"* (7:1). In other words, the earth is about to receive a great blast of destruction, probably the kind described in the events of the sixth seal, as well as those which we'll see with the trumpets and vials.

At this point in the Revelation, the events of the seven trumpets have not yet occurred. They seem to be impending destruction. With that knowledge, God moves to seal His servants to protect and keep them through the ominous and foreboding events about to happen. The angel with *"the seal of the living God"* (7:2) cries to the four angels with *"a loud voice"* (indicating that he speaks by God's authority) not to start the awful proceedings until he has completed his work. This angel represents Jesus and the authority granted Him by the Father. He is the only one who can delay the destruction until His servants are sealed.

The Sealed of Israel (7:3-8)
Who are these servants which are sealed by God? Some

have concluded that they are only a select group of Hebrew people in the last days who will be used to evangelize the earth. It is more natural to see these servants as the Church of Jesus Christ of all time.

The New Testament teaches that we become servants of God when we submit ourselves to the new life of the Spirit. Jesus said to the disciples, "Blessed are those servants, whom the Lord. . .shall find watching" (Luke 12:37). The apostle Paul taught the same principle of service. "Let every man abide in the same calling wherein he is called. Art thou called being a servant? Care not for it: but if thou mayest be made free, use it rather. For he that is called in the Lord, being a servant, is the Lord's freeman: likewise also he that is called, being free, is Christ's servant" (1 Cor. 7:20-22). We are the servants of Christ, called to serve in love and humility. We are the ones who have been sealed by God as illustrated in Revelation 7.

The servants of God are said to be sealed. The Scriptures say, "He which stablisheth us with you in Christ, and hath anointed us, is God; Who hath also sealed us, and given the earnest of the Spirit in our hearts" (2 Cor. 1:21-22). If we are in Christ, God has sealed us by the Holy Spirit, the very sealing process described in our text. Paul told the Ephesians the same thing, "After that ye believed, ye were sealed with that holy Spirit of promise" (Eph. 1:13), and "grieve not the holy Spirit of God, whereby ye are sealed unto the day of redemption" (Eph. 4:30).

Every member of the universal Church who is born again is sealed by the Holy Spirit. The Revelation is not referring to only a select band of Israelites in the end times who will be sealed.

Some commentators have felt that those sealed have to be physical Jews because of their description as from "all the tribes of the children of Israel" (7:4). Israel, however, is the Church (cf. chapter 4). It is a people of God rather than a political nation on the earth.

The Lord chose the original nation of Israel to prepare the way for the Messiah. The Hebrew people rejected, however, the New Covenant of grace through Jesus Christ (cf. John 1:11-13). The Lord then expanded Israel ("the rule of God") to the Gentiles also. To use Paul's analogy in Romans 11, the heathen Gentile people (wild olive branches) were grafted into the good olive tree (Israel), of which the Lord God and especially His Son, Jesus, is the root. The natural branches (the Hebrew people) were broken off because of unbelief. Now if they believe in the Lord Jesus, they can be grafted back in, "For if thou [the Gentiles] wert cut out of the olive tree which is wild by nature, and wert grafted contrary to nature into a good olive tree [Israel, the people of God]: how much more shall these [the Hebrew people], which be the natural branches, be grafted into their own olive tree?" (Rom. 11:24-25). What can they be grafted back into? Israel, the people of God, not the political country.

One confusing issue might be the symbolic numbers. They are not to be taken literally. The number 1,000 is the highest number which can be represented by the Greek alphabet. To indicate higher numbers, increments of 1,000 had to be employed. In this book of symbolism and signs, the number 12,000 for each tribe is merely representative of those from that tribe. The fact that there are twelve tribes causes the total which John heard to be 144,000 (12 times 12,000).

The terminology of *"tribes"* may be another confusing element. The original twelve tribes were the backbone of Israel, the framework from which grew the people of God, Israel. Each tribe was so named for one of the twelve sons of Israel (Jacob), through whom the seed of Abraham and sons of the promise would come. On his deathbed, Israel (Jacob) summoned his sons to prophesy over them (Genesis 49). As he spoke, he named them one by one and related what their future would hold in light of their nature or character. For instance, he said, "Gad, a troop shall overcome him: but he shall overcome at the last. Out of Asher his bread shall be fat. . . . Naphtali is a hind let loose: he giveth goodly words. Joseph is a fruitful bough" (Gen. 49:19-22). Thus he does with the other sons. The summary of all these prophetic descriptions paints a picture of the diversity which would exist in Israel, the people of God, who would eventually comprise a people from *"every kindred* [tribe], *and tongue, and people, and nation"* (Rev. 5:9).

The tribal system no longer exists in the country of Israel, for that matter. It is now a form of democracy, a political system from which Jesus said His kingdom would not be fashioned (John 18:36). The use of tribal terminology is foundational only.

It is in a highly illustrative way that the Lord revealed the redeemed of Israel to John. We should not be confused by the tribes or the numbers. Israel is a great cross section of people from all over the earth, including those of the Hebrew race who believe on the Lord Jesus Christ.

These 144,000 symbolize Israel in its fullness. God chose to represent the wholeness of Israel and its variety through the original twelve tribes. These are the sealed of God. They are not all sealed at the same time but as they receive the Lord Jesus through faith (cf. Eph. 1:13). And they will not be harmed by the impending destruction wrought by judgment and wrath, nor by any other disaster or calamity, past, present or future (cf. Rom. 8:35-39).

The Great Multitude (7:9-17)

What follows next in our text further reveals those who would be sealed. John now sees that "sealed" group with

151

his own eyes, *"after this I beheld, and, lo, a great multitude, which no man could number, of all nations, and kindreds, and people, and tongues"* standing before the Lord ascribing praises to Him (7:9).

The group of worshipers is so large that no "man" could number them. But God could. He who knows the flight of every sparrow and can account for every hair on our heads also knows the number of His redeemed. He revealed it symbolically and then showed John the great multitude as a way of confirmation.

John had previously seen the twenty-four elders, who represent the Church as a whole, before the throne. Now he sees the entire Church, including the symbolic elders, round about the Lord. There can be no doubt that this is the Church (Israel, the redeemed, the sealed) because of the description given. They are *"clothed with white robes"* with *"palms in their hands"* (7:9). They are blessing and worshiping the Lord. No other descriptions could better identify them.

One of the elders queried John, knowing fully well the answer, *"What are these which are arrayed in white robes? and whence came they?"* (7:13). John defers to the elder and receives the answer, *"These are they which came out of great tribulation, and have washed their robes, and made them white in the blood of the Lamb"* (7:14). Notice the elder doesn't say "the" great tribulation. He just says *"great tribulation."* There is a difference. He also says, *"these are they which came out."* The Greek is more accurately rendered "are coming out," making the statement continually present tense.

The Scriptures teach that all of the Church goes through great tribulation. Jesus said it would, "In the world ye shall have tribulation: but be of good cheer; I have overcome the world" (John 16:33). Our day-to-day survival as Christians facing sin and temptation is tribulation in itself. It is not easy to be overcomers when the world, the flesh and the devil continually try to strip us of our faith. Granted, there are those who have been martyred for the faith in every century from the first until now. But their number would not constitute the great multitude John saw. Only the entire Church of all time could possibly be represented by this great crowd of diverse people who weathered the trials and tribulations of earthly life to become overcomers.

Their robes are washed and made *"white in the blood of the Lamb."* Every saint's robe is washed, and all are a part of this great multitude.

Those of that great multitude are *"before the throne of God"* (7:15). They are very much in His presence. Jesus made it possible to enter God's presence now in the Spirit. We do not have to wait until we physically die or until the Lord's second coming to worship and praise Him as depicted here. If we are children of God and have begun to walk in the Spirit, we are part of this assembly and should praise the Lord in spirit and in truth (see comments on 4:9-11).

The saints are not only before the throne, they also *"serve him day and night in his temple"* (7:15). What is God's temple? The Scriptures say that we are , "Know ye not that ye are the temple of God, and that the Spirit of God dwelleth in you" (1 Cor. 3:16)? The elder says, *"he that sitteth on the throne shall dwell among them"* (7:15). And did not Jesus say this of kingdom life? "The kingdom of God cometh not with observation: . . . the kingdom of God is within you" (Luke 17:20-21), or "in the midst of you," as the American Standard Bible translates the verse. We should not visualize heaven in terms of grandiose visions of a great temple and other similar earthly structures. The spiritual realm is not like that of the earth. If we are in the Lord, however, He abides in us, and we have an eternal abiding place in Him. We must trust God that we'll always be with Him in the Spirit no matter what form that takes.

The elder goes on to say, *"They shall hunger no more, neither thirst any more. . . . For the Lamb which is in the midst of the throne shall feed them and shall lead them unto living fountains of waters"* (7:16-17). Jesus, the Lamb of God, is the living bread upon which the saints of God feed (John 6:51), and the Holy Spirit is that fountain of living water (John 7:38; Rev. 22:1) proceeding from God and the Lord Jesus. Natural hunger and thirst are not in view in this passage. The inner spirit-man hungers and thirsts, and Jesus abundantly satisfies our inner longings.

"Neither shall the sun light on them, nor any heat" (7:16), for there is *"no need of the sun, neither of the moon. . . for the glory of God did lighten it, and the Lamb is the light thereof"* (21:23). Every need we have is fulfilled in Christ Jesus. As we view this great multitude, we see a people having every necessity met with the presence of God dwelling in their midst. He is their bread, water, light and heat. They are protected and kept through any and everything, because they are sealed with the Holy Spirit and they are the redeemed of the Lord, washed in the blood of the Lamb.

Refer again to the diagram on pages 132 and 133. What are the saints doing during the calamities which the seals represent? They are being sealed, and as we've learned in this seventh chapter of the Revelation, they are worshiping and devoting their attention to God, specifically the Lamb of God, Jesus. We who are "sealed" in Christ can rejoice that, come what may, we are in the Lord, He is in us, and nothing can separate us from His love.

16

Sounding of the Trumpets

(8:1-9:21)

The opening of the seventh seal begins a long sequence of events which are climaxed by the return of Jesus. What John is about to see concerning these events is so dramatic and literally earthshaking that even the heavenly host, sensing the outcome, becomes silent, standing in awe of the impending judgment. The silence, according to John, lasted *"about the space of half an hour"* (8:1).

The significance, if any, of the half-hour time span is not clear. This could pertain to thirty minutes of time during the experience of John's vision as he was receiving it, but it more likely represents a symbolic amount of time, short in duration, which silences those in heaven who know what is about to happen. The mention of their silence underscores the gravity of the situation.

Jesus, who in a priestly function served the Lord by opening the seals revealing the redemption plan, now initiates the sounding of the trumpets, which declare his authority as King. Though the seven angels are used to sound the trumpets, it is Jesus who opens the last seal permitting them to act. Jesus is not only the High Priest of salvation for mankind but is also granted the right to execute judgment on the earth. He is proclaimed in Revelation 8 and 9 as King.

With the first advent of Jesus, judgment of mankind by God was openly declared through the crucifixion of the Son of God on the cross. It was completely provided for on Calvary (Col. 2:13-15). Every sin and act of unrighteousness was judged. The only way that mankind can escape the destruction associated with that judgment is to be covered by the blood of the Lamb, just as the children of Israel were protected by the blood of the passover lamb in Egypt. Whereas the provision for judgment was made at the cross (as was salvation) with the first advent of Jesus, the completion of that judgment begins here with the sounding of the trumpets announcing events which will have a devastating affect on all who are not covered by the blood of Jesus and specifically sealed by the power of the Holy Spirit.

It was a voice *"as of a trumpet"* that spoke with John in Revelation 1. It was the voice of Jesus, the same voice that now proclaims judgment. As the writer of Hebrews relates, "God . . . hath in these last days spoken unto us by His Son" (Heb. 1:2). Jesus now trumpets the message of judgment from God to an unrepentant earth. All the while, those of the Church of Jesus Christ on the earth remain safe, "under the shadow of the Almighty" (Ps. 91:1).

The seven angels who are to be used in sounding the trumpets are seen standing before God. They are given their instruments (8:2) and prepare to sound them (8:6). Before the trumpets are blown, however, John observes one more thing. *"Another angel came and stood at the altar* [in heaven], *having a golden censer; and there was given unto him much incense, that he should offer it with the prayers of all saints upon the golden altar which was before the throne"* (8:3).

This other angel represents Jesus. It may not be Jesus himself but surely reveals Him with regard to His ministry for the saints. Using His golden censer, a vessel used to burn incense, He offers His incense along with the prayers of the saints. The smoke of that incense, filled with saintly prayers, reaches the throne of God and comes before Him. This is a beautiful and symbolic way of portraying the intercessory ministry of Jesus for the saints. The book of Hebrews says, "He is able also to save them to the uttermost that come unto God by him, seeing he ever liveth to make intercession for them" (Heb. 7:25). It is this type of saving intercession, coupled with the sincere prayers of each saint, that will keep every believer from harm or destruction, particularly that which is brought forth through the judgments of God.

This angel representing Jesus then fills his golden censer with fire from the heavenly altar and casts it to the earth, amidst voices, thunderings, lightnings and an earthquake, all of which serve as warnings for the impending judgment.

This casting down of heavenly fire inaugurates the purging of the world, the flesh and the devil. These happenings could represent natural or spiritual phenomena, or both. If we view them spiritually, we will see that many have already been initiated. What we must remember is that the Church will be able to endure this judgment, whether natural or spiritual, as have the children of God throughout all history.

One: Hail, Fire and Blood (8:7)

As the first trumpet is sounded, *"hail and fire mingled with blood"* were *"cast upon the earth,"* burning up *"the third part of trees"* and *"all green grass"* (8:7). In the natural, this would be a damaging blow. Not only would the appearance of the earth be greatly marred, but the ecological balance with the destruction of some trees and all grass would be severely disrupted. Erosion and lack of fuel would be the immediate and most serious affects among many.

These things will in all probability happen literally. We should, though, remain open to seeing a spiritual side of these happenings. They may occur literally and then spiritually or in concert with one another. Because of this, we will explore the spiritual potential for each of the trumpets where applicable. The term *"third part"* throughout the Revelation means "partial" and should be applied with the events of these trumpets.

Spiritually, this first trumpet may refer to the trial by fire to which "every man's works" must be subjected (1 Cor. 3:13-15). The works of every man will be tried by the "fire" of the Spirit of God, who knows every man's heart. If the works are built on Jesus, they will remain. If they are built on anything else, they will be destroyed by the "consuming fire" (Heb. 12:29) of God.

Two: The Burning Mountain (8:8-9)

The second trumpet produces the vision of a *"great burning mountain"* being *"cast into the sea,"* upon which one-third of the sea becomes blood, one-third of the living sea creatures die, and one-third of the ships on the sea are destroyed.

Whereas things upon the land were destroyed by the first trumpet catastrophe, the oceanic life is now the target of this second trumpet. A great *"burning mountain,"* or what appeared to John as such, fell into the sea to produce the havoc described. Imagine one-third of the sea turning to blood, a virtual nightmare in itself! Yet the results of the blood produce death to one-third of all sea life. Beyond that is the destruction of the ships and, presumably, all those on board those ships.

The spiritual side of this trumpet event may relate to the judgment which God's Word will bring upon the earth. The great *"burning mountain"* might symbolize Mount Sinai, described in Heb. 12:18 as one which could not be touched and "that burned with fire." It was the site upon which Moses and the children of Israel received the law (Exodus 19).

The law was given by God as "holy, and just, and good" (Rom. 7:12). But in the flesh, man was unable to keep the law. Paul said, speaking of fleshly attempts to live by it, "The motions of sins, which were by the law, did work in our members to bring forth fruit unto death" (Rom. 7:5). But we were delivered from the law through Jesus Christ, who, sending the Holy Spirit, wrote the law upon our hearts, "not with ink, but with the Spirit of the living God; not in tables of stone, but in fleshly tables of the heart" (2 Cor. 3:3).

Apart from Jesus and the liberty of the Spirit of God, the law can only work death. The great *"burning mountain"* depicted in the second trumpet just might typify the working of death as a symbolic "Mount Sinai" falls to the earth causing destruction. The law works death to those who do not accept its fulfillment in Jesus Christ.

Three: The Fall of Wormwood

When the third trumpet sounded, *"There fell a great star from heaven, burning as it were a lamp, and it fell upon the third part of the rivers, and upon the fountains of waters; And the name of the star is called Wormwood: and the third part of the waters became wormwood; and many men died of the waters, because they were made bitter"* (8:10-11).

As a natural occurrence, this seems to touch the fresh waters of the earth, where the second trumpet had its impact on salt water. The implication is that a *"great star from heaven"* fell upon the rivers and fountains of waters, contaminating them and causing many to die as a result of its poisonous blow.

Even if this does happen in the natural, the spiritual lesson is so much stronger with this trumpet than the first two. The *"great star from heaven"* which was seen falling to the earth represents Satan. Most translations definitely show the name of the star as a proper noun, capitalizing it and giving it personality—Wormwood. The use of a *"star"* to represent an angel was already established in Rev. 1:20 where Jesus said, *"the seven stars are the angels of the seven churches."* This star called

Wormwood is not one of those seven but is one which fell from heaven to the earth. It is a fallen angel. Who could it be? It is Satan!

He falls upon the rivers and fountains of waters of the earth, which most likely represent our spiritual life. In fact, Jesus said, "He that believeth on me . . . out of his belly shall flow rivers of living water" (John 7:38). Satan's influence on our spiritual life is geared toward making us like him, a rebel and an outcast of God. His impact recorded here shows that one third of the spiritual life of earth became *"wormwood,"* or like him.

Wormwood is also a family of strong-smelling plants which produce a bitter-tasting, dark-green oil. The use of the name *"Wormwood"* for Satan shows his bitter mastery of lives not fully committed to God. He causes the sweet taste of divine spiritual blessings to become bitter in taste. Given full control, he will cause us to choke and die upon the wormwood, tainted "rivers of living waters."

The third trumpet reveals this happening. The effect reaches one-third of the earth, many men dying from *"waters"* made bitter.

Four: Sun, Moon and Stars (8:12)

The fourth trumpet proclaims again celestial events which affect the earth. *"The third part of the sun was smitten, and the third part of the moon, and the third part of the stars; so as the third part of them was darkened, and the day shone not for a third part of it, and the night likewise"* (8:12).

In the natural this appears to be a great heavenly upheaval, the balance of space near to the earth being greatly disturbed. Such events would have disastrous results, as the sun and moon in particular have great influence upon the earth's climate, oceans and general well-being.

Spiritually discerned, this fourth trumpet seems to

signify spiritual warfare. Drawing from Gen. 1:16, the sun, known as the "greater light to rule the day" is symbolic of Jesus, or more generally of the Godhead. The moon is representative of the Church, "the lesser light to rule the night." The moon has no light of itself. The illumination it produces is a reflection of the sun. The light which the Church shines forth is that of the Light, Jesus Christ. The stars are indicative of angels. Forces of all three realms are *"smitten"* during this conflict, even some who may have thought themselves to be aligned with Jesus Christ. Without him they are smitten down and rejected as is Satan and his host of fallen angels.

Whether natural or spiritual, these trumpets of judgment are permitted by God in the purging process of His redemption plan, which revolves around Jesus. We need not be concerned about them or their impact on the earth if we're in Him.

More to Come (8:13)

It would seem that the earth would be staggering from these blows of judgment, unable to take any more punishment. Yet we find, after the fourth trumpet, an angel proclaiming that there is more to come. What is about to happen will be cause for even more woe to the *"inhabiters of the earth"* (8:13).

The effects of the first four trumpets gripped the earth and some of its inhabitants. The remaining trumpets would sound even greater woe and would take their toll on mankind itself.

Five: The First Woe (9:1-12)

This fifth trumpet or first woe to mankind is both frightening and devastating. The star which falls to the earth is again an angel. This angel opens the bottomless pit with a key which is given him. What comes forth from the pit is deadly to mankind.

First, we must understand that the bottomless pit is hell. It was fashioned for the creatures of darkness. Jude declares that "the angels which kept not their first estate, but left their own habitation, he hath reserved in everlasting chains under darkness unto the judgment of the great day" (Jude 6). The trumpets are the judgments of God in that "great day." Here we see those reserved in "chains under darkness" permitted to go forth, with the sounding of the fifth trumpet, to maim and injure.

It's equally as important to comprehend that Satan and his army of fallen angels and even those who align themselves with the powers of darkness are locked into the bottomless pit of hell and are only permitted to venture from there when God allows them. Satan does not have the rule of this earth. Even though he and the other fallen angels are "principalities, . . . powers, . . . rulers of the darkness of this world" (Eph. 6:12), they are not the rulers of the kingdom of God on earth or in heaven which, through Jesus Christ, was made new. Demonic forces can only bind us if we subject ourselves to the places of darkness through sin and disobedience to God. Other than that, Satan and all other rebels of God are chained in darkness, impotent to touch the children of Light!

Before Jesus bowed His head on the cross and gave up the ghost, He said, "It is finished" (John 19:30). He could have meant His earthly ministry, and most likely did. But the depth of that statement may very well include the defeat and utter abolition of unrighteousness from the new order of the kingdom of God which Jesus came to establish on the earth. Jesus "spoiled principalities and powers, he made a shew of them openly, triumphing over them" (Col. 2:15). Does that sound like there is more to do? Does that indicate that Jesus has to conquer them again here in the Revelation? Of course not! Jesus did it on the cross! Let's stop giving Satan the rule in areas in which he has been defeated! Any power which we see unleashed in the Revelation is given by God only for a season and for a judgmental purpose. It is to that end that the fifth trumpet attack on mankind must be viewed.

Satan is allowed to send forth a demonic attack on the earth. He is the king of the bottomless pit who is known in Hebrew as *"Abaddon"* and in the Greek as *"Apollyon"* (9:11—destroyer, i.e., Satan). The prelude is *"smoke"* (9:2) rising from the bottomless pit, which darkens the sun and the air. The essence of the attack comes from the locustlike creatures which are manifested from the smoke.

The creatures are described in detail in 9:7-10. This passage symbolically describes the work of Satan. He and his demonic agents are bent on destroying mankind, not the earth itself. *"It was commanded them that they should not hurt the grass of the earth, neither any green thing, neither any tree; but only those men which have not the seal of God in their foreheads"* (9:4). Who will be harmed by these ghastly creatures? Only those who are not sealed by God, sealed and preserved by that precious Holy Spirit. If you are in that group of God's sealed, this trumpet, the other trumpets, the vials or any other force of destruction cannot hurt you, because you are in Christ!

Now many are not in Christ. They will be subjected to the punishing harassment of these locustlike creatures who will sting like scorpions and inflict great torment. Many will seek death to avoid them but will be unable to find it. The locusts will be given power to do this for five months, probably symbolic of a God-ordained period of time not necessarily restricted to five calendar months.

However or to what extent these creatures inflict their torture, physically or spiritually, they spell grave trouble for anyone not of the Lord. You have nothing to worry about if you're in Him!

Six: The Second Woe (9:13-21)

The sixth trumpet sounds the second woe to mankind, a woe far greater than the first. In fact, they become incrementally worse. The last trumpet, or third woe, ushers in the seven last plagues, even yet more horrible. In this act of judgment, God permits four angels, specifically prepared for this occasion, *"to slay the third part of men"* (9:15).

Actually, the four angels who are loosed lead or represent *"an army of horsemen"* (warriors) numbering 200,000,000 (9:16). These warriors are not specifically identified, but they don't appear to be of the earth. Their horses had heads *"as the heads of lions; and out of their mouths issued fire and smoke and brimstone"* (9:17). Instead of debating their origin, let's again look at the result of their ministry.

One-third of all men are consumed by the fire, smoke and brimstone coming from the mouths of the horses. This just happens to be the way God chose to reveal their demise. Many people without the knowledge of God will be consumed by the fire of God, whatever method that employs. Death awaits the unsaved. Life abounds for the redeemed of God. Here, death catches up with one-third of unrepentant mankind.

The remaining sector of the unsaved world, coldhearted and rebellious in its way, continues to refuse to repent of its sin—idol worship, murder, sorcery, fornication and theft (9:20-21). How much at odds with the will of God can those be who refuse to repent in the face of these calamities? The continuation of judgment for those who remain will be completed in the seventh trumpet (third woe), which is fulfilled in the seven last plagues. Before we see that happen, several intervening chapters of the Revelation will be covered first.

17

Eat the Little Book

(10:1-11)

Upon viewing the events of the sixth trumpet, John saw *"another mighty angel"* (10:1). It was no ordinary angel; it was *"mighty."* From the description John provides, we can again see Jesus revealed. This is not Jesus being manifested but Jesus being represented by the angel, another of many ways in which Jesus has been revealed in the Revelation.

Look how well the account relates Jesus and His authority. The mighty angel was *"clothed with a cloud."* This could refer to a literal cloud of the variety we might see in the sky but more likely relates to the cloud of witnesses spoken of in Hebrews 12 (cf. comments on 1:7). The saints of all time which comprise the "cloud" of witnesses are the Body of Christ, of which Jesus is the Head. His Body, arrayed in white raiment by His blood, provides the illusion of clothing Him.

"And a rainbow was upon his head," the type of bow God designated as an everlasting sign of His commitment not to destroy mankind again (Gen. 9:8-17). That bow now finds its fullness and completion in Jesus Christ. When we are in Christ, God looks upon Him, observes the bow of His covenant and cannot destroy us because of His Word. We are safe and complete in Christ.

"And his face was as it were the sun," an indication of the great Light that Jesus is, the eternal illumination of the redeemed creation (cf. Rev. 21:23-24). *"And his feet as pillars of fire,"* a description similar to that given in 1:15. These characteristics are too coincidental for them not to represent Jesus. He is to be seen in this *"mighty angel."*

"He had in his hand a little book open" (10:2). Nothing more is said of the little book or what it might be until later in the passage. Many would venture that it is the seven-sealed book of Revelation 5, which has now been fully opened. But if that were the case, it seems John would have said so. But he does not. The sealed book and its content is now no secret. John sees and describes *"a little book opened"* which, in the hands of one representing Jesus, most likely represents the Word of God.

With the exception of the Revelation which John was now receiving and would subsequently record, most of what would become the written Word was now complete. Only canonization, which would eventually place all the holy writ between two covers, remained. So the *"little book"* in the hand of the mighty angel characterizing Jesus is, in all likelihood, the Scriptures available and open to all of mankind. More evidence to that end will be presented directly. But let's finish our examination of the mighty angel.

As a sign of his great authority and dominion of all the earth, he is observed with one foot upon the sea and the other on the earth. He is a stately figure of power and might. He then *"cried with a loud voice, as when a lion roareth"* (10:3), further proof of his representation of Jesus. It is Jesus who, earlier, had been called *"the Lion of the tribe of Judah"* (5:5).

The nature and character of our Lord Jesus and all that God has made Him comes through loud and clear in this description. Through His obedience to the Father, Jesus will always be *"mighty"* in this universe. And so we have another disclosure of Him given in the mighty angel standing atop the world.

The Mystery of God (10:3-7)
"And when he had cried, seven thunders uttered their voices" (10:3). We are not told whether they all uttered

166

one message in unison or separate messages. No doubt, even if there were seven separate messages, they had the same theme. The use of the number seven shows the spiritual perfection or completeness of the message. They must have uttered something so exciting and revolutionary that John hastened to write down what he had heard. But the Lord spoke to John in *"a voice from heaven"* and said, *"Seal up those things which the seven thunders uttered, and write them not"* (10:4).

Now what could John have heard that God did not want revealed directly through writing? If we go a little further, we see that *"the mystery of God"* is mentioned (10:7). John apparently heard *"the mystery of God"* revealed. Though God would have every person to know and comprehend that mystery, He would have them know it by seeking Him diligently and by coming to Him with an open heart ready to apprehend spiritual truth rather than merely by seizing it intellectually by being told. In 1 Corinthians 2 Paul explains how to grasp spiritual truth. Our spirit must receive these truths by the Holy Spirit (1 Cor. 2:10-11).

The uttering of *"the mystery of God"* follows the appearance of the mighty angel holding the little book, which is God's Word. And it is through that Word that the mystery is revealed. God fully exposes it to those who draw close to Him through the Word.

What is the mystery of God? If you have been born again you know. The Word reveals that it is Christ (Col. 2:2), and more specifically, "Christ in you, the hope of glory" (Col. 1:27). That is what John heard and wanted to write. But the Lord wanted mankind to understand the mystery through a desire for righteousness.

After John was stymied in his attempt to record *"the mystery of God,"* the mighty angel declares to the Lord *"that there should be time no longer"* (10:6). In other words, the angel was entreating the Lord to close the age of grace, that time would be no longer for this era of universal history, when the Church of Jesus Christ is swelling its ranks with people from all over the earth. We can sense that the mighty angel is a spokesman for the whole creation, which is groaning, "waiting for the adoption, to wit, the redemption," waiting "for the manifestation of the sons of God" (cf. Rom. 8:18-23).

It is said in the next verse (and it is not too clear who reveals it) that *"the mystery of God should be finished"* (10:7) when the seventh angel begins to sound. It is the sounding of that last trump that signals the end of the age as we know it now. Then will the period of grace be complete. Then will all of God's judgments have been accomplished upon the earth. Then will the kingdom of God be complete. Then will the Church which remains on the earth be translated fully into the spiritual realm with the rest of the Church (cf. 1 Cor. 15:51-57; 1 Thess. 4:15-18).

The prophets of old have declared it, the Son of God revealed it, the Church has anxiously awaited it, and now we see the total fulfillment of it made known in the vision to John. It will surely be finished *"in the days of the voice of the seventh angel, when he shall begin to sound."* All the while, God has again provided for His people.

Provision for the Saints (10:8-11)

What is given to John next is an indication of what we must do as we await the completion of the divine events triggered at the last trump. We must eat the Word of God, a tremendous provision for the saints.

John is instructed from heaven to ask the mighty angel for the little book. He obeys, and having received the little book, he is asked to eat it. *"It shall make thy belly bitter, but it shall be in thy mouth sweet as honey"* (10:9). All of this comes true as John eats the little book and, as a closing remark for this segment of the vision, John is told to *"prophesy again before many peoples, and nations, and tongues, and kings"* (10:11). Now what does all of this mean for us? How is it a provision for the saints?

The little book is the Word of God, as we have already discerned. We, as John, must eat it. It is the bread of life, that *"hidden manna"* for the overcomers in Christ Jesus (2:17). It will give much-needed strength as we await the appearing of Jesus.

We are not literally to eat the book. Not many would incorrectly interpret this and attempt to swallow the pages of their Bible. What is spoken of here is a spiritual ingestion of the truth recorded in the Scriptures, which are the Word of God in print. We must eat, as such, and make it part of us, delighting in it and meditating upon it day and night (cf. Ps. 1:2; Psalm 119).

As we do this, the Word will taste as sweet as honey in our mouths. It is delightful and delicious to taste. Yet, when we are serious with God and feed upon that Word, taking it into our inner parts, it becomes bitter within us, because it demands a total yielding and submission to the righteousness and divine ways of God, to which the fleshly man is opposed. For that reason it becomes bitter in our belly.

But we need it nevertheless. It is one of God's provisions for the saints. He has given the Holy Spirit and the Word (we will explore this further in the next chapter). We need them in conjunction with one another to remain strong spiritually, to endure the trials and temptations of life on this earth and to proclaim the gospel message to all the earth, even as John is instructed to prophesy to the multitudes. And that brings us to our last point.

The Church is visible on the earth during all of these happenings. It has not been raptured. It is still there, "eating the Word" to grow and mature. It is "eating the Word" in order to fulfill the Great Commission. Take another look at the diagram on page 132. After six seals were broken, the Lord revealed His Church as the sealed multitude (Revelation 7). They were being sealed and kept through the power of the Holy Spirit. Now after six trumpets are sounded, the Church is instructed to *"eat the little book"* (Revelation 10), through the example of our brother John. The Spirit and the Word are the greatest provisions God could have given to keep the Church through the perilous times described. And it is no coincidence that Revelation 7 and 10 provide the Church with those lights of hope and help in the midst of a dark hour upon the face of the earth.

We need not allow our hearts to be overcome by fear of the seals or the trumpets. The Spirit and the Word will see us through!

18

My Two Witnesses

(11:1-14)

The same mighty angel that told John to eat the little book now tells John to *"measure the temple of God."* To accomplish the task, John was given a *"reed like unto a rod"* (11:1). This rod was a type of measuring device, like a ruler or yardstick of today. It has an important spiritual meaning, which we will see directly.

What was the temple that John was requested to measure? Many feel that it is the building which will be built upon the site of the original temple in the city of Jerusalem in Israel. After all, many would say, "Doesn't the Old Testament predict that the temple is going to be rebuilt?" The fact is that the prophecy of a rebuilt temple has already been or is being fulfilled. If you study the Old Testament you will find that the physical temple of God in Jerusalem, originally built by Solomon, and destroyed by invading armies, was rebuilt when the people of Israel returned there from exile, around 520-15 B.C. In fact, if you study history, you will find that Jerusalem was seized time after time. It's no telling how many times the temple there was partially rebuilt or repaired as a result of aggression against Israel the nation.

In view of Israel's rejection of Jesus, He predicted the temple's final destruction. As His disciples marveled at the temple, He said, "See ye not all these things? verily I say unto you, There shall not be left here one stone upon another, that shall not be thrown down" (Matt. 24:2). Approximately forty years later, around A.D. 70, the Roman empire literally fulfilled that prophecy and completely destroyed the temple in Jerusalem, along with

171

most of the rest of the city. And if Jesus said there would not be one stone left upon another, we can be sure that that's exactly the way it was.

The destruction of the physical temple of God was inevitable. Jesus prophesied it and it came to pass, never to be built again. No New Testament Scripture implies its reconstruction. However, the New Testament does give us some information about a temple, the kind that John was probably being asked to measure. It is the totality of all believers, who comprise the New Testament temple of God, the Church (cf. comments on 3:12; also see chapter 4, "The Household of Faith").

With Jesus all things became new (Rev. 21:5). Through Him the priesthood, the city of Jerusalem and the temple became new. They had prefigured what was to come in the covenant of grace in a spiritual sense. The Aaronic priesthood gave way to the priesthood of all believers, who minister and serve God and one another. The city of Jerusalem was to become the New Jerusalem, the Church, described in Revelation 21 and 22. And the temple, whose walls and stately appearance had been ravaged again and again, would find its spiritual counterpart in all the saints, who comprise the dwelling place of God, the New Testament temple.

The New Jerusalem of God does not have a natural or physical temple. Later, when John is given a glimpse of her glory, he says, *I saw no temple therein: for the Lord God Almighty and the Lamb are the temple of it*" (Rev. 21:22). Are you in Christ Jesus? Then you are a part of the temple of God!

The temple, even under the Old Covenant, was a dwelling place for the Lord. His presence abode in the Holy of Holies, the innermost part of the temple edifice. With the New Covenant, all believers, individually and corporately, have become the dwelling place of God, His temple. "Know ye not that ye are the temple of God, and that the Spirit of God dwelleth in you?" (1 Cor. 3:16). We must rightly divide the Word about this very important issue. The temple of God is a grand and glorious spiritual abiding place for the Holy Spirit, which gives it life. It is this temple that John is instructed to measure in the Spirit.

The mighty angel says to *"measure the temple of God, and the altar, and them that worship therein"* (11:1). In essence he was being asked to determine the size and stature of this spiritual place and how full it had become with the saints of God. The impression is given that God wanted to check on how close it was to being complete. To determine this, he would have to measure the inner court, which included the Holy of Holies (cf. Matt. 27:51), the place we now have the privilege to enter through Christ (cf. Heb. 9:11-14).

"But the court which is without the temple leave out, and measure it not; for it is given unto the Gentiles: and the holy city shall they tread under foot forty and two months" (11:2). The word "Gentiles" is symbolic of those who are not real Jews. Gentiles are those who have not been grafted into the "olive tree" (that is, Israel—cf. Romans 11). We have already seen that the true Jew, or chosen person of God, is one who is circumcised in the heart, a spiritual or inward Jew (chapter 4; cf. Rom. 2:28-29). All others are "Gentiles," a term synonymous with the unrighteous of the world. They are outside the temple, in the outer courts of God's presence. They *"tread under foot"* the *"holy city."* They mock and scorn all that is spiritual and they who have drawn close to God, i.e., the real Church of Jesus Christ. The *"forty and two months"* are merely symbolic of a period of time, like the seventy weeks of Daniel, and probably relate to the time from Pentecost to the Second Coming.

To measure the temple of God under the New Covenant would equate to identifying the saints or, in another sense, how much the saints of God had conformed to the image of Jesus Christ. How can we identify the saints? How can they be measured? They are measured by the yardstick that is Jesus himself, into whose image they are being conformed (cf. Rom. 8:29; Phil. 3:20-21; 1 John 3:2). God does not need to have buildings measured. His temple is measured in terms of perfected saints who, having been fashioned into the likeness of His Son, are permanent "lively stones" of the house or temple of God, Jesus himself being the "chief corner stone" (1 Pet. 2:5-6). All others (Gentiles) cannot be measured as part of the temple of God.

The Spirit and the Word (11:3-4)

In conjunction with "measuring" the temple of God, which is His dwelling place, John is told about God's two witnesses who would be given power to *"prophesy a thousand two hundred and threescore days, clothed in sackcloth "* (11:3). The speculation which has developed concerning the identity of these witnesses is phenomenal. Everyone from Enoch to Moses to Elijah has been suggested as a possible candidate to fit the description. A close examination of the details, however, reveals that these two witnesses are not human personalities at all but spiritual instruments used to witness to the plan of God, and specifically to Jesus Christ.

The two witnesses are described as *"the two olive trees, and the two candlesticks standing before the God of the earth "*(11:4). Right away we have an apparent problem. The two witnesses are described both as two olive trees and as two candlesticks, which gives the impression of four witnesses. The dual description of each witness, however, is most likely given to represent the measure with which they are presented to the people of the earth. God sent the two witnesses with each of them given in a double portion.

Elisha received a double portion of the Holy Spirit

(2 Kings 2). It is that measure of visibility and availability which is also given to the two witnesses of Revelation 11. Each of them is presented in a double portion. We must draw upon the symbolic teaching of the Scriptures to really understand who they are. God is not describing two men, nor even two angels, in using the symbolism of the olive tree and the candlestick.

The olive tree is used to describe the first witness because of the fruit and subsequent main product derived from it, olive oil. Olive oil was used over and over again throughout recorded Scripture in the act of anointing. When Saul was anointed for the work God had for Him, Samuel poured a vial of oil upon his head (1 Samuel 10). What was the symbolism of the oil and the anointing process? It represented the anointing of the Holy Spirit.

Therefore this first witness represents the Holy Spirit. The one witness is described as two even as God is represented in a Trinity yet is One. The Holy Spirit has been poured out upon the earth to witness to the love and power of God. It was given to draw men to God by witnessing Jesus Christ to their hearts. Jesus said of the Holy Spirit, "But the Comforter, which is the Holy Ghost, whom the Father will send in my name, he shall teach you all things, and bring all things to your remembrance, whatsoever I have said unto you" (John 14:26). That is the work of this great witness sent by God to testify of Jesus.

The second witness is said to be *the two candlesticks.* The plurality of this witness is again indicative of the double portion with which it is given. We've already seen the use of the candlestick in John's vision. In 1:20 John was told that the seven candlesticks (or lampstands) represented seven churches. The same Greek word is used here in Revelation 11 to denote the candlestick, or lampstand. The witness of the candlestick is that of the Church. The Church is the lampstand of the pure Light of Jesus, the source of illumination to the people of God (22:5). But the way in which the Church witnesses to the world and gives it Light is by holding up the Word of God and living it in their lives. It is God's Word prevalent in the Church that constitutes the second witness.

The Word of God is not necessarily printed material. It is not so much the Bible of which we speak. It is the will of God, the directives of our heavenly Father. The very Word of God was most clearly represented in His Son, Jesus. He was the Word made flesh (John 1:14). He was God's perfect will manifested to the world. And it is in that context that we must understand the witness of the Word in the Church.

God's perfect will can be manifested in the Body of Christ, the Church, as it was in the Lord Jesus. In fact, we are to be conformed to His image (Rom. 8:29). We are to show forth the will or Word of God by the nature of Jesus which dwells in us. We are to bear witness to Jesus Christ not only as we speak the Word, but as it is made alive within us as a witness to the earth.

The two witnesses are the Spirit and the Word. At another time, John recorded that "there are three that bear witness in earth, the Spirit, and the water, and the blood: and these three agree in one" (1 John 5:8). Here, we see two of the three, the Spirit and the Word (cf. Eph. 5:26, where water is linked with the Word). The third witness of 1 John 5:8, blood, speaks of "the blood of the Lamb" shed by Jesus during His earthly ministry. The Spirit and the Word are the two witnesses symbolically represented to John as *the two olive trees, and the two candlesticks.*

The length of time given by God for the ministry of the Spirit and the Word is given as *a thousand two hundred and threescore days.* These 1260 symbolic "days" are the same as the forty-two months described earlier (11:2). They represent the time from Pentecost (the beginning of the Church age) to the second coming, or at least a time just before the second coming when the ministry of the Church would be "finished" (11:7).

Their Ministry (11:4-6)

They stand *"before the God of the earth"* (11:4) and move over the face of the earth as His witnesses. They have great power to perform their ministry, as do the Spirit and the Word. Harm which might be inflicted upon them is repelled by *"fire"* proceeding out of their mouths (11:5). No human agents could do that. In explaining this as a "spiritual fire" proceeding from the mouth of such men as Moses or Elijah, many Bible expositors undermine their own position of literalism and add weight to the belief that these are "spiritual" witnesses. They are the Spirit and the Word, not mortal men or their spirits walking the earth.

The Spirit and the Word have *"power to shut heaven, that it rain not"* and *"have power over waters to turn them to blood and to smite the earth with all plagues, as often as they will"* (11:6). It does not say how often this power is executed, but it certainly is available to be used by God. The power is not human power but the power of God.

The Spirit and the Word are jointly the most powerful force at work to win people to the Lord. The Lord may use the Church as the vessel, but it is the potency of these two witnesses that makes the difference. They are the *"two olive trees, and the two candlesticks"* (11:4). They are God's two witnesses to show His might and power as well as His love and compassion.

One Final Show of Power (11:7-14)

The Spirit and the Word have been bearing this witness ever since Pentecost. It is only when God is about to close the age of grace that their testimony comes to an end, by His own decree. It is then that the Lord allows *"the beast that ascends out of the bottomless pit"* (which we will examine in detail in chapter 21) *"to make war against them, and shall overcome them, and kill them"* (11:7).

How can the beast, representing all that is evil, be capable of or be allowed by God to overcome and kill the Spirit and the Word? How can these things be rationalized in signs and symbols?

First, it would seem that the language of *"overcoming"* and *"killing"* is merely a representation of a time when God will permit the work of these two witnesses to be completely halted in the public arena, giving the impression that they have been overcome and killed. We must understand the deep symbolism here. In a manner of speaking, unrighteousness seems to the world to have overcome and "killed" the righteousness of God which it has rejected. Can't you imagine how happy the unrepentant people of the world would be if the Spirit and the Word, which continually attempt to draw them away from sin and the "pleasures" of the fleshly life, would, all of a sudden, be cut off? John was told that they would *"rejoice . . . and make merry, and . . . send gifts to one another"* because their torment was over (11:10).

Secondly, their dead bodies lying in the street is strictly a symbolic way of describing their inactivity at this God-appointed time. The *"great city"* (11:8) where they are killed and upon whose *"street"* they *"lie,"* apparently dead, is not Jerusalem. Later we'll see that the *"great city"* is *"the woman"* (17:18), or "Babylon the Great, the Mother of Harlots and Abominations of the Earth" (17:5). She represents all the rebels of the world who oppose God and refuse to acknowledge Him. It is upon the "street" of the world that the Spirit and the Word lie "dead," "killed" by the wickedness of the powers of darkness, where they are suffered not to be put in "graves." In other words, spiritual things are not just forgotten, they are publicly mocked.

Spiritually, the great city is called *"Sodom and Egypt,*

where also our Lord was crucified" (11:8). One immediately thinks at this point of natural Jerusalem. Indeed Jesus was crucified there. But, using the same spiritual interpretation, Jesus was crucified in the *"great city,"* that much larger "metropolis" representing the wicked world. Spiritually it is called *"Sodom and Egypt,"* terms synonymous with sin and rebellion. It was on the "streets" of the world system that Jesus was mocked, rejected and eventually crucified, as are the Spirit and the Word. But also in like manner, they are raised up.

With one final show of power for the people of the earth, God causes the *"Spirit of life"* to enter into them after a short period of time described as *"three days and a half"* (11:11). They are raised up as was Jesus. This powerful miracle of God is visible to the world and causes great fear to fall upon those who once again see the Spirit and the Word, who once again experience their powerful presence on the earth.

Taking this all one step further, not only are the Spirit and the Word crucified and resurrected like Jesus, they also ascend into the heavenly realm by divine invitation, where all their enemies behold them (11:12). This could be interpreted to mean that the Spirit and Word are withdrawn briefly just before the appearing of Jesus. This symbolism makes as much sense in the Spirit as it does trying to visualize it happening to mortal men in the natural. This event, like some we've already seen and others yet to come, paints a literary picture for us of God's work upon the earth in the last days before the second coming. It is powerful and dramatic.

A great earthquake occurs, and one-tenth of the city falls (11:13). A portion (one-tenth) of the world (the great city) is cast down and some die (7,000 is probably a symbolic number) in the midst of these earth-shaking events.

One last point of interest is the *"remnant"* (11:13). This *"remnant"* might represent that small sector of people who remain faithful to God. We see here the saints still remaining on the earth, awaiting the return of Jesus. They are frightened by all these happenings but look to the heavenly realm and give the God of heaven glory and praise. What they see transpiring around them is traumatic and intense, but the kingdom of which they are a part "cannot be shaken" and "cannot be moved" (Heb. 12:27-28). In this they are comforted.

If we miss the spiritual view and content of this eleventh chapter of the Revelation, the remainder of the vision becomes equally difficult to formulate in our spiritual understanding. Chapters 12, 13 and beyond are equally symbolic. These are spiritual circumstances described in earthly terms. They are given in signs such as the measuring rod (Jesus), the temple (saints of God), the outer court (the unsaved) and the two witnesses (the Spirit and the Word) for our spiritual comprehension. If we see them as such, they will be a blessing to us.

"The second woe is past; and, behold, the third woe cometh quickly" (11:14). Much has occurred since the sixth trumpet of 9:13. It foretold the events of the second *"woe"* to the earth and was followed by the descriptive and instructive tenth and eleventh chapters, which elaborated on important themes. Now the seventh or last trumpet is about to sound. The remainder of the Revelation concerns itself with the reviewing of great spiritual themes already established and concludes with the appearing of the Lord Jesus himself.

180

19

The Last Trump Sounds

(11:15-19)

With the close of the eleventh chapter of the Revelation we find the sounding of the seventh or last trumpet. This is the last one. There are no more. This trumpet signals the appearing of Jesus Christ.

Though the last trumpet is sounded here, the more familiar events of Jesus' coming will not appear until we get to chapter 19 of the Revelation. There we find the actual appearing of Jesus on the white horse, the marriage of the Lamb and the final purging of all evil. Some of the events recorded in the intervening chapters are very specifically part of the seventh trumpet happenings. Other events, as we shall shortly see, are given as review, repeated and told in a different way, with fresh symbolism, to support and strengthen the total message of God's redemption plan for the earth. Revelation 12 and 13 are good examples.

"And the seventh angel sounded" (11:15). With the exception of some "flashback" text (chapters 12 and 13), the remainder of the Revelation relates directly to the second and only coming of Jesus. The sounding of the trumpet here corresponds with 1 Cor. 15:51-52 and 1 Thess. 4:16-17. They both mark the return of Jesus and the "visible" establishment of the kingdom of God. Those who see the seventh trumpet of the Revelation as different from the "last trump" of Corinthians and Thessalonians are attempting to validate their concept of two comings of Jesus—one to "snatch away" or rapture the Church and the other to bring the Church back to earth for a "millennial" reign. The Revelation, however, which deals

with past, present and future provides only for one coming. Christ's coming is signaled by this last trump.

"The kingdoms of this world are become the kingdoms of our Lord, and of his Christ; and he shall reign for ever and ever" (11:15). The kingdom had been established through the finished work of Jesus at Calvary, yet it was not observable with the eye of the flesh. It has only been observable in the Spirit by those who have been born again (cf. Luke 17:20-21). With the return of Jesus, however, the rule of righteousness is visibly established for all to see. The kingdoms of the world were not really the Lord's kingdoms until this point. They were political in nature and filled with those who had no desire to worship and serve the one true God. Now they will be purged to establish a complete and righteous theocracy, with Jesus Christ as Ruler and Lord.

"And the four and twenty elders, which sat before God on their seats, fell upon their faces, and worshipped God" (11:16). The Church in the heavenly realm, symbolized by the twenty-four elders, worships the Lord and gives Him thanks for what is happening. That which the saints of all time have hoped for is finally coming to pass. They magnify God for exercising His power and securing His reign.

At the same time, *"the nations were angry"* (11:18). Why? Because God, as part of the seventh trumpet events, is going to pour out His wrath and pronounce judgment upon the wicked and unrighteous while, concurrently, rewarding those who have been faithful to Him. God is about to *"destroy them which destroy the earth"* and exalt *"them that fear thy name"* (11:18).

Jesus is seen in the midst of the Church in the heavenly realm. *"The temple of God was opened in heaven, and there was seen in his temple the ark of his testament"* (11:19). Jesus is the *"ark."* Under the Old Covenant the ark contained the Mosaic tablets, Aaron's rod and the golden manna pot, all representing the fundamentals of that covenant (and prefiguring Jesus as the fulfillment of the law, His resurrection from the dead and Jesus as the Living Bread, respectively). Under the New Covenant, Jesus is the focus. He is our "ark" and is revealed as such in our text.

So these events bring us to the second coming and provide the framework in which we will examine the remainder of the vision. The seventh trumpet turns our attention to the second coming and all that is associated with it. Let's begin with the interesting twelfth and thirteenth chapters.

20

Wrestling with Principalities, Powers and Rulers

(12:1-17)

This chapter cannot be viewed as a chronological sequence to Revelation 11. The time span which it covers reaches from before the birth of Jesus to the second coming events marked by the last trump. The insertion of this beautiful overview at this point in the vision serves to put everything into perspective. It takes all of the small sequences which John has experienced and pulls them together, showing them in a different way.

In order to understand the content of this chapter, we must first examine the main characters. After identifying the *"woman,"* the *"dragon"* and the *"man child,"* we will look at the plot of the story, an extremely fascinating view of spiritual history.

The Woman (12:1-2)

The *"woman"* which John saw is Israel. It is not so much the nation of Israel but the Israel of history, the people of God. It is true that Jesus, the Son of God, was brought forth in the flesh through the Hebrew people. It is with that thought in mind that many assume this woman to be the nation of Israel. However, at the time of Christ's birth, they were the only people of God. They were a nation and did produce Jesus in the flesh. But they were only the first of many "families of the earth" to be blessed (Gen. 12:3). Through Abraham, the father of faith, and his descendants would come forth a nation (Israel) which would be as difficult to number as the stars of the heaven (Gen. 15:5).

That has been one of the primary points of this

commentary (cf. chapter 4, "The Household of Faith"). Israel ("the rule of God") is a long succession of faithful people to God. It was begun in the Hebrew flesh but broadened with the first coming of Jesus and the descent of the Holy Spirit of God at Pentecost. Israel became a broad and universal base of saints, just as Abraham had been promised. It is that Israel that brought forth Jesus and is, in the Spirit, still bringing forth Jesus. Paul told the Galatians, using the same symbolic language, that he travailed "in birth again until Christ be formed" in them (Gal. 4:19). Israel, the household of faith, is the woman of Revelation 12.

The woman was *"clothed with the sun"* (2:1), an illustrative way of indicating she shone with the brightness of Jesus, the Light of the world. Indeed Jesus clothes the people of God with white raiment and the pure light of his righteousness. The moon was *"under her feet,"* which indicates she was standing on the firm foundation of the Church, a reflection of the Sun (Jesus). The "lesser light" which rules the night, a term used for the moon, represents the Church, which has been granted all power and authority over spiritual darkness (night). Israel, the people of God, is standing on that firm foundation. The Church is victorious over any spiritual force which opposes God, even death. *"And upon her head a crown of twelve stars"* (2:1). This is a crown for our Lord Jesus, the Head of the Church and the focus of the Revelation. The twelve stars represent either the twelve tribes of Israel, the apostles of Christ or both. In any case, they characterize the government of God in Israel, the Church.

"And she being with child cried, travailing in birth, and pained to be delivered" (12:2). The Romans were told that "the whole creation groaneth and travaileth in pain together until now" (Rom. 8:22). In both texts, the idea is this: the people of God are suffering the birth pangs that come before delivery. They are having Christ formed

within them. They are dying to self. They are decreasing that Jesus may increase. They are putting off the old man and putting on the new (Eph. 4:22-24; Col. 3:9-10). These things are as painful as the contractions of birth. They make the people of God cry out in pain.

The Dragon (12:3-4)

This is probably the easiest of the characters to identify. He is specifically identified in verse 9 as Satan. In other places called the serpent, he is here called *"a great red dragon"* (12:3). That red dragon is Satan and, more specifically, the manifestation of Satan upon the earth. The color red may be used to represent his bloody aggression against God's children and the creation in general.

He had *"seven heads and ten horns, and seven crowns upon his heads"* (12:3). The very same description is provided in Revelation 13 for the "beast" (13:1). It is there that we will find just how this accurately describes the work of Satan on the earth. The dragon is Satan, whether you see him as a person or in the activities of his manifested presence on earth.

"His tail drew the third part of the stars of heaven, and did cast them to the earth" (12:4). This is another way of saying that there were many angels who also fell with the rebellion of Satan (or Lucifer). He rejected the authority of God and, in the process, influenced a sector of the heavenly populace. All of these were cast down from the heavenly realm. Jude 6 supports this amply.

"The dragon stood before the woman which was ready to be delivered, for to devour her child as soon as it was born" (12:4). Satan wanted no part of Jesus nor His ministry, for he knew that it meant the end for him. He was ready to pounce upon Jesus as soon as He was born. He made a futile attempt to snuff out His life through Herod (Matthew 2). He tried desperately in the wilderness to

destroy the Son of God, but Jesus turned him back with the Word of God. He repeatedly labored through the Pharisees and the Sadducees to put an end to Jesus but was unsuccessful. This dragon is definitely Satan, who sought to kill Jesus and still looks to abort the forming of Jesus within the body of Christ, the Church.

The Man Child (12:5)

"And she brought forth a man child, who was to rule the nations" (12:5). This *"man child"* is Jesus. He came forth from the people of God and continues to do so in the Spirit. The logical extension of Jesus is the Church. God has abolished "the law of commandments contained in ordinances; for to make in himself of twain one new man, so making peace" (Eph. 2:15). He has taken the faithful of the Old Covenant and merged them with Gentile believers to form one new "man." That is the mystery of the ages, "Christ in you, the hope of glory" (Col. 1:27).

Whether initially in the flesh or spiritually in the midst of His people, the man child is Jesus. Having been introduced to the cast of characters found in our text, let us now examine the story plot revealed in the remainder of the chapter.

The Plot (12:5-17)

The people of God brought forth the Savior, Jesus Christ. Though He was fully divine, He was fully man. He accomplished his ministry on the cross, where He in obedience to the Father erased "the handwriting of ordinances [sin] that was against us" (Col. 2:14). Jesus did that in spite of Satan's attempts to destroy Him.

The Revelation text says that the woman's *"child was caught up unto God, and to his throne"* (12:5). That equates to the ascension. After the resurrection and a short period of time following it, Jesus was caught up to the heavenly places to sit at the right hand of the Father, to begin the rule and reign He was destined to have. Revelation 12:5 takes us from Jesus' birth to His ascension in thirty short words. What we have is a great panoramic spiritual overview given in a short but sweet spiritual analogy.

With Jesus in the heavenly realm, the people of God, characterized by the woman, *"fled into the wilderness, where she hath a place prepared of God, that they should feed her there a thousand two hundred and threescore days"* (12:6). In the absence of Jesus, the woman would have to be cared for in that place prepared by God. That place is the abiding that we have in God in the Spirit even while we are here on earth. This time in the "wilderness" covers the same time frame given in Rev. 11:3—1260 symbolic days, most likely from Pentecost to the return of Jesus. Upon what does the woman *"feed"?* She feeds upon "every word that proceedeth out of the mouth of God" (Matt. 4:4), as did Jesus when he was in the wilderness (cf. Luke 4). She is sustained by the Word and protected by the Spirit. To the world it is a *"wilderness."* To the people of God, it is a *"place prepared."*

The Church and individual believers are safe as long as they remain in that abiding place. They are only vulnerable when they venture out from that protection. Many saints do just that and find themselves at the mercy of Satan and his temptations, instead of abiding "under the shadow of the Almighty" (Ps. 91:1).

Revelation 12:7-10 relates heavenly warfare, a confrontation between the forces of Michael the angel and the forces of the dragon. In context of the plot that is developing, this comes on the heels of Jesus' ascension and the flight of the Church to the wilderness. It seems to portray the defeat and casting down of Satan and the other fallen angels concurrent with Jesus' ascendance to heavenly rule. The finished work of Jesus signals the defeat of Satan. He and his associates are removed from the heavenly realm with the cleansing of that place by the blood of Jesus (cf. Heb. 9:22-28). Satan may have had access to the courts of heaven before the cross (Job 1:6-2:1; Zech. 3:1), but not so after the work of atonement was finished.

We can deem this true, as John was told, *"Now is come salvation, and strength, and the kingdom of our God"* (12:10). The finished work of Jesus brought about salvation and strength. Jesus ushered in the kingdom and established it with "power" on the day of Pentecost. The perpetual accuser of the brethren was cast down. Paul told the Colossians that Jesus "spoiled principalities and powers, he made a show of them openly, triumphing over them in it" (Col. 2:15). Jesus' completed earthly ministry made all of this possible.

Though Satan is cast down to the earth and is in the process of seeking to destroy and devour, we must remember that he was defeated. He has no power. It was stripped from him when he was cast down. He and his demonic friends are like mad dogs who have been muzzled. They can growl and foam at the mouth even in the presence of the saints of God, but they cannot bite or spiritually harm them. Many people do not realize that fact and succumb to their deception. The knowledgeable people of God do not have to put up with them.

Our text says, *"They* [the people of God] *overcame him by the blood of the Lamb, and by the word of their testimony; and they loved not their lives unto the death"* (12:11). Here we see the full overcoming power of the Church available now, not a special anointing for a select few in the future. Demonic spiritual forces may be all around us, but we overcome them by the blood of the Lamb and by testifying to the lordship of Jesus in our lives. "We are more than conquerors through him that loved us" (Rom. 8:37).

Satan *"knoweth that he hath but a short time"* (12:12).

189

The world is full of people who submit themselves to Satanic powers. Satan uses these people to physically harm the saints. That is why it says that, even though they overcame by the blood and their testimony, *"they loved not their lives unto the death"* (12:11). Witches, Satan worshipers and other individuals rebellious to the will of God are used by Satan every day in an attempt to adversely influence and destroy the lives of Christians, e.g., suggesting suicide.

A tremendous spiritual conflict is going on that we cannot even see. Paul said, "We wrestle not against flesh and blood, but against principalities, against powers, against the rulers of the darkness of this world, against spiritual wickedness in high places" (Eph. 6:12). We can be assured that these evil forces rule only the "darkness" and the areas in which they are given control. But we have the victory in Jesus, who is already ruling and reigning in the heavenly realm. We can reign with Him even now by being overcomers (cf. Rom. 5:17). We must abide in Him. And though the conflict might even threaten our physical lives unto death, nothing can touch us spiritually. If we are born again by the Holy Spirit of God, nothing "shall be able to separate us from the love of God, which is in Christ Jesus our Lord" (Rom. 8:39). Not even death.

The dragon, recognizing that he is cast down to earth and only has a short time, is persecuting the people of God. Jesus amply warned us that it would be so (Matt. 5:10-12; John 16:33). That is why we must be on spiritual guard. We must put on "the whole armour of God, that ye may be able to withstand in the evil day, and having done all, to stand" (Eph. 6:13). The paradox is this: we are troubled on every side, death itself staring us in the face, yet we have already won the victory in Christ (cf. 2 Cor. 4:8-12).

All of this turmoil is not the wrath of God. It is merely

the persecution and tribulation which every saint endures to some degree as a part of maturing and growing in grace. We will discuss the wrath of God in our comments on chapter 16, where the vials are poured out. What we are addressing here is persecution which emanates from the evil one. It is being permitted by God until the return of Jesus.

Verses 14 through 17 of our subject text reviews again this persecution. This time the safety and protection afforded the saints of God is described as being lifted up on an eagle's wings. She was *"given two wings of a great eagle, that she might fly into the wilderness, into her place, where she is nourished"* (12:14). These two wings might be prayer and praise. An absence of both in the life of a believer leaves him "grounded," and an absence of one or the other leaves him lopsided and flying in circles. Amidst the persecution and struggle which Christians must face, God has made provision for us to be lifted out of it in the Spirit. We can soar like the eagle above the problems of the earthly plane, because we have the elevating power of the Spirit of God within us.

Not all the saints use their wings to carry them into the lofty places with God. But they could and should. God wants us to draw close to Him and, when we do, Satan must flee from us (James 4:7-10). Isaiah the prophet said it this way, "They that wait upon the Lord shall renew their strength; they shall mount up with wings as eagles; they shall run, and not be weary; and they shall walk, and not faint" (Isa. 40:31). Like many of the promises God has made to those who believe and are faithful to Him, we cannot benefit from this unless we recognize it is there, appropriate the gift and use it. The Lord wants us to "fly" in the spiritual realm with Him, not crawl in the dust of the earth like Satan, who was condemned in the Garden to such an existence (Gen. 3:14).

Our safety in the Lord is shown yet another way. This

191

time *"the serpent cast out of his mouth water as a flood after the woman, that he might cause her to be carried away of the flood"* (12:15). The *"water"* coming from the mouth of Satan could be interpreted as demonic words or thoughts. Water is used in the Scriptures symbolically and is associated in several places with the Word of God (Eph. 5:26; 1 John 5:7-8). Since the "water" in this instance is proceeding from the mouth of Satan, it would conversely be an evil word or thought. The "water" could also represent the flood of circumstances in which Christians find themselves (cf. Matt. 7:24-27). Satan would love to drown us in situations which would make us turn from God. Regardless of the precise nature of the "water," God thwarts Satan's efforts.

Even the earth helped the woman. *"The earth opened her mouth, and swallowed up the flood which the dragon cast out of his mouth"* (12:16). Here we have a description of the help given the saints by God. With His power, the faithful are spared, as these evil words, thoughts or circumstances are swallowed by the earth. In symbolic terms we are given comfort in the assurance of God's care.

Because of his failure to destroy the Church, *"the dragon was wroth with the woman"* (12:17). He hates his station in life. Try as he may, he cannot touch that which is rightfully God's. We are the Lord's property, redeemed by the blood of Jesus, a price that only God could pay through His Son. Unable to destroy the early church that brought forth the "man child," Jesus, Satan prepared himself to *"make war with the remnant of her seed, which keep the commandments of God, and have the testimony of Jesus Christ"* (12:17). Satan has continued his attack on each generation of the Church, but the enemy of our souls will have no greater luck in defeating any of God's children now or in the future than he has in the past! Why? Because he is the one that is defeated!

This entire chapter of the Revelation describes a wrestling match, a spiritual conflict in which we must see ourselves the victors in Christ. We have already won the match. Satan has been "pinned" on his back for eternity. He can only make a reversal and takedown on us if we leave the harbor of safety in Christ who is our strength. Let us reckon ourselves "to be dead indeed unto sin [and the unrighteousness into which Satan is endeavoring to draw us], but alive unto God through Jesus Christ our Lord" (Rom. 6:11).

21
The Two Beasts
(13:1-18)

To begin our study of the beasts, let us first establish that our text is not necessarily chronological in relation to the seals, trumpets and vials. It covers a broad span of history, revealing the existence of the "beast" in all generations and not just in the perceived "end times" or future history of the world. We have been in the last days ever since Jesus' first earthly appearance. The works of the "beast" have been prevalent throughout and even before the first advent of Jesus. If we can keep this in mind, the Holy Spirit will be able more easily to teach us the great spiritual truth about this chapter.

Secondly, and just as important in our understanding of this text, is that the "beast" is not the "Antichrist." In fact, the word *antichrist* as a proper noun can be found nowhere in the Scriptures. Neither is it implied anywhere as being manifested in any one individual personality. "Antichrist" is a spiritual conglomerate of all who oppose God.

The Scriptures clearly speak of many who might consider themselves to be the Christ in the last days. But anyone claiming to be such is called a "false Christ," not "Antichrist." Jesus said, "Many shall come in my name, saying, I am Christ. . . . For there shall arise false Christs, and false prophets, and shall shew great signs and wonders; insomuch that, if it were possible, they shall deceive the very elect" (Matt. 24:5, 24). These false Christs are just that—imposters, wolves in sheep's clothing, who live to malign the saints. But they are not the "Antichrist," a world power figure, as many teach.

The Scriptures do declare "antichrists" and a "spirit of antichrist." The prefix "anti" means against. Coupled with the word Christ, it means any one who is against the Christ, our Lord Jesus. "Anti" also means "instead of" and is used quite often to denote substitution. The antichrist spirit is not only against Christ but also offers a religious substitute in His place. In that category would be the cults and heresies of the world, which have deceived many.

Following are the five sole uses of word "antichrist" in the Scriptures, all found in four verses of John's epistles: "Little children, it is the last time: and as ye have heard that antichrist shall come, even now are there many antichrists; whereby we know that it is the last time" (1 John 2:18). "Who is a liar but he that denieth that Jesus is the Christ? He is antichrist, that denieth the Father and the Son" (1 John 2:22). "And every spirit that confesseth not that Jesus Christ is come in the flesh is not of God: and this is that spirit of antichrist, whereof ye have heard that it should come; and even now already is it in the world" (1 John 4:3). "For many deceivers are entered into the world, who confess not that Jesus Christ is come in the flesh. This is a deceiver and an antichrist" (2 John 7).

From these verses we can see the scriptural definition and usage of the word. It speaks of those, many who already existed in John's time, who oppose Christ and specifically deny that He ever came in the flesh, another way of denying His divinity and lordship. The spirit of antichrist has been in the world ever since Christ was born and will continue to be until His return. But there is no superstar "Antichrist," no isolated individual leading the "down with Christ" movement in the last days! The beast of this chapter is real, and it definitely opposes Christ and the kingdom of God. But it is not a mere man. It is a spiritual attitude universally resident in all creatures at enmity with God.

The First Beast (13:1-4)

The first beast that John saw rose *"up out of the sea"* (13:1). Those lacking spiritual discernment might envision a slithering, grotesque sea creature, like the Loch Ness monster, raising its ugly head from one of the major oceans of the world. We must recognize the symbolic, spiritual vocabulary of John to visualize the true meaning of the beast. It is actually a long succession of earthly kingdoms, whose purpose and charter is economic growth and dominance, a characteristic of those who oppose Christ. They would rather be rich and prosper than to enter into the kingdom of God through Jesus.

The fact that the beast came *"out of the sea"* is explained by examining the use of the word *"waters"* later in the vision. *"Waters,"* a word synonymous to that of *"seas,"* are said to be *"peoples, and multitudes, and nations, and tongues"* (17:15). With that understanding, we can see the origin of the beast. It came from among the various peoples of the world, earthly kingdoms reared up with Satan at the helm. If Jesus is not Lord of peoples' lives, Satan quickly moves to assume that role. For the seven kingdoms that arose among the people of the world, this was the case.

The beast is described as having *"seven heads and ten horns, and upon his horns ten crowns, and upon his heads the name of blasphemy"* (13:1). The seven heads represent seven kingdoms throughout history, from which an eighth kingdom, comprised of many with a spirit of antichrist, develops. But they are all intertwined and related. The ten horns are earthly kingdoms not empowered at the time of the vision but which receive power with the beast. Jointly they embody the beast which, if anything, could be called the antichrist of the world. But, again, this antichrist is much more than one person calling the shots. It is a parade of world figures under the dominance of Satan and his realm. (For more on the heads and crowns of this beast, see 17:7-18 and the comments upon that passage.)

The beast that John saw was *"like unto a leopard, and his feet were as the feet of a bear, and his mouth as the mouth of a lion: and the dragon gave him his power, and his seat, and great authority"* (13:2). The three animal descriptions may very well represent the first three earthly kingdoms of the seven involved in the beast. Together, then, they provide an overall illustration of the speed, strength and majesty of the whole beast. There may be some question as to which earthly kingdoms they specifically represent, but that is less significant than their meaning. The beast is quick and cunning like a leopard, strong and awesome like a bear, noble and dominant like a lion. These characteristics prevail to some degree in all the earthly kingdoms which have been, are now or shall be part of the beast.

The common feature is that he (they) receives his power from the dragon, which has been identified as Satan. Satan has been involved with all the nations of the world at some time or other. He has, however, used certain specific nations to carry out his evil plans. The Roman empire is, in all likelihood, one of the seven *"heads"* of the beast. Greece, Persia, Babylon, Assyria and Egypt are also possibilities for these past kingdoms. And who could doubt that Russia, with its great influence and imposing military strength, might be one of the seven *"heads"* in existence now, or even the eighth mentioned in 17:11. The key is that Satan provides the power, position and authority for these kingdoms of the earth. He spurs them on to their devious work.

"And I saw one of the heads as it were wounded to death; and his deadly wound was healed: and all the world wondered after the beast" (13:3). This tells us, in a token manner, that one of the kingdoms will come back to life and appear whole after once being defeated and apparently "dead" as far as the world is concerned. Some suspect this

to be the Roman empire which, in the minds of many scholars, has never really died out, though it has no officially recognized world rule. Frankly, it could be any one of the past nations of the world which have been part of this beast. But there is one possible candidate for this resurrected "head" which should at least be considered.

From John's point of view, the nation of Israel could have qualified as part of the kingdom of the beast. As a political/religious system, they were adamantly opposed to Jesus the Messiah and His messengers. Before the Jewish leaders teamed up with the Romans to put Christ to death, Jesus predicted their national destruction. Around A.D. 70, His prophecy was fulfilled—the nation was "wounded to death."

Then in 1948, the nation revived, to the amazement of the world. As a nation, they are no more favorable to the Messiah now than they were 1900 years ago. Whether or not Israel the nation will fulfill the role as the wounded and resurrected head of the beast, Christians should at least be careful not to show favoritism to any nation outside of Christ. Israel the nation included, God is "no respecter of persons" (Rom. 2:11, in context—cf. chapter 4, "The Household of Faith").

It is noted that the world *"worshipped the dragon which gave power unto the beast: and they worshipped the beast, saying, Who is like unto the beast? Who is able to make war with him?"* (13:4). The world has always *"wondered after the beast"* (13:3). By the word *"world"* is meant people who have rejected the kingdom. Refusing to bless and praise God, the creator, they naturally worship and marvel after the "prince of the power of the air" (Eph. 2:2).

The first beast is a political entity. It is a group of nations—past, present and future—which have been used by Satan throughout the centuries to work unrighteousness in the world and draw people away from God. The identity of past participating nations is not so important as recognizing the contemporary participants which impact our lives. If we are in Christ and walking in the Spirit, we will be able both to recognize the *"beast"* and to be safe from it.

Works of the First Beast (13:5-8)

What is the prime function of this beast? He speaks *"great things and blasphemies. . . . against God . . . his name, and his tabernacle, and them that dwell in heaven"* (13:5-6). His initial attack is oral, the voicing of opposition to God and His very existence. The intent seems to be one of making Christians doubt their faith. Through the rebellious and worldly people of the earth, he has done a good job, because many believers have been sidetracked in the faith and fallen prey to his deception. For this, the beast will pay.

In concert with his oral attack, he makes *"war with the saints,"* trying desperately to *"overcome them"* (13:7). This is the wrestling and spiritual struggling we have already discussed (12:5-17). Satan, through this beast, is endeavoring to draw the sheep from the sheepfold. He accomplishes it through spiritual propaganda, demonic oppression and possession of the mind. The faithful of God, however, will remain the overcomers through *"the blood of the Lamb, and by the word of their testimony"* (12:11).

It is important to see that Satan has this power only because it is given to him. Somehow in the divine plan of God, he is granted permission to carry on his work. Apparently, under the oversight of God, this persecution accomplishes a "weeding out" and "pruning" that must take place among the people of God. The branches that are not bearing fruit are removed so that the fruit-bearing branches can flourish. Satan is working through the beast for *"forty and two months"* (13:5). This is the same 1260 symbolic "days" preceding the return of Jesus that was mentioned in 11:2-3 and 12:6 and 14 (42 months times 30 days equals 1260 days, or three and a half "years"—"time, times and half a time").

Only they *"whose names are not written in the book of life of the Lamb slain from the foundation of the world"* worship Satan and the beast (13:8). True saints of God can never pledge allegiance to them or anything of the world. The children of God already have someone to worship. He is the Lord God, Immanuel, the eternal Spirit of life.

Words of Comfort (13:9-10)

Sandwiched between the description of the first beast and that of the second, we find some words of comfort and explanation. Our heavenly Father, wanting us to understand completely His redemption plan, says by the Spirit, *"If any man have an ear, let him hear. He that leadeth into captivity shall go into captivity: he that killeth with the sword must be killed with the sword. Here is the patience and the faith of the saints"* (13:9-10). Two points seem to stand out.

First, the Lord is saying, "I am in control; these things must be. For the perfect maturing and gathering of my people, these events will, by my authority, take place." There is some solace in the face of this world's troubles in comprehending that God is in command. All that occurs can only happen if He allows it. Even if we as saints are physically killed, the Lord has not forsaken us, for He has caused us to have eternal life. In Him, we can never die! We need not be impatient or lacking in faith as persecution and tribulation come to pass in our lives.

Secondly, the Lord is saying, "Those that would lead you astray and into bondage, those that would kill you with the sword, will in the same manner go into captivity and be killed." The emphasis here is, "Vengeance is mine; I will repay, saith the Lord" (Rom. 12:19; cf. Deut. 32:35).

We need not concern ourselves with striking back or taking revenge into our own hands. God will mete out judgment according to the works of every individual. We must be full of faith and patience, even if physical death should come our way.

The Second Beast (13:11)

"And I beheld another beast coming up out of the earth; and he had two horns like a lamb, and he spake as a dragon" (13:11). We are told that this beast came *"out of the earth"* or, in other words, rose up from among the people of earth. His is an earthly origin, though it is probably Satanically motivated and energized.

He had only *"two horns,"* versus the ten which comprised the first beast. We can assume that this means two kings or kingdoms, using the same definition of Rev. 17:12. But whereas the kingdoms of the first beast seem to join together in a political force, this beast seems religious in nature (13:12-17).

His horns, or kingdoms, were *"like a lamb."* His appearance to the world was *"like"* an innocent lamb, but he was really something else. Jesus is called the Lamb in the sense of His sacrifice to take away sin. This "beast" appears just like a lamb but is really a "wolf in sheep's clothing." With all his appearance as a lamb, he still *"spake as a dragon,"* revealing his true kinship with Satan.

This beast might represent a great "spiritual" movement in the world. The two horns or kingdoms might represent two major "faiths" or cults which join forces in unrighteousness and deceit. It is not quite as easy to identify them as it was to speculate on the kingdoms of the first beast. What is important to understand is that they exist. They comprise this second beast, which is religious in design.

Works of the Second Beast (13:12-17)

This beast works in conjunction with the first. It *"exerciseth all the power of the first"* (13:12). It wielded the same strength and had a similar sphere of influence as that of its political ally. But his ministry was slightly different. Instead of blaspheming God and harassing the saints, he caused *"the earth and them which dwell therein to worship the first beast, whose deadly wound was healed"* (13:12).

Not all who worship direct their praise to the one Creator-God. There are some who worship the evil forces of the universe, with specific attention given Satan. In the United States alone there are numerous cults and movements which openly worship Satan and other demonic forces. The work of the second beast, who parades around as a lamb, is to get the world to worship the political alliance established in the first beast.

Throughout the existence of the kingdoms of the first beast, many people of the world have been persuaded to worship their country and its political action. To esteem a political nation above the Lord God is to worship the same. That is what this second beast is doing. He is causing people to take their eyes off of the Lord and focus them on worldly affairs, particularly in the realms of trade, finance and general commercial endeavors. He easily accomplishes this with many because of their love of money and other material wealth. Later on we'll see the practical application of these truths as we observe the fall of Babylon which affects the commerce of the world (Revelation 18).

The beast at this point is qualified as the one *"whose deadly wound was healed"* (13:12). The nation fulfilling that role is only one of seven kingdoms involved in this political conglomerate. The qualification, however, does seem to shift the emphasis to that particular nation.

The second beast also *"doeth great wonders"* (13:13). Fire from heaven is mentioned, but many other miracles are implied (13:14). Satan had great power but was stripped of it. What he is allowed to do here through the second beast is only permitted as the Lord grants it. With his given power, he deceives many people of the earth.

Having done so and capturing their attention and devotion, he persuades some to *"make an image to the* [first] *beast"* (13:14). If we are correct in identifying the first beast as political nations heavily involved in commercial enterprise controlling the world, these "images" of the beast might be private enterprises or businesses which are modeled after the wealthy-minded nature of the worldwide beast. And the same power and life that exists in the beast is also given to these images of the beast.

All who refuse to "worship" or give their allegiance to these global and private enterprises find themselves unable to buy or sell. In fact, those who won't participate in the economic quest of the world are *"killed"* (13:15). Most interpret that literally and may be correct. This death should also be seen as symbolic, in that nonparticipants are as good as dead. Unless they align themselves with this worldly plot, they can neither buy nor sell.

"And he causeth all . . . to receive a mark in their right hand, or in their foreheads" (13:16). This mark could be a literal signification required in the hand or on the head, but it is more likely a "mark" that God can see, as He could the one placed on Cain (cf. Gen. 4:15). Earlier in the Revelation we saw the saints sealed, or marked, and that mark was invisible (7:3). A visible mark on either the hand or forehead has not been seen in the past or at the present. Yet the work of this beast and the world's involvement with it has been going on for quite some time.

The Greek word from which we translate "mark" could indicate, along with everything else we see concerning this, servitude. In this case it would mean servitude to a world system which controlled all the resources. This "mark" is recognizable by the beast and those who worship him. Anyone without it cannot buy or sell. They cannot participate wholly in the commerce which the beast controls.

For the people of the world, it comes down to a choice. We can either be "marked" as a supporter of the beast, who lives through the trickery and deceit of Satan, or we can be "sealed" with the Holy Spirit of promise which gives us eternal life in the Lord. If we are sealed by God, nothing can harm us.

The Number of a Man (13:18)

This chapter has served to introduce the two beasts. More will be shared later concerning their identity and plight as the Revelation draws to a close. One last item is the number associated with the beast. Verse 18 says that it is 666, which is *the number of a man.* The number that is given to John as a clue to the beast's identity does not refer to any one specific man. The beast is not one man, and neither does the number reflect it.

The Greek alphabet is also the number system. Each letter has a numeric value. The beast's name when totalled up in the Greek language equals 666. The name could be something like "World Trade" or "The International Monetary System," but it is most likely not a proper name for an individual.

John's reference to the number of a man is probably understood by the fact that the number of man or humanity in the flesh throughout the Scriptures is six. It represents him and his imperfection. As an example, man was created on the sixth day and is appointed to work six days because of sin. Many words related to man in the Scriptures (like 666) total up to six or multiples thereof. The number 666 is the ultimate representation of man and his imperfection in that it is triple six. It is the total of some name given the beast which is the sum of imperfect men driven by Satan.

It might be noted that the number 666 was associated with the tax burden imposed upon the people of God by Solomon (1 Kings 10:14). He used the gold he collected for his own sumptuous and showy life style. Might there be a spiritual connection to the beast of Revelation 13? Do not all those associated with the beast blatantly reject the God of creation for the god of mammon? Do they not use their "gain" on luxurious life styles? Do not the merchants of the world weep when the fall of Babylon brings this lucrative trade to an end? The story of Solomon in 1 Kings 10 has a very specific relationship to the number 666 here in the Revelation.

22

The Lamb and His Company

(14:1-20)

This chapter documents as many as six miscellaneous events which occur in the spiritual realm. Even though John saw them one after the other in the succession recorded in Revelation 14, they appear to be events which parallel each other rather than follow a precise timetable. These happenings, once again, review the truths we have learned so far in yet another symbolic way.

The main focus of Revelation 14 is the first five verses, where we see a vision of the Lamb (Jesus) standing on Mount Zion (in the presence of God) with the redeemed from among men (the Church). Despite the events which depict judgment, the fall of Babylon and *"the great winepress of the wrath of God"* (14:19), we can take comfort that the saints of God are seen in the presence of God with Jesus, untouched as all the culminating events of history take place.

Redeemed from Among Men (14:1-5)

In our study to this point we have already identified the characters of Rev. 14:1-5. The *"Lamb"* (14:1) is obviously Jesus Christ (cf. John 1:29, 36; 1 Pet. 1:19; Rev. 7:10). The company of 144,000 which stands with Jesus in this heavenly scene has been identified as the Church of all time, whether in heaven or on earth. The number is merely representative of the vast multitude of faithful souls that has grown from Abraham, the father of faith. The Greek language has no value high enough to number this great company (7:9; cf. comments on 7:4-8).

What we find in this passage is confirmation of who this multitude is. It is a vast group of individuals that praise God with one *"voice from heaven, as the voice of many waters, and as the voice of a great thunder"* (14:2). What people in all the creation could possibly do this besides the true Church of Jesus Christ? They sing a new song before the Lord and play their instruments in His presence (14:3). They are excited and seem extremely grateful to God. Only they who have been saved through Jesus Christ and know it can get this excited and be so grateful. Only they would want to learn the new song of praise to the Lord.

"These are they which are not defiled with women" (14:4), a qualification more spiritually oriented than physical. These people did not commit adultery against God. They are chaste in a spiritual sense, spiritual "virgins." They did not go "a whoring" after other gods. Only the true saints of God could fit that description.

"These are they which follow the Lamb whithersoever he goeth" (14:4). Jesus is their Great Shepherd. They follow Him as He leads. Having committed themselves to His complete lordship, they walk in His very footsteps (Ps. 37:23). Only the Church is willing to do that.

"In their mouth was found no guile: for they are without fault before the throne of God" (14:5). How can anyone be without guile or fault before the Lord? Have not all "sinned, and come short of the glory of God"? This multitude stands before the Lord without fault or sin because of their Savior, who has taken away their sin (cf. Col. 2:13-14). He gave His life that they may live without sin (cf. Matt. 5:45; John 3:16-17). Only the Church can make such a boast.

Finally we note the most convincing qualification. *"These were redeemed from among men, being the firstfruits unto God and to the Lamb"* (14:14). Who are the redeemed? The children of God are the redeemed! Jesus is the Redeemer, "who gave himself for us, that he might redeem us from all iniquity, and purify unto himself a peculiar people, zealous of good works" (Titus 2:14). We are redeemed *"From among men."* We are the "called-out-ones," the *ekklesia*, the Church. And no other group can fit that description.

In this portion of the vision, John is seeing a picture of the Church, standing with its Savior in the security of the presence of God. He is not seeing the literal Mount Zion upon which part of Jerusalem is built. He sees the Mount Zion of which the writer to the Hebrew speaks (Heb. 12:22).

All of us who are born-again Christians stand in this number right at this very moment. Because we stand with Jesus, have chosen not to be "marked" in unrighteousness and have made the choice to be "sealed" in the Holy Spirit, we can sing the new song of praise to God while all the other events of Revelation 14 transpire.

Judgment by the Word (14:6-7)

After seeing the redeemed multitude again, John *"saw another angel . . . having the everlasting gospel to preach unto them that dwell on the earth . . . Saying with a loud voice, Fear God, and give glory to him; for the hour of his judgment is come: and worship him that made heaven, and earth, and the sea, and the fountains of waters"* (14:6-7). Keeping in mind the first scene of Jesus with his household, we observe here a proclamation of the gospel message to all people of the earth. Every person that has ever lived has received that gospel in some form and at some time. Here we are being assured that God's Word is being preached. All have the opportunity to join the great multitude of saints on Mount Zion. Unfortunately, not all do.

Not everyone is willing to confess his sin and submit to the Lord Jesus. But all have had their chance. The gospel is being proclaimed in every conceivable manner. The angel says, *"Fear God, and give glory to him . . . and worship him."* And though the Church is the vessel for proclaiming it, the Word of God, particularly the written Word, contains the message. It judges the people of the earth. The truth is made known to the world through it. If the world chooses Jesus, it is redeemed. If not, it stands condemned in sin.

These two short verses beckon to all who would follow after righteousness and join the heavenly throng. It is a message of the gospel being proclaimed throughout the earth. It calls the world to come and stand on Mount Zion with the Lamb and His company.

Announcing the Fall of Babylon (14:8)

In another short sequence, John sees a second angel saying, *"Babylon is fallen, is fallen, that great city, because she made all nations drink of the wine of the wrath of her fornication"* (14:8). This seems to be an announcement of what happens later in Revelation 18, where the full details of the fall of "Babylon" are given. We will examine this thoroughly at that point, but an introduction to it seems in order here.

Babylon, the great city, is a title given to the "religious" people of the world who, having a form of religion, really do not know the Lord God at all. This would also include what we might call the apostate church, those that did know God at one time and yet turned away from Him. She is called the woman, the whore, "THE MOTHER OF HARLOTS AND ABOMINATIONS OF THE EARTH" (17:5). She is called that because of her unfaithfulness to the Lord. She is comprised of many who once may have known God but chose to go a whoring after other gods and the wealth of the world. She is the "MOTHER OF HARLOTS" because she produces other harlots through her own sin. What is being proclaimed here, even before it happens, is her demise. She may be riding high on the luxury and wealth of the riches gleaned from the "merchants" of the earth, but her fall is sure and soon to come. Each man can choose to fall with her and the rest of unrepentant mankind, or he can choose to stand with Jesus and His house on the mountain.

A Serious Warning (14:9—11)

A third angel is seen in this part of the vision. It comes before John proclaiming, with a loud voice, the wrath of God which will be incurred by anyone who worships the beast and receives his mark. *"The same shall drink of the wine of the wrath of God, which is poured out without mixture into the cup of his indignation"* (4:10). The unsaved of the world who reject the love of God will have no reason to complain when the Lord pours out His wrath, for He has given us all a choice between righteousness and unrighteousness, as well as a period of grace in which to make the choice and plenty of warning of what will happen if we refuse to know Him through Jesus.

Chapters 15 and 16 of the Revelation go into the details of the wrath of God. These verses in chapter 14 are but a warning, a very serious warning, to the world. The Lord loves all of His creation and would have every one of His creatures live eternally with Him. But in order to purge the wickedness of the earth, He will pour out His wrath. *"The smoke of their torment ascendeth up for ever and ever: and they have no rest day nor night"* (14:11). Great is the agony associated with the wrath of God. It is an eternal torment, which allows the recipients *"no rest day nor night."* How terrible all of this sounds. How difficult it is to imagine any people of the earth choosing this fate over eternal rest in the Lord. But we have all been warned by the Word of God. Jesus has voiced it, the Scriptures proclaim it and the Church has been faithful in passing it on. None will have the excuse "I didn't know." The essence of Rev. 14:9-11 has been broadcast to mankind. The decision lies with us.

More Words of Comfort (14:12-13)

Two reassuring statements are made between the announcement of God's wrath and the bloody vision of the harvest of the earth. They are inserted here as words of comfort to the saints of God.

The first says, *"Here is the patience of the saints: here are they that keep the commandments of God, and the faith of Jesus"* (14:12). In remaining faithful in the midst of all that transpires, the saints will develop patience, *"Here* [in obedience and faithfulness amidst tribulation] *is the patience of the saints."*

We are reminded of the instruction Paul gave to the Romans along these lines, "We glory in tribulations also: knowing that tribulation worketh patience; And patience, experience; and experience, hope: And hope maketh not ashamed; because the love of God is shed abroad in our hearts by the Holy Ghost which is given unto us" (Rom. 5:3-5). In this succession of events which leads from tribulation to total hope in the Lord and the love of God in our hearts by the Holy Ghost, patience is the first milestone after tribulation. The sorrows and troubles of this world work patience in the saints and strengthens them. Tribulation is not pleasant, but it should not be feared. If we *"keep the commandments of God, and the faith of Jesus,"* we will not only be established in patience, but we will continue to grow and mature to a point where we will be able to withstand anything that comes along, because of our love for the Lord.

"Blessed are the dead which die in the Lord from henceforth: yea, saith the Spirit, that they may rest from their labours, and their works do follow them." (14:13). Happiness and blessing are promised those who "die" in the Lord. The heavenly voice is primarily offering

encouragement concerning those who physically give their lives for the gospel's sake. Many in the history of the Church have done so. Perhaps also implied, however, is an encouragement to those who simply "die" to sin and the flesh, who give themselves to a new life in Jesus Christ and find *"rest from their labours."* Their works, like all the saints, will be examined before the judgment seat of Christ (Rom. 14:10). *"Their works do follow them."* God knows their faithfulness and loyalty, and they will be rewarded.

We can take heart in these words of comfort. The Spirit of God abides in us, is working patience in us through tribulation and will sustain us and bring us into the presence of God, who knows the desires of our heart. We are safe in Him.

The Harvest (14:14-20)

The last section of this passage tells of the purging that God is bringing about. Even as the righteousness of God abounded in the creation at one time, so shall it be restored by our righteous God. It is His intent to remove the unrighteous from His presence. This will be ultimately realized at the coming of our Lord Jesus.

This passage summarizes and sets the stage for a fuller explanation of God's wrath detailed in Revelation 15 and 16. The content of this introduction and subsequent results of God's wrath being poured out is consummated in Revelation 19 and 20, with the specifics of Christ's return.

The symbolism of this text centers around the analogy of a harvest, a gathering in of the "crop" at the appropriate time. Two harvests are pictured, which concern themselves with the gathering of souls rather than farm crops. The first harvest occurs in verses 14-16. The "harvester" is said to be upon a white cloud, a golden crown on his head and a sharp sickle in his hand. He was *"like unto the Son of man"* (14:14).

This first harvester is representative of Jesus. He was *"like unto the Son of man."* The *"white cloud"* upon which he sat is the Church, which is equally involved in the first harvest. The *"golden crown"* on his head is a token of the pure righteousness and complete authority granted to Jesus by God as King of the kingdom of God. The *"sharp sickle"* is used to perform the harvest, a symbolic tool for a spiritual act.

This first harvest with Jesus and the Church is one of gathering the faithful unto God. This harvest has actually been taking place since the first advent of Jesus and will continue until His return. Jesus told the disciples while on the earth that the fields were "white already to harvest" (John 4:35), indicating the vast number who were ready then to give themselves to God. Through Christ and the Church, many of those souls and millions more would be gathered unto the security of God.

Notice that no mention of a "rapture" is made. *"The earth was reaped,"* John records (14:16). The crop of a harvest when reaped is always collected and taken to storage. In this harvest, the "crop" of souls is collected and taken into the storehouse of God's care. The Lord does this without removing one saint from the earth.

The second harvest is quite different. Verses 17-20 provide the details of a very bloody harvest, one that surely speaks of the "end" for those who refuse to know God. Two angels are involved in this harvest. One holds the sickle and the other, *"which had power over fire"* (14:18), commands the harvest to begin. The sickle is thrust into the earth, and the grapes are gathered and ultimately cast *"into the great winepress of the wrath of God"* (14:19).

This is surely a harvest of the unrighteous. Paul told the Thessalonians that "God hath not appointed us [saints] to wrath, but to obtain salvation by our Lord Jesus Christ" (1 Thess. 5:9). The obtaining of salvation is seen in the first harvest. The second involves God's wrath, described as a "winepress," the symbolic tool for executing justice, as God has always promised to do.

"The winepress was trodden without the city, and blood came out of the winepress, even unto the horse bridles, by the space of a thousand and six hundred furlongs "(14:20). Based on the spiritual perspective developed to this point, the "city" is the New Jerusalem, the household of faith. *"Without the city,"* or outside its walls, is the place where the unrighteous come face to face with God's settled anger. It is outside the presence of God into which the people of the second harvest come.

It is hard for some to imagine God doing such a thing. But we cannot ignore the fact that He has promised to commit the unrepentant to everlasting punishment. This second harvest introduction portrays that judgment symbolically.

These harvests find a parallel in the teaching of Jesus recorded in Matt. 13:37-53. In His teaching on the kingdom of God, He uses several parables to indicate the "harvest" of the righteous and the infliction of God's wrath on the unrighteous. Jesus sends "forth his angels, and they shall gather out of his kingdom all things that offend, and them which do iniquity; And shall cast them into a furnace of fire: there shall be wailing and gnashing of teeth" (13:41-42). Notice that it is the wicked that are cast out, that are removed from the presence of the children of God and God himself. God doesn't have to remove the kingdom dwellers to do it. He merely removes the unrighteous, while leaving the saints untouched. This is a key point in understanding "end times" teaching.

Jesus declares this truth in yet another way, using the analogy of fishing with a net, which "gathered the good into vessels, but cast the bad away. So shall it be at the end of the world: the angels shall come forth, and sever

214

the wicked from among the just, And shall cast them into the furnace of fire: there shall be wailing and gnashing of teeth. . . . Have ye understood all these things?" (Matt. 13:47-51). The events of the last days must be aligned with all of God's Word, particularly that which Jesus taught.

We should keep these principles in our hearts as we read on into the specifics of God's wrath. The vials which we are about to see declare the judgment of God. But they are not meant for us who are in Christ Jesus. They are meant for the wicked.

23

The Vials of Wrath

(15:1-16:21)

Revelation 15 and 16 will be examined together, as they provide us the details concerning the wrath of God. This sequence begins when John observes seven angels with vials containing seven last plagues, *"another sign in heaven, great and marvellous"* (15:1).

The vials are symbolic, as were the seals and trumpets. These vials contain awesome plagues which are to be poured out on the earth. They represent the wrath of God against all who oppose Him. What we must understand as we study this is that the wrath of God is not an uncontrolled temper but a settled or controlled anger. The wrath with which we are most associated is that of uncontrolled feelings and emotions which have laid dormant within us and are suddenly discharged in a burst of rage. But the Greek word used throughout the Revelation, which translates "wrath," when seen as an attribute of God, has a fuller meaning of "controlled anger."

God has put up with the sin and unrighteousness of man ever since his fall in the garden of Eden. Century after century, men have rejected Him and openly blasphemed His name. But He is a God of love and has patiently been executing a plan of salvation which was designed to reconcile himself to man. Some have responded. Others have not. At His appointed time, these "vials of wrath" will be poured out upon those who turned away. But it will not be in a burst of rage, as we find ourselves doing many times. It will be because He has thought it through, carefully designed His actions and justly dealt His anger in a series of controlled events. There is a big difference between deliberate action and wild, emotional fury.

Scripture holds no room for a doctrine of "universal salvation." Such Scriptures as Matt. 24:12-22; Luke 13:1-5; John 3:36; and 2 Pet. 3:7 remove any doubt as to what God is going to do. The truth is that God will, as it is clearly noted in Revelation 15 and 16, pour out His controlled wrath on all who will not draw close to Him.

The Church Victorious (15:2-4)

In addition to seeing the seven angels with the vials of wrath, John saw all of the people who were victorious *"over the beast, and over his image, and over his mark, and over the number of his name"* (15:2). These are the people of faith who have their victory in Jesus Christ (1 Cor. 15:57). They have been more than conquerors over the world-ruling political powers, the associated false religious systems and the attempts that Satan has made in trying to get them to be identified with these "beasts." They are the Church victorious.

"They sing the song of Moses the servant of God, and the song of the Lamb" (15:3). This strongly suggests the diversity of individuals who comprise the Church, the household of faith. They can sing *"the song of Moses"* (Exodus 15), which proclaimed their deliverance from Egypt by God's mighty hand. That song prefigured the deliverance that saints of God would have from the "Egypt" of sin and oppression. But they can also sing *"the song of the Lamb,"* which tells of their victory in the Lord, a song announcing the completed victory of Christ, of which the song of Moses was only a shadow (15:3-4). And every person who believed in the Lord by faith, from those on the shores of the Red Sea with Moses to those standing on the *"sea of glass"* in the Revelation (15:2), are able to praise the Lord with one voice, male and female, Greek and Jew.

It is the Church victorious. They have gotten the victory. They will not suffer the wrath of God, even though they had to endure the tribulation which surrounded them throughout their lives. Jesus told them, "In the world ye shall have tribulation" (John 16:33), but they were also assured that "God hath not appointed us to wrath, but to obtain salvation by our Lord Jesus Christ" (1 Thess. 5:9).

The saints on earth will not be harmed by the wrath of God. Remember the children of Israel in Egypt. The plagues were poured out strongly upon the Egyptians while the Israelites remained unharmed. The same thing will happen when the wrath of God is *"poured out without mixture* [not diluted or watered down] *into the cup of his indignation"* (14:10). The Church is victorious over sin and death. Surely the wrath of God will not harm them.

Jesus as Judge (15:5-8)

We have previously seen Jesus as Priest (seals) and King (trumpets). As the vials are about to be poured, we see Jesus as Judge. His power and authority is observed in the seven angels, who come forth from the *"temple of the tabernacle of the testimony in heaven"* (15:5). They are *"clothed in pure and white linen"* and have *"their breasts girded with golden girdles"* (15:6). They represent the majesty of the Lord Jesus, who is being revealed.

We are also told by John that *"no man was able to enter into the temple, till the seven plagues of the seven angels were fulfilled"* (15:8). So great and awesome is this show of power by God that no one is able to endure the pure presence of God until His settled anger is completed.

The "vials" which we are about to see are grueling and dreadful, whether perceived as literal or spiritual. Many literal explanations have been written. The text itself could be considered very understandable in the natural. Literal explanations do seem possible for some of the vials and, no doubt, God could bring them about in the natural as described. We shall, however, explore some possible spiritual interpretations in line with the symbolism of the Revelation. Let us now examine each one briefly.

One: Upon the Earth (16:1-2)

The first portion of God's wrath is poured out *"upon the earth,"* causing a *"noisome* [injurious and possibly foul-smelling] *and grievous sore upon the men which had the mark of the beast and upon them which worshipped his image"* (16:2). What this says is that all those who align themselves with the world political and religious systems rather than developing a relationship with God, his Creator, will suffer the agony and stench of the sin in which they wallow. God will allow them to have the "sores" of rebellion, giving "them up to uncleanness," giving "them up unto vile affections," and giving "them over to a reprobate mind" (Rom. 1:24, 26, 28). Those kinds of "sores" are very *"noisome and grievous."*

Two: Upon the Sea (16:3)

The second vial is poured out *"upon the sea,"* causing it to become *"as the blood of a dead man: and every living soul died in the sea"* (16:3). The "sea" has been identified as the peoples of the world (Rev. 17:15). This vial tells of the death of every soul not in communion with God. They are lifeless, having the *"blood of a dead man."*

"The life of the flesh is in the blood: and I have given it to you upon the altar to make an atonement for your souls: for it is the blood that maketh an atonement for the soul" (Lev. 17:11). Through Jesus' blood, atonement is made for those souls who have salvation. Rejecting the blood covering of Jesus, all other souls find themselves in a "sea" of humanity that is dead and without life, which can only be found in the Blood (cf. Eph. 2:1; 1 Tim. 5:6).

Three: Upon the Rivers (16:4-7)

The third share of God's wrath is poured out *"upon the rivers and fountains of waters; and they became blood"* (16:4), probably the same lifeless blood described in the second vial. Who or what are these *"rivers and fountains of waters"*? Verse 6 says that they are the ones who *"have shed the blood of saints and prophets."* You see, they are not really natural bodies of water but symbolic "rivers," representing spiritual forces outside the realm of the Holy Spirit, the *"river of water of life"* (Rev. 22:1). This vial actually proclaims death being poured out on those who persecuted and *"shed the blood of saints."*

We can see a pattern developing. The first three vials are extremely similar when we understand the symbolism. God's wrath is eternal punishment for the unrighteous. What we have seen are the different ways or variations of describing it. Punishment is proclaimed to the unsaved in general and to certain select groups in particular, like those who *"shed the blood of saints."* This pattern should be kept in mind as we go on.

The voice of the angel and other heavenly voices announce that God's judgments are *"true and righteous,"* that they are not unfair and are but an equitable retribution for the evil done (16:5).

Four: Upon the Sun (16:8-9)

The fourth vial is poured out *"upon the sun"* which, to this juncture, has represented the illumination and righteousness of Jesus Christ. The wrath is not meant for Jesus or any aspect of God's righteousness but is merely poured out upon the "sun" prior to the angel using its rays to *"scorch men with fire"* and great heat (16:8).

Paul said the same thing. "Every man's work shall be made manifest: for the day shall declare it, because it shall be revealed by fire; and the fire shall try every man's work of what sort it is. . . . If any man's work shall be burned, he shall suffer loss: but he himself shall be saved; yet so as by fire" (1 Cor. 3:13, 15). This part of God's wrath seems to burn away the evil, "religious" and false works of men, leaving them "naked" and standing truly as they are before God, with only their final judgment remaining.

Yet with this punishment, they refuse to repent or give Him glory. So the Lord continues pouring out His wrath.

Five: Upon the Seat of the Beast (16:10-11)

With the emptying of the fifth vial *"upon the seat of the beast,"* his *"kingdom was full of darkness; and they gnawed their tongues for pain, And blasphemed the God of heaven because of their pains and their sores, and repented not of their deeds"* (16:10-11). The political and religious beasts of the earth may have offered a temporary "light" to the world, but they have their lights put out by God. They are enveloped in darkness as the seat of the beast (the base or place where it was established) is destroyed.

Satan and his demonic band could be considered the *"seat of the beast,"* yet this more likely represents the earthly operation of Satan's power permitted in the political and religious realms. They are defused and shut down, their efficacy nullified. The granted power to control any of mankind is eliminated. Yet they still blaspheme the God of heaven.

Six: Upon the Great River Euphrates (16:12-16)

The sixth vial is poured out *"upon the great river Euphrates"* (16:12). In the natural, the Euphrates (which means the "good and abounding river") is a river that flows from the mountains of Armenia to the Persian Gulf. Biblically, it constituted the eastern boundary for Canaan (cf. Gen. 15:18; Exod. 23:31; Deut. 1:7). It represents a boundary wherever it is found in Scripture (cf. Gen. 2:14; Deut. 11:24; Josh 1:4). On its banks was also built the city of Babylon, the zenith of rebellion against God. Spiritually, this river might represent one of the "borders" of the spiritual Canaan land, into whose rest the people of God come. It also denotes a symbolic line of separation between the realm of the Spirit and that of the flesh (or the world). On one side of the "river" dwell the people of God, while on the other side dwell the unrighteous, typified in Babylon.

As the sixth vial is poured out, it dries up that "border," preparing the way for *"kings of the east"* (16:12). Jeremiah had a prophecy against Babylon (Jer. 51:60-64), which included casting the Word of God into the midst of the Euphrates. As the Word of the Lord sank out of sight into the water, so the Lord said Babylon would be destroyed, never to rise again. We see the fulfillment of that prophecy as the triumphant saints of God (*"the kings of the east"*) are allowed full power over all God's creation with the final fall of Babylon. She had represented confusion, error and bondage. When destroyed, she and her boundaries disappear, allowing the children of God to come into the perfect law of liberty in the Spirit.

The "way" for the *"kings of the east"* (saints) was prepared by Jesus. The sixth vial shows the removal of the limits placed on the people of faith by anything which Babylon represents. They are no longer influenced by her sinful ways.

Satan is greatly distressed with the victory that saints have and subsequently sends forth *"three unclean spirits,"* proceeding from *"the mouth of the dragon, and out of the mouth of the beast and out of the mouth of the false prophet"* (16:13). What is it that they do? It says they work *"miracles"* (16:14). They probably work them through individuals and groups open to their deception. Whenever such things occur, many will follow after the "miracle workers," and that is what happens in this sequence. The devil has been allowed to deceive the world, even crossing the borders of Canaan land (the people of God) and deceiving the elect, if it were possible. In Matt. 24:24 Jesus said, "There shall arise false Christs, and false prophets, and shall show great signs and wonders; insomuch that, if it were possible, they shall deceive the very elect."

How does God's wrath come into all of this? The purpose of God allowing all of this to happen is to destroy "Babylon" and specifically to gather those who are opposed to God to the battleground of Armageddon. Literal teaching would place this in the vicinity of Megiddo, an ancient, strategically centered, fortified city of Israel which has been the site of numerous battles throughout history. Its location was important with respect to the ancient trade routes which went from Egypt to Syria. Countless lives were lost in the endless fighting that occurred there, and it has subsequently become symbolic of war. But the "Armageddon" of Rev. 16:16 is not taking place near that city.

In the symbolic language of the Revelation, "Armageddon" appears to be the spiritual battleground where Satan and all who follow after him are defeated. But all the world is "Armageddon." Every time a Christian stands on the Word of God and acts against the Satanic realm in the authority of Jesus Christ, part of Satan's army is crushed in that symbolic "valley." The wrath of God seems to be poured out upon the unrighteous on the battleground of earth, on which the saints already stand victorious in Jesus.

There may be one more great spiritual battle at the coming of Jesus, which we could call "Armageddon" (cf. Rev. 19:11-12), but this battle is happening even now as we daily put on the whole armor of God and stand against the "wiles of the devil" (Eph. 6:10-18). Even now, we can issue a foretaste of God's wrath against the rebellious spirits of the creation.

Seven: "It Is Done" (16:17-21)

The pouring out of the seventh vial is very significant. It marks the end of God's wrath as described in the vision and brings us to the appearing of Jesus in Revelation 19. Chapters 17 and 18 appear to describe in further detail the fall and destruction of the great whore, or Babylon, which is completed with the seventh vial (16:19).

We know that the wrath of God, and possibly all of the plan of salvation, is complete with this vial when, with its flow into the air, a great heavenly voice declares, *"It is done"* (16:17). Before Jesus bowed His head on the cross and gave up the ghost, He said, "It is finished" (John 19:30). That meant that His earthly ministry was complete and the plan of salvation had been fully set into motion. The heavenly announcement here with the seventh vial means that the plan of salvation is concluded. The time of grace, when anyone could partake of God's love and favor through Jesus, is over. The universe is finally going to be rid of all unrighteousness, by God's choice.

The wrath of God is manifested in two different ways. First, *"a great earthquake,"* of a magnitude never before experienced by the earth, shakes the world and all who dwell upon it (16:18). The writer to the Hebrew people foresaw this event. He recorded, "See that ye refuse not him that speaketh [God]. For if they [the first Israelites] escaped not who refused him that spake on earth [God on Mount Sinai], much more shall not we escape, if we turn away from him that speaketh from heaven: Whose voice then shook the earth [at Mount Sinai]: but now he hath promised, saying, Yet once more I shake not the earth only, but also heaven [the Rev. 16:18 shaking]. And this word, Yet once more, signifieth the removing of those things that are shaken [the unrighteous], as of things that are made, that those things which cannot be shaken [kingdom dwellers] may remain. Wherefore we receiving

224

a kingdom which cannot be moved, let us have grace, whereby we may serve God acceptably with reverence and godly fear: For our God is a consuming fire" (Heb. 12:25-29).

That passage again confirms the biblical position of permanence for the kingdom of God. It is unmovable. It is God in the midst of His people. All who do not fit into that scheme or do not wish to commune with God must be removed. The sons of God, the joint-heirs of Jesus, remain stationary, built on the rock of Jesus Christ. It is only the hardhearted and unrepentant sector of the world's population that will "wing its way to worlds unknown" where "there shall be wailing and gnashing of teeth" (Matt. 13:50).

With the earthquake we see the division of the great city (Babylon) into three parts, the fall of the cities of the earth, the fleeing away of every island and the disappearance of the mountains (16:19-20). All of this will be explored in depth in the next two chapters. Basically, one thought is being conveyed. Anything man-made, such as cities, organizations or the works of men, will be removed or destroyed, with only the things of eternal and spiritual value remaining.

The second manifestation of God's wrath in this seventh vial is the plague of giant hailstones, which cause mankind to blaspheme God (16:21). The Egyptians were pummeled by hailstones (Exod. 9:22-26). God could do the same thing in the last days. But in Ps. 18:13, "hailstones and coals of fire" are the symbolic expressions of the voice of God. It is His voice which is *exceeding great* and unbearable for those who refuse to submit their lives to righteousness.

Of course these hailstones, as well as the other measures of wrath meted out in our subject text, could very well be literal in nature. However, parallels in the Word indicate they also have spiritual implications. Regardless of how they are manifested, you have nothing to be concerned about if you are a child of God, a kingdom dweller. We are part of a kingdom which cannot be shaken or moved while all else is being destroyed around us.

24
Judgment of the Great Whore
(17:1-18)

What begins in Revelation 17, identified as the *"judgment of the great whore"* (17:1), continues through Revelation 18, where the details of that judgment are spelled out. We shall address each chapter separately because of the extent of detail.

It will be helpful to understand, as we look at both chapters, that the titles Woman, Harlot, Great Whore, Babylon the Great and the Great City are all synonymous. Each refers to the same group of unfaithful people, using names significant of her disloyalty. Each may relate to a specific aspect of her life, e.g., religious, economic, social; but corporately they identify the same entity.

The Woman Identified (17:1-6)
In order for John to comprehend more fully what he was seeing, the Lord sent to him one of the seven angels used to pour out the vials of wrath. The angel said, *"Come hither; I will shew unto thee the judgment of the great whore that sitteth upon many waters: With whom the kings of the earth have committed fornication, and the inhabitants of the earth have been made drunk with the wine of her fornication"* (17:1-2).

Regardless of what title you choose, the great whore is that body of people which knew God and turned away from Him. Some would call her the Apostate Church, which wrongly implies an organized entity against God. It is highly probable that many associated with the organized and institutional churches of the world are part of this great whore, but that does not mean that there is an intentional, structured, worldwide formation to carry on this blasphemy against God. She, similar to the true, universal Church of Jesus Christ, is comprised of individuals from every nation, kindred, people and tongue.

Consider for a moment the analogy that is drawn for us. A harlot does not necessarily have a personal vendetta against her husband or some other man. She became a harlot by turning away from that which was right and moral and by turning to that which was wrong and immoral, through the passions and lusts of the flesh. The great whore became what she is in like manner. In fulfilling the lusts of the flesh, many people around the world turned away from what is right in the Lord and turned to the corrupt and adulterous life of the flesh.

The true Church of Jesus is scripturally identified as the Bride, the pure, spotless virgin who is to be wed with the Bridegroom, Jesus. Anyone who chooses not to be or remain a part of this virgin Bride, by indulging wholeheartedly in sin, becomes a "harlot" against God, joining themselves to the great whore.

The terminology of adultery and fornication to represent a turning away from God is not new in the Revelation. All through Scripture we are presented this illustration. The most famous might be the writings of Hosea the prophet. He outlines his own personal sorrow over an adulterous wife and then, by the Spirit of the Lord and experience, prophesies the whoredom and adultery of Israel, who were the children of God. Hosea chapter 4, in particular, emphasizes strongly the harlot aspect of Israel's backsliding. It is that same aspect of spiritual harlotry which is addressed in the Revelation. Those who play the "harlot" against God are part of this great whore.

The *"great whore"* that John was to see sat *"upon many waters."* The *"waters"* are clearly identified in verse 15 as *"peoples, and multitudes, and nations, and tongues."* They are a cross section of all the world's population, not restricted to any particular group of people. It is from that setting that the great whore emerges. She is universal.

The great whore is one *"with whom the kings of the earth have committed fornication, and the inhabitants of the earth have been made drunk with the wine of her fornication"* (17:2). Her great sin is boldly declared. She has caused whole nations (the kings of the earth) to commit "fornication" against God. Because these people turned away from God after once knowing Him, other large groups of people were influenced not to worship the one true God. This could apply to countries such as the Moslem nations of the world, or to any country in which the leaders endorse a false religion and thus persuade the general populace to worship other gods.

The general population of the world is made drunk *"with the wine of her fornication."* This refers to the people who were not part of the Bride or the harlot but, through the "intoxication" of the harlot's fleshly influence, made a choice to serve unrighteousness. As such, the great whore, i.e., all who comprise her, are a stumbling-block to the earthly populace. Jesus said, "It were better for him that a millstone were hanged about his neck, and that he were drowned in the depth of the sea" (Matt. 18:6). That is why the judgment of the great whore will be so great.

For John to see the great whore, he again had to be carried away *"in the Spirit into the wilderness"* (17:3). To perceive the spiritual truth, he had to be in the Spirit. Once there he saw *"a woman sit upon a scarlet-coloured beast, full of names of blasphemy, having seven heads and ten horns"* (17:3). The "beast" upon which she sat is the one we have already examined in Revelation 13. The beast in chapter 13 had seven heads and ten horns, descriptions given to represent the kingdoms involved in this worldwide political machine. The harlots of the world associated with the great whore get a piggyback ride on the beast. They (she) ride securely on its back until their judgment.

This woman (the great whore) *"was arrayed in purple and scarlet colour, and decked with gold and precious stones and pearls, having a golden cup in her hand full of abominations and filthiness of her fornication "* (17:4). This is the attire that is expected of a harlot. She is decked out in wild-colored apparel and is adorned with the costly jewels and stones earned by her fornication. The world, having made "love" to her, gave of its wealth and economy to improve her financial situation. Most people are aware of the individuals and groups of people who have made it their aim to become rich through false teaching and preaching. They make huge financial gains through the proclamation of a "gospel" which does not lead people to salvation through Jesus Christ. These are some of the harlots who are part of the "woman."

But she is not only recognizable by appearance. She is identified by names that are written on her, *"MYSTERY, BABYLON THE GREAT, THE MOTHER OF HARLOTS AND ABOMINATIONS OF THE EARTH"* (17:5). They all clarify who she is, the woman of ill repute. She is a *"MYSTERY"* to all who cannot see through her facade. She is *"BABYLON THE GREAT,"* a title associated with heathen Babylon of old and, even before that, with Babel, the city which rejected the authority of God (cf. Gen. 11:1-9). Verse 18 says she *"is that great city* [Babylon, Babel], *which reigneth over the kings of the earth."* And she is *"THE MOTHER OF HARLOTS AND ABOMINATIONS OF THE EARTH."* She has birthed other harlots through her own lewd lifestyle. She has raised up cultic sects throughout the earth who practice such things as witchcraft, mind control and fortunetelling. These are abominations to God (cf. Deut. 18:10-12). She is the *"Mother"* of them. They all have their root in the exaltation of self, the lust for power, which is the satanic nature of the great harlot.

She is *"drunken with the blood of the saints, and with the blood of the martyrs of Jesus"* (17:7). She has taken her toll upon the saved and the unsaved of the world. This may be symbolic "blood," but it truly speaks of the slaughter she has inflicted as she has caused countless millions to be doomed to destruction. Is it any wonder that all who are associated with her must face the awful judgment of the Lord?

In summarizing her description, she is definitely a universal creature. A diversity of mankind composes her being. She once knew God and turned from Him. But even worse, she caused many others to fall, too. For this she will be judged harshly.

The Beast Identified (17:7-18)

Our understanding of the beast is greatly enhanced in verses 7 through 18. The angel asks John, *"Wherefore didst thou marvel? I will tell thee the mystery of the woman, and of the beast that carrieth her"* (17:7). The angel then proceeds to instruct John concerning the beast, who has a direct connection to the woman already described.

The beast carries the woman. The lust for power and wealth that is the nature of the woman is carried out through the Kingdom of the beast. Having already seen that the beast is really a succession of earthly kingdoms, we can see how they could make it easy for sin and immorality to be spread. The hearts of wicked men justify themselves and eventually make sin acceptable in the sight of people who are blinded to its consequences.

Satan's involvement is stated in verse 8. *"The beast that thou sawest was, and is not; and shall ascend out of the bottomless pit, and go into perdition."* The verse goes on to say that they *"that dwell on the earth shall wonder, whose names were not written in the book of life from the foundation of the world"* (the unsaved), but the saints, being familiar with God's Word, will not have to wonder, because they see Satan's trickery and recognize his deceit. Satan is called the "son of perdition" (2 Thess. 2:3). He comes right out of the pits of hell (the bottomless pit) to effect this final assault on the authority of God.

The beast is described as having seven heads. These *are seven mountains, on which the woman sitteth"* (17:9), which are *"seven kings: five are fallen, and one is, and the other is not yet come; and when he cometh, he must continue a short space"* (17:10). This conglomerate of kingdoms is made up of five from the past which are no longer in existence, one which existed at the time of John's vision (probably the Roman empire) and another which would be established after that time.

It is difficult to pinpoint the seventh kingdom whose life is to *"continue a short space."* Was it Hitler's Germany? Is it Russia? Certainly their posture with regard to human rights and divine authority would make them candidates for the seventh kingdom of short duration. Or perhaps Russia is the eighth kingdom which *"is of the seven, and goeth into perdition"* (17:11). At any rate, we know that a series of political powers influenced by Satan are the subject of the beast's identity.

It is the eighth kingdom, most always prophesied for the future and associated with the mythical "Antichrist," that gets all the attention. But that last kingdom is but a product of the first seven. For those who lived under the dominance of the first six or seven, life was just as difficult. "Spiritual wickedness in high places" is something that people have had to wrestle with throughout all history. The eighth kingdom, which may now be in existence, just happens to be the last one to have these Satanic characteristics.

The beast is not just an end-times phenomenon. These eight empires are spread out in time from early history to the final purging of all evil at the coming of Jesus. The eighth kingdom may be the final one in existence at the appearing of Jesus, and it may be more horrible than all the other seven put together, but it is only one of a series which have been reality in the life of mankind.

"The ten horns which thou sawest are ten kings, which have received no kingdom as yet; but receive power as kings one hour with the beast. These have one mind, and shall give their power and strength unto the beast" (17:12-13). These ten kingdoms did not exist at the time John received the vision, which means they did not coexist with the first six major political kingdoms of the beast. It would appear that these ten smaller kingdoms were to be raised up together at some point in time, probably near the coming of Jesus. Their *"one hour"* reign is symbolic of a short time span. It is possible that some or even all of them exist today. Many people strongly suggest these ten horns represent the nations of the European Common Market, and perhaps they do.

When these ten nations begin their alliance, they will be of one accord, having *"one mind, and shall give their power and strength unto the beast."* Their whole purpose will be to support the work of the last empire in the beast's historical line. As you put the "periscope" up and look around the world, the most obvious candidates today for these ten kingdoms would be either the countries about to become the European Common Market or the Soviet-aligned countries around the world, all of whom would give their power and strength to the Soviet Union. Of any nations that would fit the descriptions of Revelation 17, these seem to qualify best. But we cannot be dogmatic about the identity of these kingdoms. We must continue to be spiritually perceptive and discerning, because they might arise from the least expected circles of global influence. They could yet arise from the most innocent-looking of nations. We must "be sober, be vigilant; because your adversary the devil, as a roaring lion, walketh about, seeking whom he may devour" (1 Pet. 5:8).

These ten kingdoms appear to attain their strength

and power with the help of those who have turned away from God, i.e., the whore. The ungodly and unrepentant will give all they have to these nations, seeking their own gain and security, only to be headed for destruction. For the ten horns (kingdoms) *"shall hate the whore, and shall make her desolate and naked, and shall eat her flesh, and burn her with fire. For God hath put in their hearts to fulfill his will, and to agree, and give their kingdom unto the beast, until the words of God shall be fulfilled"* (17:16-17).

The ten kingdoms will use the whore until they have reached the pinnacle of their reign. They will then turn on all who are part of the whore and destroy them. All of this is in the will of God, as we see in our text. God utilizes the ten kingdoms to bring judgment on the whore. The particulars of her fall, desolation, being naked, having her flesh eaten and burned with fire, are symbolic and will be explored in greater detail in the next chapter. But we can understand that God, in fulfilling His purposes, will use these nations to accomplish His divine plan.

Most likely at the return of Jesus, the ten kingdoms will *"make war with the Lamb, and the Lamb shall overcome them"* (17:14). When we study Revelation 19, we will see the complete story of the destruction of the beast, the ten kingdoms and those that received the mark of the beast.

Hopefully this chapter has been helpful in establishing the possibilities of who comprise the woman and the beast. Even if we cannot completely comprehend the whole picture, the guidelines presented here should be beneficial in the days ahead. We have nothing to fear, because we are joint-heirs with Jesus Christ. The beast and associated kingdoms cannot overcome us in Christ, because we are overcomers in Him. If we remain sober and alert in the Spirit, we will fully understand the events related to the plan of salvation in the past, at the present time and in the future.

25

The Fall of Babylon

(18:1-24)

If there's one thing that we should be "snatched" out of it is the great city, "Babylon, Mother of Harlots." All who are a part of her have become a disgrace to God, initiating the greatest "Abominations of the Earth." God does not want any of His children to be associated with her for the judgment that shall come.

The powerful angel that *"lightened"* the earth with his glory (18:1) surely represents Jesus with His great strength and overwhelming illumination. The angel proclaims with a strong voice, *"Babylon the great is fallen, is fallen, and is become the habitation of devils, and the hold of every foul spirit, and a cage of every unclean and hateful bird"* (18:1). The angel has described the state of those among her ranks. She is *"fallen"* into the depths of sin and depravity. She is fallen from the good graces of God.

Imagine how disgusting and abhorrent this group of rebellious people must be to God. In their sedition and sin, they have allowed devils and foul spirits (demons) to seduce them and live freely in their lives. This actually means that they have become demon-possessed through Satan worship and the entertaining of the spirit world outside the realm of the Holy Spirit. They are, in a symbolic sense, a *"cage"* for *"every unclean and hateful bird."*

Babylon, the sinful system apart from the kingdom of God, is a *"habitation"* not only for those associated with the occult but also for all others who are still spiritually dead. The spiritually dead are not always atheists. In fact, they are usually very religious, on the surface, finding great comfort in their own lifeless and self-righteous religion. The religion of the spiritually dead may talk of God, but it is materialistic and self-sufficient. Outside the realm of religious ritual, the spiritually dead see no need for a real reliance on God. Many have been "caged" in the fallen Babylon through self-rightous religions.

Through this reckless and unrighteous living, Babylon has caused three things to happen. The first says that *"all nations have drunk of the wine of the wrath of her fornication."* That means that people from every nation in the world have taken part in her depravity. Secondly, *"the kings of the earth have committed fornication with her."* They have participated in her "fornication" and have defiled themselves with the same sins. And lastly, *"the merchants of the earth are waxed rich through the abundance of her delicacies"* (18:3). If there's a dollar to be gained, someone with an eye upon earthly treasure will seize it. The people of "Babylon" delight to have all the luxuries of life, gaining the whole world, if possible, at the expense of their souls. The merchants of the earth gladly make capital gain on her foolishness.

Because of all this, a voice from heaven sounds the commandment to *"come out of her, my people, that ye be not partakers of her sins, and that ye receive not of her plagues. For her sins have reached unto heaven, and God hath remembered her iniquities"* (18:4-5). The people of God must not have fellowship with darkness (2 Cor. 6:14). They must not participate in the sinful practices which God so clearly detests. This is a real problem for many weak Christians who, not being firmly established in the Word, yield themselves to fleshly lusts and passions and involve themselves in occult activities which God hates. To these God says, *"Come out of her."*

The reason for this plea is simple. God is going to pour

236

out on her the plagues already described. He does not want any of His people to be touched by the judgment He will issue. That makes it very clear that true Christians will be on earth when the plagues of God's wrath are poured out. But if they are not involved with *"Babylon the great,"* they will not be burned by the wrath and vengeance which God will measure out. The stench of her sin has reached the nostrils of God, and He has *"remembered her iniquities." Come out of her, my people . . ."*

Downfall of the Harlot (18:6-8)

Even as Babylon has performed her works and seduced the people of the earth, she shall be rewarded *"double according to her works"* (18:6). The "cup" of wretchedness which she has filled will be doubly filled for her. Her glorious and sumptous living will be replaced by *"torment and sorrow"* (18:7).

She, like the unfaithful people at Laodicea (cf. Rev. 3:17), *"saith in her heart, I sit a queen, and am no widow and shall see no sorrow"* (18:7). And because of this arrogance shall her *"plagues come in one day,"* not necessarily a twenty-four hour period but certainly in a short span of time. She shall taste *"death, and mourning, and famine; and she shall be utterly burned with fire: for strong is the Lord God who judgeth her"* (18:8). She will be completely laid to waste by the "consuming fire" of God. Her downfall is sure.

These words are given to us to show that we cannot live in the eternal salvation and victory of the Lord Jesus if we fool around with the sins of Babylon. Her fall is certain even as you read these words. And if You partake of her sins, you will fall with her.

Political Sorrow for Her Destruction (18:9-10)

With the fall of Babylon we are told that *"the kings of the earth . . . shall bewail her, and lament for her"*

(18:9). They will be shocked and amazed with the swiftness and completeness of God's wrath. They will be in remorse for her loss. Why? Because they committed the same sins she did and *"lived deliciously with her"* (18:9). They, who probably never knew the Lord or even desired to know Him, had become very close to Babylon who had known the Lord yet turned away. Their's will be great empathy at the loss of a "sin partner."

We might also assume that the world, at this point, might also recognize that the hand of God had performed Babylon's destruction. They would have seen the quick downfall and perhaps have a semirepentant heart. Their tears are most likely shed in sympathy and in fear. But with all the sorrow and grief, there still appears to be no true repentance, no yielding to the Omnipotent God.

Economic Sorrow for Her Destruction (18:11-19)

If the kingdoms of the world mourned the fall of the apostate city, the merchants of the world mourned even more. The loss they sustain at the purging of Babylon is financial. They could probably care less about the lives or personalities involved. What makes them *"weep and mourn over her"* is the sure prospect that *"no man buyeth their merchandise any more: the merchandise of gold, and silver, and precious stones"* (18:11-12).

This addresses the economic aspect of the fall of Babylon. When God judges her sin and destroys everyone involved, world trade surely suffers. The merchants, shipmasters, sailors, traders and others involved in trade who *"were made rich by her, shall stand afar off for the fear of her torment, weeping and wailing"* (18:15).

Babylon is made up of individuals who left a knowledge of God for the pleasures of the world. She fell in love with the riches of the world and sinful sensuality instead of the Lord God Almighty. Many in the world today are part of Babylon. Whether or not they are part of some organization or institution, their main objective is the building of their own little "kingdoms," the accumulation of wealth, the erection of buildings and great edifices, the possession of costly goods. And who provided all these things? The merchants and tradesmen of the world. No wonder they wail the loudest at her fall.

God is going to judge Babylon. *"Come out of her"* He tells His people (18:4). Take no part in earthly kingdoms. Refuse to defile yourselves with her sin. Don't throw your money away on worthless, worldly ventures but, instead, invest it wisely in the proclamation of the gospel or for the care and feeding of the poor. Why make the merchants of the world rich when all of these earthly efforts are going to fail?

Permanence of Her Fall (18:20-24)

The finality of the judgment on Babylon is declared by another mighty angel who *"took up a stone like a great millstone, and cast it into the sea, saying, thus with violence shall that great city Babylon be thrown down, and shall be found no more at all"* (18:21). God symbolically shows John and us the permanence of her fall.

Verse 22 describes the fact that no life would be found in her any more, no sound of music or work of the craftsman. Verse 23 goes on to say that *"the light of a candle shall shine no more at all in thee."* Any last glimmer of light that existed will be snuffed out. Even the light which radiated from true Christians witnessing in her midst will be no longer, because they have come out of her by the instruction of God.

"And the voice of the bridegroom and of the bride shall be heard no more at all in thee" (18:23). This is the most serious statement and reaffirms the absence of any "light" in Babylon. Jesus (the bridegroom) and the Church (the bride) no longer have a voice in her. They can no longer be heard in her sinful presence. The bride has

been gathered unto Jesus who, in turn, has led them away from Babylon. The angels of God did the same for Lot and his family before Sodom and Gomorrah were destroyed (cf. Genesis 19).

Three reasons are given for Babylon being deserted and destroyed. The mighty angel said, *"for thy merchants were the great men of the earth; for by thy sorceries were all nations deceived. And in her was found the blood of prophets, and of saints, and of all that were slain upon the earth"* (18:23-24). These are the reasons for her fall. God is putting an end to her deception, murder and sinful influence. She is truly fallen!

The fall of Babylon is permanent. Some day it will be complete. Her defeat was set in motion at Calvary. Every time the Church takes authority over Satanic influence, refuses to have fellowship with the children of the night and proclaims the gospel with power and strength in Christ Jesus, Babylon falls a little further. At the coming or appearing of Jesus, she will be no more.

Revelation 18 gives us the symbolic details. What actually happens to complete her fall may not occur in the way we think it might. Her likeness as a city is symbolic. Her "burning" is figurative language indicating her end by the "fire" of the Spirit of God which shall consume her. *"Babylon the great is fallen, is fallen."* And all that remains is the City of God, the New Jerusalem, the Church, the household of faith.

26

The Marriage Supper of the Lamb

(19:1-21)

For God's just and equitable judgment on all who had fallen away in apostasy, the heavenly host praises God and hails His actions. For so long, the corruption and murder of the great whore had gone unavenged. But with her fall complete, the faithful rejoice and say unto God, *"Alleluia; salvation, and glory, and honour, and power, unto the Lord our God: for true and righteous are his judgments"* (19:1-2).

The rejoicing is not so much over the death and destruction of the disobedient as it is for the correct judgment of God and the fulfillment of His Word. His judgments are true and righteous. They cannot be questioned and should be praised. The Church (twenty-four elders) and all the creation, including the four beasts *"fell down and worshipped God that sat on the throne, saying, Amen; Alleluia"* (19:4). And as if to say that God appreciated the praises of His people in His judgments, *"a voice came out of the throne, saying, Praise our God, all ye his servants, and ye that fear him, both small and great"* (19:5).

It is interesting to note that the "alleluias" of 19:1, 3, 4 and 6 are the only ones in the entire New Testament. Hallelujah (praise the Lord) is the Old Testament counterpart. It seems they were reserved for this special occasion—the downfall of Babylon (18:20).

This is but a continuation of the praise that, even today, the saints offer up for the righteousness and honor of God. We praise Him now for the victory of the cross, where the fall of Babylon was instituted in the first place.

Her downfall is occurring little by little, and each time we praise God for His power and authority, we can picture ourselves in this scene of heavenly worship to which God has raised us (cf. Eph. 2:4-6). No wonder the saints of all time praise Him then for the completion of the work begun.

Eternal Fellowship with the Lord (19:6-9)

Concurrent with this setting of praise, we find rejoicing for the marriage of the Lamb which is about to occur. A great multitude *"as the voice of many waters* [peoples], *and as the voice of mighty thunderings, saying, Alleluia: for the Lord God omnipotent reigneth. Let us be glad and rejoice, and give honour to him: for the marriage of the Lamb is come, and his wife hath made herself ready"* (19:7).

The unified voice that speaks this praise is loud, because many have become part of the bride to be wed. Their acclamation sounds the fullness of joy at the prospect of having eternal life with Jesus Christ. The One they have known in the Spirit through faith for so long they are now going to see manifested in their presence, never to leave their side. He was there all along and they knew it, but His impending manifestation in their midst is reason for great comfort and delight.

Jesus (the Lamb) is about to appear with His wife-to-be (the saints). The second coming, full of mystery to the world and long anticipated by the Church, has finally arrived.

This marriage, or union, between Christ and the Church is not going to take place without an engagement period. Their "courtship" has been one which developed in love and has become strong through getting to know one another. Jesus has been ready for the marriage. It is the Church that had to be prepared and made ready. It is the Church that had to work out its own salvation with

242

fear and trembling (Phil. 2:12). It is the Church that had to "study to shew thyself approved unto God" (2 Tim. 2:15). It is the Church that had to learn to "praise God in his sanctuary . . . in the firmament of his power" (Ps. 150:1). With these things done, the wedding is about to occur.

Though many years have been involved in this courtship, the marriage will be for eternity. And just as the Lord would have us carefully choose a faithful mate on earth and develop a bond of love before marriage, He has taken the time to prepare the bride of Christ, to get her ready for eternity in the heavenly places.

Only those who are born again will be part of the bride. One's name on a local church membership role and attendance at Christmas, Easter and communion services will not make him a part of the bride. Only those who have prepared themselves will clasp hands with Jesus in the heavenly realm. Only those devoted to the Lord will experience the honeymoon. Only the faithful will spend eternity in the home of the newlyweds.

"Blessed are they which are called unto the marriage supper of the Lamb" (19:9). It will be an eternal feasting with the Lord. The glory of knowing the Lord while on earth will expand to unimaginable heights of ecstasy. And we can only experience it if we are part of the bride and prepared.

This is an important matter. Many who fancy themselves to be part of the Church are not so, and many who are have not prepared themselves. Jesus is not marrying someone He does not know. He is espousing himself to those who have thoroughly acquainted themselves with Him. He will marry no strangers. John saw the bride *"arrayed in fine linen, clean and white: for the fine linen is the righteousness of saints"* (19:8). Those who have prepared themselves will wear the fine linen, white, spotless and without blemish.

The specific word *"righteousness"* used in verse 8 comes from the Greek word *dikaiōma* and means "righteous act." It is different from the imputed righteousness of Jesus (*dikaiosunē*) in that it represents the excellencies of the saints, as the garment is woven thread by thread, each act or deed being a "thread" (cf. 45:13-14).

The wedding has been acclaimed and blessings have been announced for those who are fortunate enough to attend the eternal wedding supper of the Lamb. Who will attend? If we know Jesus personally and prepare ourselves through the reading of the Word, prayer and praise, our seats at the banquet table are being prepared.

Angel Worship Rebuked (19:10)

John was overwhelmed. He wasn't exactly sure what to do. He says, *"I fell at his* [the angel's] *feet to worship him. And he said unto me, See thou do it not: I am thy fellowservant, and of thy brethren that have the testimony of Jesus: worship God: for the testimony of Jesus is the spirit of prophecy"* (19:10). This one little verse is full of truth.

First, the worship of angels is rebuked. The angel declares, *"See thou do it not."* Some promote the worship of angels by seeking to talk to them or pray to them, which is here strictly admonished. Angels are but another creature of God. They are fellowservants with the saints. They worship God as we do. It is to God the Father that our praise must be directed. We are to *"worship God."*

Secondly, we find out what the spirit, or essence, of prophecy is, *"the testimony of Jesus is the spirit of prophecy."* Prophecy, regardless of the prophet or bearer, is to testify of Jesus, to acknowledge and declare Him as Lord of all. John was imprisoned on the isle of Patmos *"for the testimony of Jesus"* (1:9). He had made known the will of God concerning Jesus as the Savior, the King of

Kings and Lord of Lords. We, too, must prophesy and testify to that end.

"The testimony of Jesus is the spirit of prophecy." The vision that John shares with us is a prophecy, a testimony of and to Jesus. It reveals Him. We must declare Him in like manner—in our speech, in our actions and generally in our lives by bearing fruit.

The Appearance of Jesus (19:11-21)

Finally, we have arrived at the second coming of Jesus. It is this next portion of Rev. 19:11-21 that provides the particulars of Jesus' appearance. But really, the details are few compared to other New Testament descriptions of His coming or to those details in the Revelation spent on describing Jesus, preparing His followers for eternity and disclosing the completed bride of the Lamb.

What John sees first is a white horse, the same one observed earlier in the vision (6:2). Its white color represents the purity and holiness of its rider. *"He that sat upon him was called Faithful and True* [adjectives already associated with Jesus in 3:14], *and in righteousness he doth judge and make war"* (19:11).

Verses 12-13 continue, *"His eyes were as a flame of fire* [cf. 1:14], *and on his head were many crowns* [cf. 6:2]; *and he had a name written, that no man knew* [cf. 3:12], *but he himself. And he was clothed with a vesture dipped in blood: and his name is called the Word of God"* (as it was in John 1:1-14). There can be no question, with all these descriptions and qualifiers, that this One on the white horse is Jesus. He is the Word made flesh, who shed His blood to take away the sin of the world. His *"vesture,"* or outer apparel, bears witness to the sacrifice He made. This is Jesus, the Christ.

"Out of his mouth goeth a sharp sword, that with it he should smite the nations: and he shall rule them with a rod of iron: and he treadeth the winepress of the fierceness and wrath of Almighty God. And he hath on his vesture and on

245

his thigh a name written, KING OF KINGS, AND LORD OF LORDS *"*(19:15-16). The sharp sword is the Word of God (Eph. 6:17), by which the world will be judged. It smites the nations. Jesus, who had been given rule of the kingdom when He ascended to heaven (Acts 1:9), will now bring the *"fierceness and wrath of Almighty God"* to destroy all wickedness. Having done that, the King and his true servants will live eternally in the new heavens and earth created by God (cf. 2 Peter 3:13).

John saw Jesus in the heavenly realm. He also observed that *"the armies which were in heaven followed him upon white horses, clothed in fine linen, white and clean"* (19:14). This army is that of the saints who follow Jesus, the same group observed in Rev. 14:4. They are with Him in the heavenly realm. Even those still physically alive on earth are part of this great army (Eph. 2:4-6). Their white horses and clean linen come from Jesus, whom they follow, and from their own deeds done in the Spirit. It is the purity of Jesus that has made them acceptable to God and joint-heirs to the kingdom. They are the saints, and were it not for the fact that the final destruction of the beast and the false prophet is told in this passage, this chapter could pertain to Christ and the Church now, who presently reign victorious and sup together in the "secret places of the Most High" (Ps. 91:1).

But we do see the final casting of the beast and the false prophet into *"a lake of fire"* (19:20). Because of this event we can be sure that this is the appearing of Jesus. The scenario of Jesus' second coming, using the Revelation and other New Testament references, is as follows: "Unto them that look for him shall he appear the second time without sin unto salvation" (Heb. 9:28). It will not be twice, three times or any other number. There is only one more coming of Jesus. He will come with the saints who have gone on before us (19:14). The armies of heaven will always accompany Him.

The saints on earth will be "caught up together with them in the clouds [of witnesses]" (1 Thess. 4:17), thus completing the bride of Christ. The marriage of Jesus to the Church will be fulfilled. The marriage supper or feast in the presence of the Lord will commence and never end.

27
The Great White Throne Judgment
(20:1-15)

In the next segment of the vision, John sees some events which take us first to the past and present before going on to the future. The past and present relate to the ruling and reigning of Christ which, in Him, we experience now. The future aspect of this passage focuses on the Great White Throne Judgment.

A Serious Look at the "Millennial Reign"

Many students of the Bible approach Revelation 20 with an eye to the future. The early portions of the chapter discuss a "thousand-year" period often called the "millennial reign" or "the Millennium." Because Satan is said to be *"bound"* for this period (20:2), it is concluded that, with all the wickedness in the world now, the thousand years have not yet begun. Moreover, Revelation 20 is most always studied in chronological sequence with respect to the second coming and is therefore relegated to the future.

First we must remember that John saw recurring sequences which focused on selected subjects. They were reviewed, repeated and shown to him in different ways with varying symbolism. Revelation 20 enables John and us to step back and see a broader span of history than the second coming events of chapter 19. If any portion of Revelation 20 could be considered to follow the second coming occurrences or be concurrent with them, it is verses 7-15. As in Rev. 19:19-21, the beast and all who associate themselves with him come up against the saints in a last futile effort, only to be destroyed forever.

Revelation 20:1-6, however, spans the time up to the second coming.

Secondly, the binding of Satan took place at the cross. All of his power to dominate lives was stripped at that point (cf. Col. 2:15). Though many people submit themselves to the influences of Satan today, he was nevertheless defeated. Calvary did not happen to secure something in the distant future. The truth is that Jesus Christ has set men free from Satan's evil grip (John 8:32). Calvary was the place that he was *"bound."* If it wasn't, the Church could never have developed from twelve ragged disciples to the millions that comprise it today. Some Scriptures that support this theme are Matt. 12:28-29; 28:18-20; Mark 3:27; Col. 1:13; and Heb. 2:14-15.

This binding is described to us in symbolic terms. The *"bottomless pit"* is symbolic of the pits of hell to which Satan has been cast down. The *"chain"* used to bind him is likewise symbolic. It is not a real iron or metal chain. It is the "chain" of restraint placed upon him by God through the cross and a victorious, reigning Church. Satan has truly been bound, like a mean dog secured on the end of a chain fastened to a large tree. He can bark and snap at you, but he is no real threat unless you approach him within the length of the chain holding him. Many have done just that. They have rejected the kingdom of God available through Jesus and have stooped to the pits of hell in sin and corruption to be bound there with Satan.

Certainly there are many people, even Christians, who are struggling with Satan and his demonic friends, but only because they choose to do so. If Satan had you bound and Jesus set you free, as we often sing, then he has no hold on your life. "If the Son therefore shall make you free, ye shall be free indeed" (John 8:36). If anything else binds you, it is probably your flesh, which needs no Satanic help to be sinful. But Satan is bound by the blood of the Lamb and the word of our testimony. If only the Church would realize it and move in the authority and power granted her in Christ Jesus!

Next, we must understand that even the *"thousand years"* are symbolic, like all the other elements of this apocalyptic passage. Why would this be literal when the key, the bottomless pit and the chain have been clearly identified as symbolic?

In discussing the time prior to Christ's return, Peter reveals an interesting fact about God's timetable: "One day is with the Lord as a thousand years, and a thousand years as one day" (2 Pet. 3:8). This period of grace in which the Church finds itself is like a day in God's sight. Likewise, any one day could be viewed by God as a millennium. In other words, time is not something God has to worry about. Within the confines of the Greek language, where one thousand is the highest number represented by the alphabet, and with the knowledge that we are dealing with apocalyptic text, the *"thousand years"* are representative of a time span in which God is dealing with man.

God could not have stated a literal number for the time of the age of grace, for that would be in direct contrast to Jesus' statement which says, "of that day and hour knoweth no man, no, not the angels of heaven, but my Father only" (Matt. 24:36). God described the Church age to John as the *"thousand years"* to confound the wisdom of this world. "The natural man receiveth not the things of the Spirit of God: for they are foolishness unto him: neither can he know them, because they are spiritually discerned" (1 Cor. 2:14). And just as Jesus used parables to hide the truths of the kingdom from robbers, thieves and the natural man, so has God given us the *"thousand years"* as an expression of the time in which the Church of Jesus Christ builds itself up while Satan is bound by the power of the cross in their lives.

250

Another argument put forth concerning the "millennial reign," where Christ returns to earth to rule physically for a thousand years, centers around a statement of Isaiah the prophet which says, "The wolf also shall dwell with the lamb, and the leopard shall lie down with the kid; and the calf and the young lion and the fatling together; and a little child shall lead them" (Isa. 11:6). There is more Isaiah text which should be read, but this one verse will suffice to make the point. Some view this passage of Isaiah as describing that future millennial reign where even the animals will live together in peace. But the timing and interpretation of this prophetic message need careful discernment.

What Isaiah was really prophesying was the kingdom life that would be ushered in with the first coming of Jesus. Isaiah envisions the righteousness and faithfulness of Jesus in this reign. King Jesus will sit on the throne in heaven while His subjects, characterized by the diversity of wild and tame animals (indicating their past and present natures) harmoniously exist together in His love. You will notice that Isaiah does not even talk about people. He describes kingdom life through the illustration of animals who by nature, like human beings, cannot coexist except that something supernatural happen. The supernatural happening is the rebirth of sinful man through the cross, which enables him to love his brother.

Jesus fulfilled the law and the prophets with his coming the first time (Matt. 5:17). The kingdom already exists, even though the world cannot perceive it with its natural eye (Luke 17:20-21). Jesus is sitting on the throne at the right hand of God. His saints are ruling and reigning with Him even now (Rom. 5:17; Rev. 5:8-10), in heaven and on earth. The future millennial reign theory only serves to weaken the victory which we should be walking in at the present. Looking again to Isaiah, Christ and the Church are an "ensign" (sign) to the world (Isa.

11:10-12), for they can live triumphantly in the midst of trouble and sorrow. Their life will never end. They are ruling and reigning for eternity. And that brings us to yet another aspect of this *"thousand years."*

John says, *"I saw thrones, and they sat upon them, and judgment was given unto them: and I saw the souls of them that were beheaded for the witness of Jesus, and for the word of God, and which had not worshipped the beast, neither his image, neither had received his mark upon their foreheads, or in their hands; and they lived and reigned with Christ a thousand years"* (20:4). The struggle many have with this verse is the impression that only decapitated Christians will sit on the thrones to rule and reign after the resurrection. Indeed, many who were physically beheaded are already reigning in the heavenly places. But many more who didn't worship the world system or receive its evil mark also sit on these thrones in the heavenly places in Christ Jesus. If we are born again, we can reign with Christ right now.

The saints in heaven and on earth are one in the Spirit. We sit with Jesus now (Eph. 2:6). We rule and reign with Him for the symbolic *"thousand years,"* and beyond that for all eternity.

It is only toward the end of this period of grace that God will loose Satan and his forces (20:6). Again, this loosing is indicative of God removing the restraints for a short period before He crushes the powers of darkness forever. They go up to *"deceive the nations"* (20:7), to assemble the wicked for one final assault on the righteous of God. From the four corners of the world they encompass *"the camp of the saints about, and the beloved city"* (20:9—the Church). But God intervenes, devours them in His wrath and casts the wicked into eternal destruction (20:10).

The millennial reign is not theology for the future. It is the kingdom rule of God, which cannot be shaken by any force (Heb. 12:25-29), which exists now and forever for those who live and believe in Christ (John 11:26).

Two Resurrections

The subject of resurrection is also addressed in Revelation 20. It, too, has been greatly misunderstood in Christian circles. Two resurrections are intimated in our text. Let's examine them both.

The first is mentioned in verse 5 and relates to those who are seen ruling and reigning in verse 4. This first resurrection is seen in John 11:25-26, where Jesus discusses resurrection with Martha, the sister of Lazarus (who is about to be raised). Jesus says, "I am the resurrection, and the life: he that believeth in me, though he were dead, yet shall he live: And whosoever liveth and believeth in me shall never die."

Mankind is born spiritually dead in sin (Eph. 2:1, 3; Ps. 51:5). Every man is in desperate need of life. Knowing that, God sent Jesus to the earth and made life possible through the cross. "God, who is rich in mercy, for his great love wherewith he loved us, Even when we were dead in sins, hath quickened us [made us alive] together with Christ . . . And hath raised us up together, and made us sit together in heavenly places in Christ Jesus" (Eph. 2:4-6). According to these verses, in Christ we have already been resurrected from the dead and have been given a heavenly position, the one detailed in Rev. 20:4. This is the first resurrection.

All who have been raised with Christ through rebirth will never spiritually die again. We may physically die, with our bodies returning to the dust from which they came. But our spirits are alive in Christ forever. *"The second death hath no power"* over us (20:14). We are alive forevermore. We are priests *"of God and of Christ, and shall reign with him a thousand years"* and for eternity (20:6).

The second resurrection applies to the wicked dead,

who do not live until the period of grace is over. That would include the wicked who are already dead and those who die during the *"thousand years." "The rest of the dead lived not again until the thousand years were finished"* (20:5). When the time comes, God raises them up for final judgment. That is the second resurrection. However, *"blessed and holy is he that hath part in the first resurrection* [by becoming part of the universal Church through rebirth]: *on such the second death hath no power"* (20:6).

The Judgments of God (20:11-15)

The final expressions of Revelation 20 we must consider are the judgments of God. John saw a *"great white throne"* (20:11). Its color represents the holiness and purity of the One sitting upon it. It is *"great,"* or mighty, in comparison to the thrones upon which the saints have been seated during the period of grace. It is the Lord, even Jesus himself, who sits on the *"great white throne"* to judge the creation, *"from whose face the earth and the heaven fled away; and there was found no place for them"* (20:11).

John observes a great judgment taking place. The Scriptures would seem to indicate that all of the creation will stand before the Lord in that day, whether good or bad. Jesus taught the disciples, "When the Son of man shall come in his glory, and all the holy angels with him, then shall he sit upon the throne of his glory: And before him shall be gathered all nations: And he shall separate them one from another as a shepherd divideth his sheep from the goats: And he shall set the sheep on his right hand, but the goats on the left. Then shall the King say unto them on his right hand, Come, ye blessed of my Father, inherit the kingdom prepared for you from the foundation of the world. . . . Then shall he say also unto them on the left hand, Depart from me, ye cursed, into everlasting fire, prepared for the devil and his angels" (Matt. 25:31-34, 41).

That is exactly what happens in Rev. 20:11-15. *"The books were opened: and another book was opened, which is the book of life: and the dead were judged out of those things which were written in the books, according to their works"* (20:12). Several books are described. It would seem that the books contain the works of every man. The book of life, identified as *"another book,"* contains the names of all who are saved, who have become "alive" in Christ Jesus. This sets them apart from those who were "dead" in sin and death.

The judgment is simple. The works of every man are reviewed by the Lord. The "goats" or ones whose names are *"not found written in the book of life"* are *"cast into the lake of fire"* (20:15). These are they which chose *"death and hell"* over life and heavenly living (20:14). The "sheep," whose names are found written in the book of life, are invited to inherit fully the kingdom which, until this time, they had only sampled.

Paul speaks of the judgment seat of Christ in Rom. 14:10-12, "We shall all stand before the judgment seat of Christ. For it is written, As I live, saith the Lord, every knee shall bow to me, and every tongue shall confess to God. So then every one of us shall give account of himself to God." The *"great white throne"* and the judgment seat of Christ are most likely one and the same. The wicked and rebellious are given eternal punishment (20:14-15). The righteous are rewarded for their commitment to the Lord and their good works which followed after them (14:13; cf. 1 Cor. 3:12-15). But both are declared from the same throne upon which our Lord sits.

The mockers and scoffers of the world cannot conceive of this happening. They laugh and make fun of anyone who proclaims it. But God assures us that all these things shall happen. We can choose to be ready to fully inherit the kingdom and abide with the sheep of the kingdom forever. If not, we will perish with the goats.

255

28

The New Jerusalem

(21:1-22:5)

In our study to this point, we have seen some spiritual facts concerning the kingdom of God, the real Jew and the nation of Israel that no doubt were completely new to many readers. This chapter is no exception, because we will be examining the identity of the New Jerusalem *"coming down from God out of heaven"* (21:2).

For many, the last two chapters of the Revelation are a composite picture of heaven located somewhere in the universe. The precisely measured walls, the sparkling foundations of precious stones, the beautiful pearl gates and the streets of pure gold are all thought to be literal. After all, didn't Jesus promise us a dwelling place in our heavenly Father's mansion?

The truth is that the New Jerusalem detailed in Revelation 21 and 22 is not a physical city floating somewhere in the far reaches of the cosmos. The walls, foundations, gates and streets are all symbolic of the spiritual composition of something far more glorious than a conceived metropolis. The New Jerusalem described in our text is the completed Church, expressed in elaborate typology.

John saw *"a new heaven and a new earth"* (21:1), for the first had passed away. He was seeing the realm and dimension in which the redeemed creation will live throughout eternity. The Lord said, *"Behold, I make all things new"* (21:5). The creative power for fashioning the new heavens and earth was inaugurated at Calvary. It is not finished yet but is fast approaching completion. Regardless, the New Jerusalem exists in that realm. John was being shown how it would look when it was completely finished, a creation not of the natural but of the spiritual, *"coming down from God out of heaven."* Apparently, those individuals who have experienced out-of-the-body visions in the Spirit, or those who have seen heaven at death but then revived to tell of it, saw exactly the same thing that John did—the completed Church in all its splendor!

As John saw the holy city descending from the heavenly places, he saw and subsequently recorded our first clue as to what the New Jerusalem is. He said the New Jerusalem was *"prepared as a bride adorned for her husband"* (21:2). The New Testament "bride" can be only one thing—the Church. This symbolism is used for no other spiritual entity created by God. To interpret it any other way would be to depart from sound biblical pattern established in the Word. It is the bride, spotless and without blemish, that will join in "wedlock" with the Lord Jesus. It is the Church.

A booming voice from heaven declares a few things about the New Jerusalem which John was seeing. *"Behold, the tabernacle of God is with men, and he will dwell with them, and they shall be his people, and God himself shall be with them, and be their God"* (21:3). The tabernacle, or dwelling place, of God is the Church, redeemed men and women who have welcomed the Lord into their lives. We are the dwelling place of the Holy Ghost (1 Cor. 3:16). Jesus is Immanuel, God with us. He lives in our midst and in our hearts now.

"And God shall wipe away all tears from their eyes; and there shall be no more death, neither sorrow, nor crying, neither shall there be any more pain: for the former things are passed away" (21:4). These things are addressed in the spiritual. They pertain to the pain, sorrow and grief of sin, which are the former things which have passed away. In Jesus, we have been set free from sin and death, which is reason for great joy, wiping away the tears and never being sorry anymore. But this verse even applies

in the natural, for when the bride of Christ is complete and in the heavenly realm after Jesus' return, none of these negative conditions will ever exist again. The Lord said, *"Behold, I make all things new . . . for these words are true and faithful"* (21:5). They apply to the Church now and in the future.

The Lord then declares to John, *"It is done"* (21:6). Every provision for becoming reunited to our loving heavenly Father has been completed. And as if to confirm that fact and present us with a choice, the Alpha and Omega, the beginning and the end of all things, says, *"I will give unto him that is athirst of the fountain of the water of life freely"* (21:6). In other words, anyone who is thirsty for spiritual truth and a life of walking in the Spirit will be freely refreshed by the Holy Spirit, the life of the Church. *"He that overcometh shall inherit all things; and I will be his God, and he shall be my son"* (21:7). There is not much doubt as to the blessings offered those who respond to God. He becomes a personal heavenly Father to them. And as joint-heirs, they are given all of the inheritance given Jesus.

For those who refuse to become part of the true Church, that is *"the fearful, and unbelieving, and the abominable, and murderers, and whoremongers, and sorcerers, and idolaters, and all liars,"* the Lord said they *"shall have their part in the lake which burneth with fire and brimstone: which is the second death"* (21:8). When put in these terms, it shouldn't be difficult to make a decision to serve the Lord. But the number of those who will not is legion.

John is given further proof that the New Jerusalem is the Church when, as he puts it, *"There came unto me one of the seven angels which had the seven vials full of the seven last plagues, and talked with me, saying, Come hither, I will show thee the bride, the Lamb's wife"* (21:9). Now we know that the bride, the Lamb's wife, is the Church. And what do you suppose John saw when he was carried away in the Spirit? He saw *"that great city, the holy Jerusalem, descending out of heaven from God"* (21:10).

The Church is the New Jerusalem! We should all know it, believe it and live in it. God will not be doing anything else with the natural city of Jerusalem. It was part of the Old Covenant and was specifically used to house the presence of God. But under the New Covenant, God dwells in the New Jerusalem, the Church of Jesus Christ, which is His temple.

It is that house or temple to which Jesus referred in John 14:1-3. Before His death and resurrection, Jesus told the disciples that there were many mansions in His Father's house. Any scholar of the Greek language will agree that the word which is translated "mansions" is more accurately translated "dwelling places."

Jesus was about to be crucified and make possible those dwelling places in the Lord. His atoning death accomplished it. "For Christ is not entered into the holy places made with hands, which are the figures of the true; but into heaven itself, now to appear in the presence of God for us" (Heb. 9:24). He did that in the period from His death until His resurrection on the third day. He cleansed the heavenly places with His blood and made it possible for us to dwell there. That is precisely what Jesus was speaking of in John 14. He went before the Lord, prepared and secured our dwelling place by His blood and returned to receive us unto himself, that where He was, we could be also. Jesus is not somewhere in space now, building homes like we know on earth. The dwelling places were prepared through His death. And we can live in them even today in the Spirit and, for sure, through all eternity.

We need not let this crush our vision of the heavenly places. The heavenly realm is real, and if we are born again of the Spirit, we are part of it. What we must adjust is our perception of *"that great city."* The symbolic characteristics are given for us to see what the Church will look like when it is completed and in its final glorious state.

Let God concern himself as to the location of heaven or the Church in heaven. It is a spiritual position that we cannot measure nor apprehend with our natural minds. And while many Christians have made heaven their ultimate goal, our earnest and sincere goal should be conforming to the image of Christ, living in Him so that we will be part of heaven forever regardless of where it is.

Composition of the City (21:10-21)

John describes the completed Church as best he can by using earthly comparisons and illustrations. He starts off by saying that it has *"the glory of God"* (21:11). It shines forth the glory like that of Moses when he came down off Mount Sinai from the presence of the Lord. The Church, however, will not lose that glory as was the case with Moses after a time. The life of Jesus Christ and the indwelling of the Holy Spirit have ensured that the Church will forever exude *"the glory of God."*

"Her light was like unto a stone most precious, even like a jasper stone, clear as crystal" (21:11). Notice that the light was "like" precious stone. He wasn't actually seeing a crystal-clear jasper stone. He was observing the light of her glory which, to him, could only be compared to something he saw on earth.

The New Jerusalem had twelve gates made of pearl, with the *"names of the twelve tribes of the children of Israel"* written upon them (21:12). The names of the tribes merely represent the diversity of those who comprise the Church, saints reaching all the way back to the Old Testament patriarchs and including the most contemporary of saints under the New Covenant. The Church is "a chosen generation, a royal priesthood, an holy nation, a peculiar people" (1 Pet. 2:9). It is the "nation" of Israel ("the rule of God") and very correctly bears the names of the tribes from which it evolved.

The symbolism of the pearls for the gates might be understood by the manner in which the inhabitants of the New Jerusalem enter therein. A pearl is formed within the oyster when a speck of sand or other irritant lodges in its flesh, causing it to secrete an insulating substance which forms around the speck. The result is a round and smooth pearl, which does not irritate the oyster. "We must through much tribulation enter into the kingdom of God" (Acts 14:22). There are many irritants in our lives which need to be covered by the working of the Holy Spirit. Only God can cause a life to have no tears, death, sorrow, crying or pain. And He does it by allowing us to go through the hard places and experience the soothing of the Holy Spirit in making our lives precious pearls in the sight of God. "If we suffer, we shall also reign with him" (2 Tim. 2:12). That is the secret of entering the pearly gates of the New Jerusalem.

"And the wall of the city had twelve foundations, and in them the names of the twelve apostles of the Lamb" (21:14). Wherein the gates had the names of the twelve tribes of Israel, the foundations of the heavenly city contain the names of the twelve apostles, signifying it was built upon their solid teaching from the Master. "For other foundation can no man lay than that is laid, which is Jesus Christ" (1 Cor. 3:11). Jesus laid the foundation in them. The Church was then subsequently built upon their teaching and instruction by the power of the Holy Spirit (cf. Eph. 2:19-20).

"And he that talked with me had a golden reed to measure the city" (21:15). This is the same type of measuring device we encountered in Revelation 11 where the temple was measured. The significance of the measurements taken indicate that it was complete. *"The length and the breadth and the height of it are equal"* (21:16). It is com-

posed of individuals from every *"kindred, and tongue, and people, and nation"* (5:9), and likely so, for our "God is no respecter of persons" (Acts 10:34). He has, in His love, included men and women from every walk of life. The New Jerusalem is truly foursquare. It is complete in the Lord.

In general, *"the city was pure gold, like unto clear glass. . . . and the street of the city was pure gold, as it were transparent glass"* (21:18, 21). John could only picture what he was seeing as pure, refined gold, a creation tried by fire, with only the purest elements remaining. *"And the foundations of the wall of the city were garnished with all manner of precious stones"* (21:19). The Church, as it was shown to John in all its glory and perfection, was a glorious sight, very close to being indescribable.

No Temple Therein (21:22)

"And I saw no temple therein: for the Lord God Almighty and the Lamb are the temple of it" (21:22). Being a spiritual creation of God, the New Jerusalem had no need for a temple of earthly construction. God the Father and Jesus, His Son, are the temple in the heavenly realm.

This may sound somewhat confusing in that the Church has been identified as the temple of the Holy Spirit. In other words, the Lord by His Spirit lives and abides in us. But Jesus prayed to His Father in the presence of the disciples that "they also may be one in us: that the world may believe that thou hast sent me" (John 17:21). Not only does God abide in us, we abide in Him. That makes the Lord the temple, into which we must enter to have life eternal.

All the teaching which says the earthly temple in Jerusalem will be rebuilt in the last days has overlooked the New Testament definition of God's temple. There is only one temple, which must get our undivided attention, and that is the Lord God Almighty and the Lamb. They are our temple!

Divine Illumination (21:23-27)

Another aspect of the New Jerusalem is its source of light. *"The city had no need of the sun, neither of the moon, to shine in it: for the glory of God did lighten it, and the Lamb is the light thereof"* (21:23). Not only are the Father and Son the temple, they are the source of illumination. *"There shall be no night there"* (21:25), for all darkness has been dispelled. *"The nations of them which are saved shall walk in the light of it"* (21:24), just as Jesus had promised, "I am the light of the world: he that followeth me shall not walk in darkness, but shall have the light of life" (John 8:12). Glory be to God who provides us divine illumination!

A River and a Tree (22:1-5)

John was shown *"a pure river of water of life, clear as crystal, proceeding out of the throne of God and the Lamb"* (22:1). This is symbolic of the abundant Word of God flowing forth from His throne. It is *"clear as crystal"* to those of spiritual persuasion and is available to all of mankind like the flow of a mighty river. Its source cannot be depleted.

In the midst of the New Jerusalem could be seen *"the tree of life, which bore twelve manner of fruits, and yielded her fruit every month; and the leaves of the tree were for the healing of the nations"* (22:2). There are all sorts of explanations for this *"tree of life."* It has even been related to a plentiful harvest in the present nation of Israel where, in some portions, crops grow year round. But the *"tree of life"* in the New Jerusalem is not a horticultural wonder. It is the Lord Jesus, whose revelation we seek.

Who has provided *"healing of the nations"*? Jesus. Who is the living manna which provides us spiritual nourishment? Jesus. Who has given us life-producing fruit for all the days of our lives? It is Jesus! He is the *"tree of life."* We must live and have our being in Him. Any other interpretation for this tree is superficial to the true meaning we find in Jesus.

As Jesus has been the focus of the Revelation, He is also the focal point and source of life for the Church, the New Jerusalem. That great city exists today for all who would know God through Jesus Christ. If you are a citizen of the heavenly places in Christ Jesus, your every need is supplied. You are complete in Him (Col. 2:10).

29

The Spirit and the Bride Say, Come

(22:6-21)

Jesus is coming again! *"Behold, I come quickly,"* says the Lord Jesus (22:7). "I come suddenly" would also be a correct paraphrase. For those who are ready, who keep *"the sayings of the prophecy of this book"* (22:7), blessings are promised (cf. 1:3). For those who are not ready, who have rejected the Lord and His kingdom, Jesus will come as a thief in the night.

"Behold, I come quickly [suddenly]; *and my reward is with me, to give every man according as his work shall be"* (22:12). It is the works of every person that will determine their eternal destiny. If we have ceased from our labors, rested in the Lord and allowed our works to be for Him, we will have great reward (cf. Hebrews 4). If we still abide in our carnal and sinful works, death and hell will greet us at the coming of Jesus.

"Surely I come quickly. Amen. Even so, come, Lord Jesus" (22:20). There is nothing to fear if you live in Christ. You can say, *"Come, Lord Jesus,"* knowing your eternal home is in Him.

New Jerusalem Inhabitants (22:14-15)

In the closing verses of the prophecy we find out who can inhabit the New Jerusalem, which is like saying who can be part of the Church. *"Blessed are they that do his commandments, that they may have right to the tree of life, and may enter in through the gates into the city"* (22:14). New Jerusalem inhabitants are they whose names *"are written in the Lamb's book of life"* (21:27). They do the commandments of God, and the first which must be heeded is to be born again. Only they shall see the kingdom of God (John 3:3). They enter the city through praising God, for "Praise" is the gate(s) (cf. Isa. 60:18).

"There shall in no wise enter into it any thing that defileth, neither whatsoever worketh abomination, or maketh a lie" (21:27). For outside the walls of that great city, beyond the periphery of its divine illumination and far off in the darkness of eternal despair, *"are dogs, and sorcerers, and whoremongers, and murderers, and idolaters, and whosoever loveth and maketh a lie"* (22:15).

The choice is simple: obey the commandments of God in Christ Jesus, the fulfillment of the law, or be cast into "outer darkness: there shall be weeping and gnashing of teeth" (Matt. 8:12).

A Word to the Wise (22:18-19)

A very serious warning is issued concerning the content of this prophecy, one which makes this author take note. *"If any man shall add unto these things, God shall add unto him the plagues that are written in this book: and if any man shall take away from the words of the book of this prophecy, God shall take away his part out of the book of life, and out of the holy city, and from the things which are written in this book"* (21:18-19).

I become very sober when I ponder those statements. I pray that I have been faithful in sharing the truth which God reveals to me about the Revelation. I have literally risked spiritual position in order to be obedient in the transmittal of God's Word. But it is worth that risk if even a small portion of what has been shared brings revelation and understanding that you didn't have before.

This warning is issued for all of us. Let us be careful that we approach this prophecy with a serious intent to reveal Jesus and the great spiritual truths contained therein. Faulty interpretation and personal theology may result in undesired consequences. "Study to shew thyself approved unto God, a workman that needeth not to be ashamed, rightly dividing the word of truth" (2 Tim. 2:15).

The Invitation (22:17)

The Revelation of Jesus Christ concludes with an invitation. *"The Spirit and the bride say, Come. And let him that heareth say, Come. And let him that is athirst come. And whosoever will, let him take the water of life freely"* (20:17).

First, the Spirit of God says, *"Come"*—not next week, next year or in a millennium. Come now! *"Now is come salvation, and strength, and the kingdom of our God"* (12:10). Now is the time to receive it. The Spirit draws us and beckons us to enter the gates of the heavenly city.

Secondly, the bride says, *"Come."* The universal Church proclaiming the mighty gospel of Jesus invites you and I into the presence of God. It is the Church's duty to say to the lost and confused of the world, *"Come."*

God offers a universal invitation to *"whosoever will."* The thirsty of the world who desire to drink of the fountain of God and of the river flowing out from His throne can come and drink freely now. *"The Spirit and the bride say, Come."*

30

In Conclusion

Keeping in mind the exhortation of Rev. 22:18-19, my concluding remarks will be brief.

The kingdom of God is hidden from the eyes of the world. It is not something that God will allow to be defiled. To enter therein, we must be born of the Spirit of God. Truly we cannot even see it until we are.

The world will not perceive nor receive the kingdom and the great spiritual truths of God, because it will not accept Jesus. It refuses to "see" Him. And as Jesus said, "No man cometh unto the Father, but by me" (John 14:6). He is the door, the gate and the entrance to the sheepfold.

The Revelation presents Jesus. It is a revealing of Him. My purpose has been to highlight those places in the text which have too often been overlooked in presenting Him. In Him the kingdom has fully come. Nothing is lacking with Jesus at the right hand of the Father. He is ruling and reigning in the heavenly realm by the authority vested by our Father. And when we abide in Him, we are there in the heavenly places as well, "heirs of God, and joint-heirs with Christ" (Rom. 8:17).

Bibliography

Bunyan, John. *The Pilgrim's Progress*. New York: Frederick A. Stokes Co., Inc., 1939.

Epp, Theodore. *Practical Studies in Revelation*. Lincoln, Neb.: Back to the Bible Broadcast, 1969.

Foxe, John. *Foxe's Book of Martyrs*. New York: Pyramid Publishing, Inc., 1968.

Gaglardi, B. Maureen. *The Path of the Just*. Burnaby, B.C., Canada: New West Press, 1963.

MacPherson, Dave. *Why I Believe the Church Will Pass Through the Tribulation*. Greenville, S.C.: Jewel Books, 1971.

Martin, William C. *The Layman's Bible Encyclopedia*. Nashville, Tenn.: The South-Western Publishing Co., 1964.

McKonkey, James H. *The Book of Revelation*. Pittsburgh, Pa.: Silver Publishing Co., 1921.

Slemming, C.W. *Made According to the Pattern*. London: Henry E. Walter, Ltd., 1938.

The author welcomes your response to this commentary. He is available for speaking engagements and teaching seminars. Please address all correspondence to:

Lerry W. Fogle
P.O. Box 1212
Frederick, MD 21701

1-800-323-6549
Relief from a Life of Bondage
Swinson